What people are saying about *Embracing Failure*

"I love this book. If you cannot embrace failure, you'll probably never enjoy success; it's part of the process."
– Bob Proctor, leading prosperity coach, best selling author, celebrity from The Secret movie, Chairman Proctor Gallagher Institute

"Embracing Failure is a vitally important, life-changing book that everyone should read. Refreshing, enlightening and impactful. This book has a lingering effect and long after you read it, you will be reflecting the author's insights and experience positive change in glorious ways."
– Peggy McColl, New York Times Best-Selling Author

"In this landmark book, Lennox masterfully captures the essential character required to succeed in any endeavor. Applying what is shared could reward you abundantly."
– Mick Petersen, International Best-selling Author of *Stella And The Timekeepers*

"I highly recommend Embracing Failure: Your Key to Success, *not just because it is a great book, but also because my own success has come by persevering through failure. I have made a strength of it, and every week challenge my three teenage boys with the question, 'What did you fail at this week?' It is a great way to build character and prepare them for life. This book will do the same for you."*
– Robert Pascuzzi, Partner, Creative Planning Services and best selling author of *The Ravine*.”

"What would you do if you absolutely knew that the failure you fear is THE lesson you required to achieve the greatest thing you desire? Would you embrace that failure? I suspect the answer is, "Yes," and, therefore, this book is a MUST read for you."
– Emmanuel Dagher, Healer and best selling author of *Easy Breezy Prosperity*

"The value of this book is inherent in the title. I highly recommend Embracing Failure: Your Key to Success.*"*
– Michael Internoscia, Principal, M&M Private Lending Group

"It's been said over and over that it's not how many times you fall, it's how many times you get up. The challenge is, no one tells you how to get back up after failure... until now."

"Embracing Failure: Your Key to Success *provides a new context for failure and the ability to keep moving forward, change your life for the better and reach the level of success you want.*"

– Jase Souder, Speaker, Author, Trainer and founder of The Prophet Factory

"I highly recommend this great work by Lennox Cornwall. Embracing Failure: Your Key to Success *will give you hope with the various trials we all experience. Life has taught me that sometimes we win by losing. '...for when I am weak, then I am strong.' 2 Corinthians 12:10*"

– Pastor Randy Carter, Set Free Ministries

"In this great work, it is to Lennox' credit and a testimony to his wisdom that he provides a unique perspective in what is a crowded space – the Self-Help and Business Genres. I strongly recommend your delving into this book – NOW!"

– Banafsheh Akhlaghi, Attorney and International Best-selling author of *Beautiful Reminders ~Anew*

"Success without failure is like a coin with heads and no tails – impossible. In this insightful book, Lennox coaches on how to use apparent failure to achieve your greatest success."

– Don Marks, CEO Pop-A-Lock, the World's Largest Locksmith Franchise

EMBRACING FAILURE

Your Key to Success

LENNOX A. CORNWALL

Published by One Truth Publishing

Copyright© 2016 Lennox Cornwall
Second Edition, 2017

No part of this book may be reproduced or transmitted in any form or by any means, electronic or mechanical, including photocopying, recording or by any information storage and retrieval system, without written permission from the author, except for the inclusion of brief quotations in a review.

Limit of Liability and Disclaimer of Warranty: The publisher has used its best efforts in preparing this book, and the information provided herein is provided "as is."

This book is designed to provide information and motivation to our readers. It is sold with the understanding that the publisher is not engaged to render any type of psychological, legal, or any other kind of professional advice. The content of each article is the sole expression and opinion of its author, and not necessarily that of the publisher. No warranties or guarantees are expressed or implied by the publisher's choice to include any of the content in this volume. Neither the publisher nor the individual author(s) shall be liable for any physical, psychological, emotional, financial, or commercial damages, including, but not limited to, special, incidental, consequential or other damages. Our views and rights are the same: You are responsible for your own choices, actions, and results.

Permission should be addressed to: lennox@lennoxcornwall.com

Publisher's Cataloging-in-Publication data

Names: Cornwall, Lennox, author.
  Title: Embracing failure : your key to success / Lennox Cornwall.
  Description: Second edition. | Great Cacapon, WV: One Truth Publishing, 2017
  Identifiers: ISBN 978-0-9994067-0-0 | LCCN 2017914243
  Subjects: LCSH Success in business. | Business failures. | Failure (Psychology) | Self-actualization (Psychology) | Entrepreneurship. | BISAC BUSINESS & ECONOMICS / Small Business. | SELF-HELP / Personal Growth / Success.
  Classification: LCC HF5386.A2 .C67 2017 | DDC 658.4/09--dc23

Editor: Nita Robinson, Nita Helping Hand?
www.NitaHelpingHand.com

Cover Design: AuthorSupport.com

Chapter Illustrations: Art & Design by R. Sauer

Layout: Anne Karklins
info@annehk.ca

DEDICATION

To Divine Intelligence:

Thank you for my life, thank you for my wife, thank you
for who I am and for what I have;
Thank you for the strength, courage, integrity, intelligence and ingenuity,
as well as the openness of heart and of mind to be who I am,
to be the best I can be, to love and serve others,
to love you, to serve you and to obey your commands.

Amen.

– LAC

CONTENTS

Dedication v

Preface: Why I wrote this book 9

Foreword: Rodney C. Flowers 11

Introduction: About This Book 13

Chapter 1: The Meaning of Life 19

Chapter 2: Understanding Values 47

Chapter 3: Embracing Failure 79

Chapter 4: Discipline – The Sovereign Road to Freedom 107

Chapter 5: Work – The Ethic of Success 141

Chapter 6: Rise to The Challenge 167

Chapter 7: Discard Limiting Beliefs 193

Chapter 8: Recognize Your Genius 225

Chapter 9: Wisdom 249

Chapter 10: Sacrifice – The Ultimate Price 263

Chapter 11: When All Is Said and Done 275

PREFACE

WHY I WROTE THIS BOOK

In 1989 I resigned my position as a Corporate Banker in the City of London with what, at the time, was the biggest bank in the world. I left behind this financially rewarding, upwardly mobile career with the Yuppie lifestyle to pursue a childhood dream of owning my own business before the age of thirty. With my thirtieth birthday looming the following year, it was simply time.

Well, I did start that business before my thirtieth birthday. It was the first thing I had failed so completely at that, for the first time before or since then, I contemplated suicide – even though it was for the briefest of fleeting moments.

Shortly after my ever so brief flirtation with suicide, this book started out as a cathartic journal to help me understand how I managed to go from Hero in a cutthroat, dog-eat-dog corporate environment to Victim in what should have been the manifestation of my wildest dreams. Journaling is powerful medication – and addictive at that. Before long, I was incredulous of the rich understanding that poured forth from my musings. If I didn't before, I certainly did believe, then, in the existence of a superconscious mind, because there is no way I could come to the incredible wisdom I had arrived at in the absence of such consciousness. Above all, I was gifted the understanding of what failure really is, and then learned to embrace and embody it in such a way that I now dared to seek it out, realizing that without it, there is no such concept, reality or truth called success. Please understand – and if you don't now, you certainly will with the guidance of this book – that this is not some esoteric metaphor to motivate you, or myself for that matter, through difficult times. It is a literal truth; one that if you do not embrace, you cannot succeed – period!

Twenty years on, having written a few books more for fun than finances, I was working with one of my mentors, Bob Proctor, and lo and behold like a bolt from the heavens the idea flashed across my mind to find my long discarded manuscript and share it with the world. I could say that it blows my mind that it didn't occur to me to do so before now, but I have learned to accept that things are as they are and we then must make of them what we will.

With a mixture of excitement and trepidation: excitement, because I knew the value of what I'd written; trepidation, because what I had written was on the hard drive of a twenty-plus-year-old computer that I hadn't booted up for perhaps the latter ten of those years and wondered if it would still be willing to come out to play. Thank God it was, and thank God the wisdom I gained from the superconscious mind can now be shared among those for whom it was meant to be.

– LAC

FOREWORD

Many people would rather avoid the opportunity to accomplish all they could ever want out of life if there's the slightest possibility of experiencing failure. Oftentimes people rank the potential of experiencing failure much greater than the current pain or suffering they may be experiencing in their lives.

Having been paralyzed from the neck down once before in my life and enduring a prolonged life-span of moments unable to move or feel the limbs of my body, I somehow can relate to the individual suffering from the inability to move from one position in life to another of much greater satisfaction and joy as a result of the fear of falling short of the destination of their choosing. My personal experience with paralysis was traumatizing and debilitating. I wouldn't wish it on anyone. However, if we were to analyze the reasons why people never experience what they really want to experience in life and the most prevalent thing that keeps people from trying to accomplish what they truly desire, we would find fear of failure as the culprit.

The fear of failure can be just as debilitating and traumatizing to one's life similar to that of paralysis or walking into a room and the only exit door slamming tightly shut behind you. All of a sudden you find yourself stuck, in a rut, with no way out. Unfortunately, many people live their lives in this paralytic state, unable to move as a result of the ideas of failure invading their hearts and minds, thereby stripping them from all productive action toward discovering their most successful selves and realizing their most desired goals.

You see, whenever we embrace the desire to accomplish something greater in our lives, we all have to make the decision to either step forward into growth and reach for our goals and dreams despite the possibility of failure, or allow our fear of failure to hold us back in a place of ill-conceived comfort and security.

Lennox Cornwall provides the remedy to this life-threatening conception of failure with this book *EMBRACING FAILURE: Your Key to Success*.

I heard a wise man say that your evaluation of a thing determines what you believe about a thing. In this case, by reevaluating and thereby redefining our perspective on failure we are able to change the idea around failure and actually use it in a positive way to help us achieve what we really want. I think it's brilliant that the author of this book has shared with us such a simple technique that can have a positive and life-changing impact on what we are able to achieve in our lives.

Think about what things you have avoided as a result of fear of failure. Think about how failure has caused you to look at life. Perhaps it has paralyzed you in more ways than one.

With this book in your personal library you never have to fear failure again. It is rich with life-changing strategies that show you how to redefine the idea of failure and embrace it, and actually use it as a launching pad toward all that you desire in life.

Get up and rise above the furrows of failure. Loosen yourself from the grips of defeat and grab hold of a new understanding. A new way of living. Your key to a successful life.

Rodney C. Flowers

International Best Selling Author
Get Up! I Can't. I Will. I Did… Here's How!, *Essential Assertions*, and *Conversations With Rodney*

INTRODUCTION

ABOUT THIS BOOK

"I am only one, but still I am one. I cannot do everything, but still I can do something. And because I cannot do everything, I will not refuse to do something that I can do."

– Edward Everett Hale

WHAT FOR?

Awake! Awake! the alarm clock shakes
Quick haste, I need toothpaste
Brush, brush, I have to rush
Toast, jam, the door I slam

Quick down the street I run
To the station with the nation sadly not for recreation
Locomotion is the notion
One more sip of coffee potion

On the train my rush in vain
Yet again, I stand in pain
All the trains in their lanes
They are old England's life blood veins

Train approaching Cannon Street
Light-footed, I do fleet
In and out of peopled streets
Little time to meet and greet

Up ahead the leaders' furthest
Now the race begins in earnest
Face aglow a red hot furnace
Carry on I have to earn this

Gathering pace I lead the race
Now the pack they must chase
Looks as though I'll win the race
After such a gruesome pace

And so to work a lowly clerk
Always treated like a jerk
The race to work my only perk
'tis my solace not a quirk.

— LAC

As a child I day-dreamed about what I would be when I grew older. I could see the house I would live in. I knew that I would be happily married. I just knew that life would afford me freedom and comfort.

I remember the great boxer, Muhammad Ali, being interviewed. He was asked what made him such a great boxer. His response, so natural, was that when he was a boy he knew he was born to be great. God had made it so. And when he knew that boxing was his purpose, it was inevitable that he would be a great boxer. The sense of destiny I felt in that moment was immeasurable. Not because I could box; I still can't, but because I felt the same certainty about my life. It was my birthright to be great. It is what God wanted. All I needed to do was determine my purpose and the rest would follow.

At the age of five my mother was preparing me for my first experience of school –primary school. It is one of the few experiences of those times that I can recall. The message was that I had to go to school because it was the only way I could get into university and that without a university education, I could not get very far in life. This is, of course, nonsense, but I thank Mom for the conditioning as it enabled me to – eventually – enjoy school life and to experience the relative freedom afforded a university undergraduate.

Did I ask to go to school? No. Did I want to go to school? No – I cried most of my first day. Of course, I'm not naïve enough to suggest that I should have been given the choice as a 5-year-old. My point is that relying on grownups, as children must, creates a disposition toward a reliance on others for what we want and also, more damningly, conditions us to live according to the dictates of others.

In fact, when I think about it, that is what I had always done. My dad wanted me to be a naval officer, my mom wanted me to be a doctor, my teachers probably couldn't have cared less so long as I behaved in their classes and achieved adequate grades. What about me? What did I want? You see, this is the problem. *Do you know what you want*? Do you <u>really</u> know what you want? And, if so, why do you want it? Have you ever given it much thought? I know you. You are me. Your physical appearance may differ. You and others may call you by some other name, but you are me.

I know you had empowering childhood day dreams. I also know, even if you cannot remember, that there were times when you felt very special. Do you feel that way now?

Reading this book can ensure that those childhood daydreams do not turn into adult nightmares, if you choose for it to do so. The epitaph of so many people is "If only..." If only I had taken that chance; if only I had had the time; if only I had listened to myself; if only I had met the right person; if only I had got that promotion; if only I could win the lottery. I know you, and so know that, given the choice, you would not choose this epitaph. This book gives you that choice.

I know you. You have your own beliefs, some of which are very strongly held. Some of which serve you well. Others of which prevent you from becoming all that you can become. They stunt your emotional growth – growth that is essential for successful living. To maximize the benefits you derive from this book, I would ask but one thing of you. Suspend your disbelief. You do not allow what you believe to be possible or not to impair your enjoyment of a novel or a futuristic sci-fi movie. Do not allow it to reduce the benefits this book is about to bring to your life.

Each chapter will introduce you to a subject with which you may or may not have some familiarity. It matters not either way. I am certain that the material is so presented to yield an optimal return on your investment of time, measured in spiritual as well as material wealth.

This book will challenge you. However, right now you know all you need to know about living life successfully. Like me, you always have. The challenge comes from the fact that this inherent knowledge for successful living is not at the level of conscious awareness. It has been suppressed over time by the powerful messages you have received from everybody else about how you should live and about what constitutes success, most of which has been false and misguided, though (often) innocently so. Reading this book can help you release that knowledge from the depths of your subconscious being to your conscious reality.

Several media have been used to communicate each concept to you. They include satirical drawings, poignant quotations from people we may regard as successful, my own poetry at the beginning of each chapter and, of course, prose with a little dialogue thrown in.

Before proceeding to Chapter 1, please meditate awhile on Edward Everett Hale's quote at the beginning of this introduction. It embodies the mindset I encourage you to adopt while reading this book, with the intention of applying its principles in your life. And so, with this first chapter begins a new chapter in your life. Embrace it!

CHAPTER 1

THE MEANING OF LIFE

"Man's main concern is not to gain pleasure or to avoid pain, but rather to see a meaning in his life. That is why man is ever ready to suffer, on the condition, to be sure, that his suffering has a meaning."

– Viktor Frankl

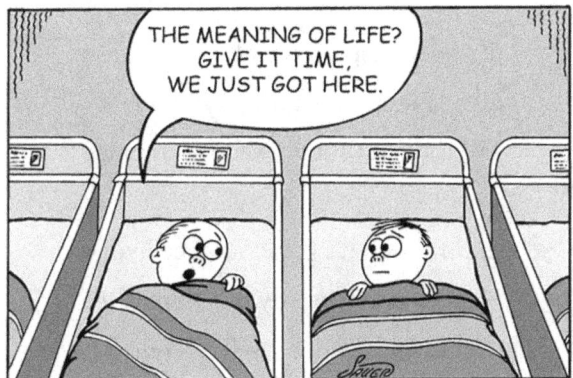

DEATH IS CHANGE IS LIFE

A tree has grown from a seed that's sown
The changing times its growth rings show
Of moments high and moments low
While the sands of time continually flow

It's been here now four hundred years
While history sped through many gears
This proud old son is still with peers
Whose wind bound seeds have lots more heirs

As time goes on its sap will seer
But who will care to shed a tear
Or make the time for soothing prayer
Who said that change was ever fair?

As man strives on our tree's now gone
It's been displaced by homes of taste
Erected in a mighty haste
Without a thought of love or grace

And though it's gone our tree lives on
Its life preserved by this here verse
inscribed upon itself of course
This paper now its new life force.

– LAC

THE MEANING OF LIFE

- What is the meaning of Life?

- What is the purpose of Life?

- Parable of the flea

- Get on purpose

- Be true to your responsible self

- Believe in yourself

- Live and let live

- Abundance vs. scarcity

- Learn to love

WHAT IS THE MEANING OF LIFE?

The best dictionary (New Standard Dictionary) definition I could find is that life is "the active principle of the existence of animals and plants…"

Is this really adequate? It fails to enlighten us as to what the very element, "the active principle" is and, therefore, brings us no closer to an understanding of the meaning of life. This is particularly true when one considers that at the quantum level animal and plant life are no different from objects regarded as inanimate, like minerals. Life, then, has to be something other than the physical mass we call our body. The active principle, life, takes the quantum material available to it and creates with it a physical manifestation of itself. Is this not what God does? I conclude that life is God. In the creation of man, God has input a creative ability. Thus, we are co-creators with the Creator. This gift of creation sets man apart from the rest of the animal kingdom. It has been gifted to us for a specific reason, that being to seek the purpose of life. It is our compass to find the way home, if you like. However, the compass did not come with an instruction manual, so our understanding of how best to use it must come from personal trial and error, until we try and succeed.

WHAT IS THE PURPOSE OF LIFE?

The purpose of life is the pursuit of success. Success, contrary to the conditioning we have received is, by its very nature, immeasurable. $1 million in net assets may lead one man to conclude he is successful where, for another, an annual income of $1 million may not satisfy his criteria for success. To yet another man, the raising of three healthy children, the love of a devoted wife, a dog named Rover and six goldfish may do the trick.

Because of conditioning, you may say that each man is a success by the criteria he has chosen to measure his success by. Success, by this definition, becomes a precarious, unstable and transient state of being. For, if the man whose only criteria for success is $1 million in net assets, suffers a misfortune reducing his net assets to $950,000, he is no longer successful. If the family of the man with the goldfish tragically dies, does this now render him unsuccessful?

To find success we must transcend materialism, and go beyond the attitude which says that "When I get X then I will be happy" or "If I had Y then I would be happy". Not only does this thinking render success a precarious proposition that, by definition, must be unstable and transient, it sets up most people for perpetual failure. Reaching beyond the material things in life that are mere representations of true success, we may ask ourselves, "What is it about these things that gives us the feeling of success?" The unequivocal answer is peace of mind. Success then, is nothing more than peace of mind. It is not physical or object. It is very much metaphysical and subject; subject to the beholder. It is an immeasurable internal state of being which impacts our external world.

Now, lest we fall into the trap of thinking that one who sets the bar of success so low that that he may find peace of mind in any bar that serves liquor, let us be cognizant of Abraham Maslow's admonition that:

> "A musician must make music, an artist must paint,
> a poet must write, if he is to be at peace with himself.
> What a man can be, he must be."

Thus in co-creation, we are called to strive, to stretch ourselves.

True success is permanent. It withstands physical losses – money, loved ones, property, et al. It is the state of being toward which all humans strive, knowingly or otherwise, in their good deeds and their bad, in their love and in their hatred, in their giving and in their taking.

It is my contention that peace of mind, happiness and freedom are all different ways of expressing success and, as such, are the same. After all, when one says I am happy, what is the happiness about? Going beyond the object, for example, passing an exam, finding a romantic partner, coming into money – the state of being promoting the feeling of happiness is success (a state of mind). Similarly, when one says "I have freedom;" freedom from what? The object may be oppression, financial difficulties, time constraints and so on, but behind the object is success (a state of mind).

The question then is: "If success is not inherent in objects, how might I pursue it?" After all, if it is just happiness, peace of mind and freedom, it is no more than a feeling, a state of emotional being. The key is in the statement that it is "a state of emotional being". As such, success is totally within our control. Events or objects may affect our emotional state, but be clear that we allow them to do so.

"Two men sat behind prison bars, one saw mud, the other saw stars." There are numerous accounts, particularly related to prisoner of war camps, clearly demonstrating that one's attitude of mind is the fundamental difference between those who survive and those who perish. Or, if you like, that freedom (success) is a state of mind, controlled by one's indomitable self and not by those who care to exert influence upon that self. To achieve a greater understanding of this, I would urge you to read (or re-read) Viktor Frankl's *Man's Search for Meaning* or Aleksandra Solzhenitsyn's *The Gulag Archipelago*.

I do not suggest that, in what one might call everyday life, the achievement of such a permanent state of mind (success) is easy. It can be a life's work. It is the purposeful pursuit of this everlasting success that is the ongoing purpose of life, and the very pursuit is the barometer of purposeful living.

It is no wonder that in meditation, or subsumed in the midst of a thick forest, people have been known to feel a sense of being with God, since such circumstances can induce a total state of peace of mind.

PARABLE OF THE FLEA

Freddie Flower was born to a family of performing fleas. Both parents' ancestries were rich with generations of performing fleas. Their home, located within a glass jar – the space in which is referred to by the elders as the universe – has been in the Flower's family for four generations.

Life in Freddie's world, Fleadom, is very sterile and regimented. It is governed by a Council of Elders. Their main reference in determining law is *The Tenets of Fleadom*, believed to be circa 1,000 years old. The Elders' strict interpretation of *The Tenets of Fleadom* leaves little scope for individuals to decide how a good citizen should live. It perpetuates the values of Fleadom's founding fathers in a language barely understood by most who read it today. Ingesting the contents of *The Tenets of Fleadom* by rote is the first and deemed most important lesson a young flea learns at school. Indeed, conscientious parents, like the Flowers, ensure that their children are able to recite whole passages from *The Tenets of Fleadom* prior to attending school.

In common with many young fleas, Freddie became disenchanted with the restrictive life he was forced to lead. Many of those he grew up with turned to a life of crime to channel their energy and relieve the boredom. Something deep inside Freddie prevented him from following this path. Rather, he sought guidance from Mr. Berry, an Elder who was a family friend he had become close to over the years. Elder Berry was a wise and inspirational figure.

One day, Freddie was feeling particularly directionless so he immediately called upon Elder Berry for guidance. "Freddie, the truth is beyond the universe as we know it. Seek solace in the dignity of your work. You are a talented flea, and, like your grandfather before you, have the ability to become the greatest performing flea of your generation. Go Freddie. Go and become all that you are capable of becoming. Channel your energies into your work." This Freddie did with gusto. In no time at all, twelve months had passed by. Freddie worked so hard that his dedication and superior talent ensured his progress to Flea Master in charge of all the performing fleas. The youngest flea ever to achieve this lofty status, Freddie rightly felt proud.

At the same time, every day, six days a week, the bell would ring, just as it has done for generations of performing fleas. On the sound of the bell, Freddie would lead his colleagues in their athletic motions – gloriously complex routines requiring the utmost agility on a plethora of apparatus. A sight to behold, it truly was.

A further twelve months went by as quickly as the first. "Elder Berry, I have been Flea Master for twelve months. I do enjoy my job; the responsibility, the challenge of improving already high standards and, above all, the camaraderie.

But this is it for me. I can go no further. I am at the pinnacle of my career. There is nothing left for me. I grow more despondent every day. What should I do?"

"Remember, young flea, the truth is beyond the universe as we know it. There are no limits, but those we impose on ourselves." This message served only to confuse Freddie. Nevertheless, he absorbed himself in his work, extracting whatever pleasures he could from it.

A decade passed and then another. Freddie received news that his great mentor, Elder Berry, was gravely ill and so to his bedside he rushed. In the two decades that had passed, Freddie had seen less and less of Elder Berry and felt guilty about this, knowing that the lower frequency of his visits to Elder Berry coincided with a greater need in Elder Berry for company as he grew older. On arrival to visit Elder Berry, Freddie was shocked at the seriousness of his condition. It was as though the life force, once so strong in this flea of wisdom, had been sucked out and dissipated into the ether. It was clear to Freddie that the great teacher was soon to be gone. Soon to shed the burden of responsibilities for the many fleas, like Freddie, who keenly sought his wisdom.

"Elder Berry, it's me – Freddie. I came as soon as I heard news of you."

Elder Berry was quick to seize on Freddie's gingerly tone.

"Young flea, is that a note of sorrow in your voice? It betrays your pity. I want no pity from you, just love. Can you do that for me, Freddie?"

"If it is what you want, yes."

"Then good. How are you these days? I haven't seen you for some time."

Oh, dear, that feeling of guilt comes rushing to the surface of Freddie's mind.

"I… I'm fine. I'm so sorry I haven't been to see you in a while, what with work and…"

"Freddie, I want you to understand something. Understand it with your heart and not with your mind. I love you. And, because I love you, I expect nothing from you. If you love me, you too will expect nothing from me. There is no need to feel guilt for what you have or have not done for me. Do you understand, Freddie?"

"Um, I think so."

"Good, that's a start at least. I am about to die…"

Freddie twitched with this cold confirmation of what his senses had been screaming at him.

"See, there you go again."

"I'm sorry, I can't help it."

"I am about to die and of this you should have no expectations."

"But I'm going to miss you."

"Precisely. You are going to miss me. You cannot see beyond the veil of your own self-interest. You know nothing of death so cannot possibly have expectations of it. What you are feeling is the result of the expectations you have about your life after my death. Can you see the folly in this, Freddie?"

"Umm...."

"Anyway, enough of this. It is not why you are here. Freddie, I believe in you and want to leave you a gift that endorses my belief. Often I have said to you that the truth is beyond the universe as we know it. Well, it is."

At this moment, Elder Berry was staring Freddie straight in the eyes, and with that passed away peacefully.

A remorseful Freddie was more confused over these words than ever he had been.

Months later, in preparation for a performance, Freddie was engrossed in his work. Suddenly the ground beneath him began to shake violently. His circus apparatus were thrown in all directions. Fleas were running for cover from what, they knew not. Amid the confusion, Freddie recalled a teaching at the hands of Elder Berry during which he was told of a great quake that shattered the world. The world in which his grandfather was known to be the greatest performing flea, with Elder Berry one of his performing pupils. In that quake his grandfather died.

Bang! Crash! The walls of the universe shattered and with that the foundations of Freddie's myopic beliefs had shattered. What he previously believed to be a perplexing metaphor was a literal truth. For what had happened was that the young daughter of the flea circus owner dropped the jam jar which housed the performing fleas, thereby shattering their world. The Universe had expanded and so too Freddie's understanding of the truth. He now knew of human beings, of dogs on which other flea tribes made their home and many other phenomena. Suddenly, his hitherto senseless existence became more palatable. Sure, he did not know everything and sure, the expanded universe raised more questions than it had answered. But this was somehow all okay. The owner of the flea circus rounded up all the fleas with the help of his hapless daughter and put them in a new jar with brand new apparatus.

It wasn't long before Fleadom got back to normal with one significant difference. Freddie's new understanding made him stand out among his fellow fleas. So much so that in increasing numbers they would seek his counsel. Inevitably, Freddie was elected onto the Council of Elders. Elder Flower was to become the most visionary and inspiring Elder Fleadom had ever known.

Can you relate this parable to your own life? Its morals include:

- Things are not always as they seem, as our understanding of what is, is limited. In the light of this knowledge, embrace new discoveries;

- Whatever skills you require to succeed are already inherent in you. It is never too late to change what you are doing or your attitude toward what you are doing. This is no different for you as an individual as it is for a company struggling to survive by producing terrestrial telephones in the face of an explosively changing market of global communications. It would have to shift its attitude from that of telephone manufacturer to that of communications company, for which its current skills are ample for it to play a significant role in the expanding market;

- What you are doing right now can propel you to success, provided you accept the necessity for change;

- Sometimes it takes a personal trauma like the shattering of Fleadom to urge us into the active pursuit of our dreams.

GET ON PURPOSE

Getting on purpose is a process of self-discovery toward success. In the remaining chapters of this book you will be given the opportunity to see life from a perspective that you may never before have considered. But like all opportunities, it does not have to be taken. That decision rests solely with you. If taken, however, it will be an aid in your progress toward success.

In getting on purpose, there are two fundamental questions that need to be asked. The first is: "Who am I?" Well, who are you? When asked the question, do you give your name? Do you tell people that you are a butcher, baker or candle-stick maker? Is what you do for a living a true representation in your eyes of who you are? Are you the letters that appear after your name? Maybe you are more elaborate in your answer. Perhaps you would say that you are a spiritual being who elected to come to earth to learn the lessons necessary to progress to the next level. Maybe so, but what lessons? What next level? There are more questions than answers. It seems the more we find out the less we know. It is not an easy question to answer and one's view of the answer may change in one's pursuit of success. That it is difficult to answer does not alleviate our responsibility to continually ask ourselves the question. Not in some tortuous way but in a calm manner expectant of an answer.

The second question is: "Why am I here?" The Spanish philosopher, Jose Ortega, says that, "We are here to write, act out and produce our own drama," which is a delightfully poetic way of saying that we are here to create our own success – peace of mind, happiness, freedom. Getting on purpose is about you, through a process of self-discovery, determining what drama you will write, act out and produce.

Self-discovery is a process of trial and error. Jesus' forty days and forty nights in the wilderness is an appropriate metaphor. It is an unavoidable part of finding success. Personal growth (positive change) is a prerequisite for success. I see it as a great adventure. Like an Indiana Jones movie, it is action-packed. You are the hero. The just outcome relies on you. You will get into all sorts of apparently dangerous scenarios. Apparent, because you know the hero always survives. You will go to places and meet people, some of whom you imagine to be helpful to you, while others are not so. In truth, they are all in the right place at the right time. Without meeting them, without their influence, you could not be who you are at any given moment. The universe is perfectly on purpose. You will experience joy, frustration, awakenings, loneliness, exhilaration, doubt, love, confusion and a host of other emotions along the way, but your courage, persistence and determination ensure a successful outcome.

So what will be the script for your particular drama? When you were a child you had a clear idea of what you wanted to be. A dancer, police officer, acrobat and so on. As you grew older, the conditioning of you by others – parents, teachers, friends, the media, politics, status, your neighborhood, fear, etc. doubted you out of it. Everyone who has achieved the success I refer to is pursuing activities that they enjoy. Like you, I know apparently successful bankers, doctors, entrepreneurs, artists, and so on who hate what they are doing but whose lifetime investment of time, emotions, education, money and other resources prevent them from ever seriously considering what else they might do. And, the criticism if they pursued their dream certainly does not bear thinking about.

Write your script around the things you enjoy. And please, don't allow ridicule and rejection to prevent you from doing so. These are inevitable. In breaking out and pursuing the dreams you want, your script may differ from the norm. People can be suspicious of that which is different. Also, you will be a constant (perhaps subconscious) reminder to others that they are leading lives of quiet desperation in which their conscience craves what their external life is not. It is, thus, congruent for them to encourage you to do what they are doing; which, if they are able to do, provides them with a degree of solace.

BE TRUE TO YOUR RESPONSIBLE SELF

Finding your internal compass (creativity) is not easy. In fact, it may be the greatest challenge that you face. Two characteristics observable in most people are that, given the choice:

1) They would rather have something for nothing than work for it; rather win the lottery than earn their millions. Most want power without the burden of responsibility. They want good health while living an unhealthy lifestyle.

    If they knew with certainty that they could either win $2 million on the lottery five years from now by simply playing the same numbers every week, or earn $2 million in five years by establishing their own business, confronting the challenges inevitable in such a venture, most would buy the $1 ticket every week. They do not subscribe to the adage, "There is no such thing as a free lunch." They believe that the worth they gained from $2 million won is equal to the worth gained from $2 million earned, and without the hard work to boot! The exceptionally important point of which they are ignorant is that the value in having $2 million goes beyond financial security and what they can buy with it. They will stop worrying about not having any money and start worrying about the stock market crashing or property prices falling or how to respond to begging letters from family and friends. They won't hear that internal voice that says the opportunity cost of buying a $1 ticket every week instead of earning their wealth is the lost opportunity for personal growth, which comes with the ups and downs of earning the $2 million, and that personal growth is a prerequisite for success. The $2 million earned would merely be the material evidence of their spiritual development in the pursuit of success. Thus, success is more about who we become than it is what we get.

We can all recall moments in our lives in which we strove to achieve something and, on reflection, the very endeavor made its achievement ever sweeter, more appreciated and more satisfying, and that, somehow having had to strive for it made us a better person. This is personal growth. It occurs when we go beyond what is comfortably achieved. If we do not perceive value and do not derive satisfaction from our endeavors they cannot bring peace of mind. The price of success is not like that for some new piece of technology, which, if we perceive to be too high, we may delay gratification in the knowledge that in, say, one year, it will fall to within an acceptable price range. It is not like the price of some trinket we may find in a bazaar where we may be expected to haggle. No. The price of success is fixed and is non-negotiable.

2) Most would shirk full and complete responsibility for all aspects of their lives. They elect governments to deliver what they think they want, the objects of peace of mind – security, money, law and order, housing, health care, and so on – and when the government doesn't deliver to satisfy their expectations, they blame them. In the meantime, they often blindly follow that same government's doctrine. They choose their enemies for them, tell them which foods are healthful and which are not, how much taxes to pay and then decide what they will be spent on.

Leo Tolstoy shares an unadulterated example of this transference or shirking of responsibility in his classic work, *The Kingdom of God is Within You*. Tolstoy asked a Russian soldier, called upon by the state to brutalize and murder the peasants from whence the soldier himself came for crimes that, if equity were a consideration, could not be considered crimes at all. "How can you kill people, when it is written in God's commandment: 'Thou shalt not kill'?" The soldier replied, "They must have found a law for it. The archbishops know as much about it as we do, I should hope." Tolstoy observes that this attitude is fortified by military code and quotes Article 87 of the then Russian army:

"To carry out exactly and without comment the orders of a superior officer means: To carry out an order received from a superior officer exactly without considering whether it is good or not, and whether it is possible to carry it out. The superior officer is responsible for the consequences of the order he gives."

What about you? Do you carry out Article 87 in the context of work or home as either the superior officer or the solider?

Most will shirk responsibility whenever they feel it safe to do so. You have to unearth your own compass and pursue your own unique path to success, and not one given to you by mom, dad, teacher, preacher, politician or guru, for, say, "A man convinced against his will is of the same opinion still."

To be so convinced is to live life contrary to the demands of your conscience which cannot bring peace of mind. Further, to conform to the two aforementioned human characteristics is tantamount to giving away your creative force, without which you will never be successful.

Our ability to abandon the search for freedom is made possible by a self-inflicted psychological inertia. This state of being reveals itself in our ignoring the truth. We convince ourselves that our lifestyle is what we want and is perfectly consistent with truth (what our conscience craves). Such self-delusion is born of the desire to shirk our personal responsibility in the struggle for freedom. This struggle is deemed to be more painful than the acquiescent submission to the life of quiet desperation which so many of us choose. The reality is that we suppress the cravings of our conscience in favor of the lifestyle we choose. So, a man may believe that he ought to stop smoking because it is damaging to good health, but convinces himself that he cannot because he is addicted to it. It is within his power to stop, but the transference of responsibility away from self to addiction makes it acceptable for him not to. The addiction is to blame and not him. He can claim no power over it. After all, the psychologists and doctors agree with him. His conscience may tell him that smoking in public is unfair to non-smokers but he convinces himself that to not smoke in public would be an infringement of his freedom. The transference of responsibility away from self to the (misguided) concept of freedom fortifies his psychological inertia and eases his conscience.

But what is an addiction? The dictionary will tell you it is the dependence upon a harmful habit. I would add to the word dependence the word submission to make it clear that the addict does have the power to overcome the addiction. To say, "I cannot give up smoking because I am addicted to it," is to relinquish responsibility for continuing to choose the habit. That way, one can blame some external power over which one may claim to have no control.

When does a smoker stop smoking? He stops when the desire for better health and greater social responsibility outweigh the desire to be a victim of his addiction. The addiction is no more. In awakening to the reality that smoking is not for him, he regains control of his ability to respond (responsibility).

With responsibility comes the duty of awareness. It is up to us to find out, if we don't know. The laws of nature are ambivalent to one's knowledge of them. They are true regardless. Jumping off a ten-story building will pretty much have the same effect on he who knows and understands the laws of gravity as it would on he who has never heard of gravity or its effects. Similar, too, are the laws and actions of man. "I did not know" is a poor defense in the hour of need.

BELIEVE IN YOURSELF

We cannot have too much self-belief. It is the elixir that picks us up when we are down. A healthy self-belief is evidenced by a positive outlook toward life. The first step toward an abundance of self-belief is to know that no one is better than you are. Each of us is blessed with talents, of which some are stronger than others. Recognizing and then developing those talents, that we know (sometimes only deep inside) will propel us toward success, is a basic essential in the journey to success. Alan Sugar, the former Chairman of Amstrad Computers and Tottenham Hotspur PLC, started his business life as a market trader. Sylvester Stallone hawked the script for Rocky around numerous film makers before achieving box office success. Mostly, he was turned down. On the odd occasion he received an offer to purchase the script, he refused. The prospective purchaser would not agree to Stallone playing the leading role. His hunger, through lack of food, was over-ridden by his hunger to become an actor. His belief in this was so strong that he held out until eventually he got what he wanted.

I was once asked by a mentor if I knew of anyone more unfit, ugly and stupid than I, but whom I regarded as more successful. The list was long. He was trying to help me to see that so called advantage had little to do with success. To believe that we are disadvantaged compared to someone else is no more than our excuse for not succeeding. We say to whomever will listen, "I would, but I haven't got enough money"; "I would, but I don't have the education"; I would, but I haven't got the time"; I would, but I have the family to think about"; "I would, but I don't know how". If you suffer from this, just make sure that every day you are doing something to go forward, no matter how small a step it might be. That way your "BUT" always remains behind you, where it belongs, and so cannot get in your way!

It is not a good idea to continually compare yourself to others. You are unique. You cannot be them and they cannot be you. Concentrate on your own abilities. Be the best you possibly can. Everything you need for success is already within. There is a story of an old African farmer, told by the late Russell Conwell. The farmer toiled on his land for many years. Not satisfied with the living it was providing, he decided to sell up and risk his entire wealth prospecting for diamonds on the hearsay of others. He traveled far to where the other prospectors were. After two years of unsuccessful prospecting, he returned home penniless to work as a hand for the new owner of the farm. One day, while digging a field, he came across an old rock which he cast aside in view of his employer. On inspection, his employer realized immediately that the rock was, in fact, a diamond. The new owner then prospected his acres of land and discovered many more diamonds, making him a very wealthy man.

Often we search for success by going out and reading the next book, getting the next degree, attending the next seminar or consulting the latest guru. Before we know it our search for that advantage, that edge, becomes procrastination. Emerson said, "Do the thing and you shall have power." By all means seek to improve yourself in whatever way you believe to be right, including being guided by, coached and taught by others. You are your best judge. But don't allow some notion of perfection or lack of knowledge to prevent you from using the talents you have right now to progress to success.

Sometimes when we look for diamonds at home we do not see them, prompting us to believe that we are less than others, and so, allow our big "BUT" to get in the way once more. If we cannot see the diamonds when we look, it is simply because we are looking for the polished, cut, finished article. Diamonds in-the-rough are not that way. They can be mistaken for pieces of worthless rock. It is our responsibility to add value to our diamonds by polishing, cutting and finishing them ourselves.

LIVE AND LET LIVE

Just think of how much time and effort we invest in being right and making others wrong; winning in the wake of others losing. Go beyond seeing just right and wrong. Choose a different perspective on what is. Given the choice, choose to be effective rather than right. In the final section of this chapter, *Learn to love*, I will show that there is no winning in the wake of another's losing. To perceive a win when another loses is to perceive an illusion of corporeal existence.

To live and let live requires immense tolerance and patience. It requires us to see all others as our equal. Everything about us is expressed in relation to other people. It has been said that 85% of our satisfaction is derived from interaction with others, while only 15% comes from personal achievements. Right now, think of one thing you would like to achieve. Now, imagine that no one but you knows that you have achieved it. How do you feel? Has it lost some if its appeal? Given that 85% of our satisfaction comes from relations with others, it must follow that the pursuit of good relationships is necessary to achieve success. Ralph Waldo Emerson said: "An individual has a healthy personality [a lifestyle congruent with his conscience] to the exact degree to which he has the propensity to look for the good in every situation," which, of course, would include looking for the good in other people. The psychologist, Brian Tracy in *The Psychology of Achievement*, refers to a psychological study from which it was concluded that, "An individual has a healthy personality to the exact degree to which he can get along with the greatest number of other types of people." Conversely, I suppose, an individual who only gets on with others of similar beliefs and lifestyle is among those with the unhealthiest of personalities.

There can be an overwhelming urge to assume that we know what is best for someone else. This occurs particularly where we allow the belief that our age, experience, special knowledge, upbringing or other trait, bestows an advantage over someone else. A common example of this is that of a parent shoehorning a child into, say, a career the child does not care for. No one can know what is best for another person unless that other person tells them. This may be so even in the case of a newly born infant. In love with the infant, we can only do what instinctively and through knowledge we believe to be right. Some mothers feed on demand, others prefer a more uniform program; some mothers are committed to breast feeding, others swear by the bottle; some mothers believe that dairy milk is best, while others choose a non-dairy alternative. So which combination of these choices is best for a child? Perhaps all we can say is that we know the child needs nourishment if he is to not perish. This, however, cannot be viewed as superior knowledge since the child knows this too! We should not confuse the need of our conscience to be responsible (in this case for the child) with our knowing what is best. Kahlil Gibran says it best in his writing on children:

> "Your children are not your children.
> They are the sons and daughters
> of life's longing for itself.

The sentiments expressed in this verse of Gibran's great poem can be applied to other relationships: employer-employee, teacher-pupil, government-citizen, to name a few. For such a relationship to exist one has to trust and be trusted, to love and be loved.

Live and let live means looking for the good in others. It means if we cannot find something good to say about someone to say nothing at all. It is perfectly reasonable to not like everything about someone we meet. However, many of us enter relationships on that basis with a secret agenda to change the things we do not like, thereby establishing the "perfect" relationship for ourselves. What we do not bargain for is that the other person may never change, which we then allow to be the source of eternal friction on the relationship or the cause of its ultimate demise. What's more, we do not stop there. We blame the other person's "faults" for our long suffering and the ruin of the relationship. Far better if we hold no expectations of another. Do not expect them to treat you well or be faithful.

Rather, replace your expectations of them with a commitment from yourself to live consistently with your conscience. Seek to treat others as you would be treated. Compliment and praise others when it is appropriate to do so. Do not castigate them when you think they have done wrong. Learn to separate their behavior from who they are. See each person as a human-being not a human-doing. Make them feel important and accepted for who they are. When we act in this way, two magical things happen:

1) People treat us in the same way; and

2) The behaviors for which we give positive feedback will be repeated. Why? Because we all like to be accepted, complimented, praised and made to feel important.

To live and let live requires us to make a positive contribution. It is common for us in our endeavors to consider what will be our gain. The phrase, "What's in it for me?" is as commonplace in contemporary society as is McDonald's, Coca-Cola and divorce, and from a psychic perspective possibly more damaging to our wellbeing than any of these. A far more productive consideration would be, 'What contribution can I make that will add value to society?" The research of Peter Drucker in the business arena has proven the beneficial nature of this outlook to those companies who adopt it. It can work with equal effect in the personal, educational, political, family and religious arenas. Let us replace the phrase, "What's in it for me?" with, "How may I serve you?"

To live and let live is to recognize the value of cooperation above competition. This is well illustrated in a business context. Let us take two bars geographically close to each other from apparently competing bar operators. In the spirit of competition, they would be loath to share ideas or to help each other in any way. The result is that each continues with its limited understanding of how best to operate a bar, each cutting prices and creating other marketing and promotional initiatives to win market-share. In such an "I win, you lose" contest each, to a degree, will harbor thoughts of loss. Each may harbor a certain degree of animosity toward the other.

In the spirit of cooperation, the two bars will share ideas on what has worked and what not. One will provide a backup source of change if the other is short, loan the odd bottle of spirit until the other's delivery arrives later in the week and so on. Each reciprocating in this way will ensure a smoother running of both bars, thereby providing a higher level of service. They may even conduct joint marketing and promotional activity to attract more customers to the area. In so doing, if one attracts, say, 10% more business while the other only 5%, they are still both better off than under the regime of strict competition. Before you cry "monopolistic practices" or "cartel", let me assure you, I'm not advocating a regime of price fixing or product standardization in any way. Remember, they are both operating under the aegis of different parent companies, setting objectives and prices separately from each other, and promoting their individual Unique Value Propositions. Customer choice is not compromised in any way.

What then, if a third, say, very much larger bar operated by a third group locates nearby? Fantastic! There is an increase in supply of market knowledge, back up change and short term loan of product, not to mention more competition which encourages each to improve its offering. We thus see another improvement in customer choice and service. What's more, if the new arrival is successful, it will attract more people into the area, some of whom will find bars one and two more suitable to their taste than bar three which originally attracted them. Everyone's a winner!

ABUNDANCE VS. SCARCITY

A belief in scarcity is a key factor in our not achieving success. The two main areas in which we allow a scarcity mentality to restrict us are opportunities and resources. We are taught that opportunity only comes around once and if it is missed that is it. While it would be folly not to seize an opportunity that you want if the circumstances are right, it is also folly to suggest that other opportunities will not arise for you. A soccer player may miss the opportunity to score a goal, but if he continues doing the right things, other opportunities to score will arise. A corporate executive may miss out on the opportunity to become CEO of his company, but if he continues to perform to the required standard, the opportunity will arise again either within the present company or another. This executive, like you, should be committed to the goal and not the means by which it is pursued.

The opportunity to establish a business in whatever field you desire is limited only to the degree to which you accept to be limited in your thinking. Market saturation does not exist. In 1979, a young barrister, Tim Martin, bought a pub in London. At that time, it is fair to say, the demand for high street pubs in London was considered to be well satisfied. However, by being different and raising standards, his entry into this market caused an explosion of new growth. His company, Wetherspoon PLC, has managed to attract people into its pubs who, hitherto, would not have dared enter the seedy, misty-windowed, smoke-filled, archetypal high street pub of the past. The implementation of service standards, cleanliness and product quality commensurate with high profile, chain store retailers brought success to the company, and importantly, expanded the marketplace. Several other new entrants followed suit. The company received a full stock market listing in 1992. At the time of writing, Wetherspoon has over 1,000 pubs with turnover exceeding $3 billion and 35,000 plus employees.

The new pub companies created in the wake of Wetherspoon include Regent Inns, Tom Cobleigh, Hobgoblin, The Magic Pub Company, Surrey Free Inns, and The Old Monk Pub Company. In turn, the traditional brewers responded by establishing their own brands such as Chef and Brewer (Scottish and Newcastle), O'Neill's (Bass), All Bar One (Bass), Festival Ale House (Allied Domecq), Friar Tuck (Greene King) and Hot Shots (Whitbread); or alternatively, have bought independents in order to participate in the revolution.

A belief in the scarcity of resources has been the main cause of war throughout the ages, with Nation States believing the most efficient way to wealth creation was through stealing it from others using aggression and colonization. This scarcity mentally exists because we crudely measure a physical resource in terms of its basic mass – X acres of land, Y tons of coal, Z barrels of oil – and determine its longevity by applying its outstanding mass to a given rate of consumption. Hence, if the world supply of oil is one hundred barrels (including expected discoveries) with an annual consumption rate of ten barrels, oil reserves will be exhausted in ten years. What the calculation does not cater for is technological advancement, which, for our purpose here, we can define as simply a more efficient way of doing things. So, if a barber using a pair of scissors and giving a maximum of twenty haircuts per working day can increase his productivity to forty per day by using an electric shaver, he has doubled his capacity through technological advancement.

In his book, *Unlimited Wealth*, economist Paul Zane Pilzer persuasively propounds an economic theory founded on the premise of unlimited resources. The one thing that all traditional schools of economics have agreed on is that we live in a world of scarce resources, and that economics is about the distribution of wealth created from those resources. One example he gives is that of oil, which, in the mid-1970s, was predicted to be running out. In the late '80s and early '90s, inflation-adjusted oil prices were lower than at any time since the 1960s with petroleum supplies overflowing. Pilzer explains that what happened was the invention of the $24 computerized fuel injector replacing the conventional $300 carburetor, doubling the fuel efficiency of new cars. This, in effect, doubled the supply of gasoline, thereby, increasing the "fixed" supply of oil. Technological advancement also impacted the ability to extract oil from sources previously unavailable with the old technology. Pilzer's conclusion is that fixed physical assets are less important than intellectual assets. Bear this in mind when reconciling your own personal balance sheet!

A source of support for this view comes from the balance sheets of many of today's most successful companies. The balance sheets of Microsoft, Apple Computers and other hi-tech companies features a significant financial value for intellectual assets. Such assets are known to boost the book value (net physical assets) of some companies by up to 100 times. Wealth, then, is being created from intellectual rather than physical assets. Andrew Carnegie might have said: "My financial wealth comes from my companies' steel mills" whereas today, Bill Gates might say: "My financial wealth comes from my companies' ideas". The former's wealth is limited by the measure of physical assets we looked at earlier. The latter's unlimited. There is a finite amount of physical matter that can be fit into a given sized glass jar. How many ideas can be fit into the same glass jar?

By the way, although it is my poetic license to ponder Andrew Carnegie saying that his financial wealth came from the ownership of his steel mills, the truth is that even they were just the material manifestation of his real wealth, the source of which, like all wealth, is spiritual.

A belief in scarcity often triggers an impulsive reaction to protect proprietary rights which can be a self-inflicted blow. Home video cassette recorders were first introduced in the mid-1970s. At the time, there were two competing systems, Sony's Betamax and JVC's VHS. Betamax was technologically superior. With this apparent market advantage, Sony's strategy was founded on preventing competing manufacturers from using its system in the hope that the consumer would select the superior product and thereby provide Sony with the biggest slice of the market. Contrastingly, JVC was aggressive in licensing hundreds of other manufacturers to produce VHS cassette recorders. The sheer volume of VHS cassette recorders available in the marketplace encouraged software manufacturers to offer a far wider selection of tapes in VHS format than in Betamax. Consequently, consumers' incentive to buy VHS over Betamax was greater still, as was retailers' willingness to stock and provide valuable shelf space to VHS over Betamax. By 1987, VHS machines had a 90% market share, and in 1988, Sony announced the manufacture of its own VHS cassette recorder.

OPEC's attempt in the early 1970s to control the supply and price of oil foundered in the wake of improved technology effectively increasing the supply of oil and, therefore, greatly reducing its price. The Hunt Brothers' attempt to control the supply of silver was thwarted when Kodak, the world's largest user, in fear of price increases developed photographic processes that used less and less silver, and sometimes none. Silver prices plunged and the Hunts were financially ruined.

So the more we believe in abundance, the greater is our propensity to share and the more everyone can have. You may say that while this is a compelling argument, in the very long run (5,000 million years) the sun is going to burn out, which signals the end for all sentient life on planet earth. While you may have to collect your winnings on "the other side" if I'm wrong, I'm prepared to wager a $1 to a penny that between now and the demise of the sun, further technological advancement will allow humankind to populate other planets. In the universe there are 100,000 million galaxies, each with a 100,000 million stars. We live in one small galaxy called the Milky Way. If we traveled at the speed of light (11,600,000 miles per hour) it would take approximately 100,000 years to get from one end of our galaxy to the other. What, then, is the probability of another planet somewhere in the universe being capable of supporting human life? Well, if only one planet in each of those galaxies had the potential for the necessary conditions to support human life, and if only one in every one million of these actually had the appropriate conditions, we would have human life supporting conditions on at least 100,000 other planets in the universe!

If we take the debate to its logical conclusion, you could counter with: "Okay, but if our sun can burn out so can all others in the universe." True, but that's okay. The latest thinking in cosmology, elaborated in several books including The Life of the Cosmos by physicist, Lee Smolin, suggests that our universe is not everything as physicists once believed, but one of many universes, each expanding from its own singularity (point of infinite density), having experienced its own big bang. Stephen Hawking and Roger Penrose established as far back as the 60's that singularities also exist at the heart of black holes. Our expanding universe is explained by the same mathematical model as a collapsing black hole, but with the opposite direction of time. The thinking is, if the diversity of our universe with galaxies, stars, planets and organic life has been created from the singularity in which it was born, within a black hole, could not something similar be happening to the singularities at the heart of other black holes? If the premise is true, it means that there is a path to other universes through black holes. Our universe is but one of a population of universes interconnected by what physicists call worm holes. How do we travel through a worm hole? I do not know, but a $1 to a penny says that the sons and daughters of future generations will know. If I am wrong, you know where to collect your winnings!

The foregoing science-speak sounds a tad like the eternity that theologians have propounded since the dawn of theology. I have but one dollar left for one more wager, and that is that those same sons and daughters of future generations will, when the penny finally drops, realize – once and for all – that science and religion have always been observing the same coin: one from the perspective of Heads, the other from that of Tails.

LEARN TO LOVE

When asked about their first recollection of love, a fair percentage may recall that first kiss behind the bike shed at school, or some similar event. But, is that feeling really love? Rather than "I love you," often it would be more appropriate in a romantic setting for one partner to say to the other, "I lust for you." It is a more accurate assessment of what they are feeling. True love is the currency of life, the ultimate medium of exchange. It is enduring and, within each of us, infinite. As the size of one's family grows, the love bestowed on each member is not proportionately diminished. In a loving relationship, the sum of the parts is greater than the parts, so we may liken such a relationship to a bridge. Together the two pillars comfortably bear the burden of the bridge, but apart would be incapable of bearing the burden of just half the bridge. The ground conditions on each side of the bridge differ so, while the pillars have to work together to support the bridge (the loving relationship), so too does each have to make decisions independent of the other to best manage the conditions in which their foundations are set.

Love is a verb, not an adjective; active, not passive. It is a commitment to the personal growth of another; the sacrificing of self for another. Love shows no favor. Shakespeare wrote, "The fragrance of the rose lingers on the hand that cast it." Equally, it lingers on the hand that caresses it.

Sadly, my first recollection of love was not behind the bike shed. In fact, I do not recall my school ever having a bike shed! For me, it is a completely different event. As a child, I was fascinated by squirrels so much so that during the run up to my 12th birthday, I demanded a squirrel as a birthday present. Mum (I grew up in England) said she would see what she could do. On the big day, a cage in the kitchen, veiled by a cloth, was rattling away with the sound of my squirrel. Excited though I was, I waited for the rest of the family to rise before the unveiling. Well, the moment had arrived and Mum whipped off the cloth.

> "What's that?" I shrieked. "It's not a squirrel".

> "No," said Mum, "it's a guinea pig. I could not get a squirrel anywhere."

> "I don't want that fat rat. I want a squirrel."

Mum, genuinely having searched the stores for a "pet" squirrel – really – was rather angry at my thoughtless, ungrateful outburst.

> "Okay, young man, your brothers can have the guinea pig and you shan't have a birthday present at all. Now go to your room."

That night I dreamed that Mum was successful in securing a squirrel for my birthday. The bushy-tailed ball of fun walked and ran around its carousel wheel, dined avariciously on the nuts I fed it, and generally did all I needed it to do to please me. In my dream, days had lapsed. I grew a little bored of the squirrel in its cage and thought, "I'm sure it would prefer being able to run about the house freely." So I released it, leaving the cage door open so it could feed whenever it so desired. My companion seemed altogether happier, exploring parts of the house even I had no knowledge of. A great thought came to me. "It's enjoying itself so much in the house, what if I let it play in the garden? After all, it is more like its natural habitat." I followed through. The back door was opened and away it went climbing trees with a verve no squirrel had exhibited hitherto. I left the cage door open as usual for it to feed. A day went by, and then two. After a week, I realized it was not coming back. I awoke from my dream in a stream of tears. As my awakening consciousness grew, I began to realize that my sense of loss was for me and not my squirrel, which was happily bounding trees and dining in the best places nature had to offer. It was happy. My feeling of loss was suddenly transmuted to a feeling of selfishness. I ran downstairs and recounted my dream to Mum. "So what have you learned?" she asked. "That love is about giving the ones you love the freedom to do as they wish, even if that means the freedom to leave you." Mum must have been impressed with this answer for she let me have the guinea pig back. This proved to be the first of three guinea pigs that my siblings and I had a loving relationship with as we grew up in the light of our parents' own love for us.

As the proverb states, no man is an island. Successful living is dependent upon each of us relating well to others. Learning to truly love others, whether they would cast the rose or caress it dearly, brings success ever closer. "Father, forgive them, for they know not what they do" (Luke 23:34). By this, Jesus was referring to the unity of all. To paraphrase his meaning would be to say, "They could not harm me if they realized that to do so is to inescapably harm themselves." In embracing the unity of all, we learn to love without favor.

There are two basic proofs of this unity; one biblical, the other scientific.

Biblical proof

From Genesis, we learn that: "In the beginning God created the heavens and the earth… Then God said, 'let us make man in our image…' God formed the man from the dust of the ground and breathed into his nostrils the breath of life, and the man became a living being… God caused the man to fall into a deep sleep; and while he was sleeping, he took one of the man's ribs and closed up the place with flesh… God made a woman from the rib… God blessed them and said to them, 'Be fruitful and increase in number'… Adam named his wife Eve, because she would become the mother of all the living."

Scientific proof

The universe was formed about 14 billion years ago from a point of infinite density known as a singularity. An explosion – the big bang – at the heart of the singularity caused the universe to expand into what we now witness as the universe. Thus, everything in the universe was born from the pre-exploded singularity and is, therefore, inescapably related to everything else in the universe.

Whether we metaphorically or literally subscribe to Adam and Eve's own "big bang" to conceive humankind or to the scientific big bang, each is a compelling proof of the unity of all. So, are we now going to go forth and love our fellow man as ourselves? Probably not. And why not? Because we cling on through psychological inertia – our unwillingness to grow – to three redundant beliefs. Our belief in:

a) Our separateness from others. We are able to accept our unity intellectually, but not emotionally;

b) In scarcity. If he has it, I cannot. Therefore, I must deprive him of it so that I may have it; and

c) In the finality of death.

These beliefs compel us to live our lives in fear, the antithesis of love. True love comes from reversing these beliefs so that we believe in:

a) Unity;

b) Abundance; and

c) Everlasting life

We are each a droplet in the ocean of life. The loss of even the smallest droplet reduces the material mass of the ocean. But what of the droplet? Interaction with other forces may change it into ice, vapor and maybe back to water. Yet no phenomenon can destroy it.

CHAPTER 2

UNDERSTANDING VALUES

"A people that values its privileges above its principles soon loses both."

– Dwight Eisenhower

FROM THE WOMB TO THE TOMB

Oh gosh, I'm born, my world is torn,
I've been thrown from home, the peace of the womb.
But now I'm blessed, suckling mother's breast,
And so to rest in my new nest;

At 14 years of age, not yet a sage, I'm filled with rage,
So difficult to gauge the next chapter or page,
Seen by so many as just a mere knave,
And, well to my parents, I'm a bloody good slave;

At 25, I leave the hive,
And to prove I'm alive, I party and jive,
In a fit of lust, I grab her bust,
So now I must make her my first;

I'm still alive at 35,
But no longer, party and jive,
Supporting five in my own hive,
Pray God, when do I arrive?

Now 44, there must be more,
If I could open some other door,
My life would not be such a bore,
And perhaps I'd not remain so poor;

At 56, who needs new tricks,
Any change is but a transient fix,
Socialize? I cannot mix,
You do not seem to get my gist;

Now 67, I contemplate heaven,
Just ten years more to 77,
It's too late now to move to Devon,
With all the other elder brethren;

And now I'm dead, I rest my head,
Under the tombstone "Here lies Fred",
And while I'm gone, I know no wrong, no right,
My being is consumed by a loving, bright light.

– LAC

UNDERSTANDING VALUES

- Two women die
- What values are
- Why we have values
- Situational ethics
- Where values come from
- Where beliefs come from
- Experiments in conditioning
- Implications of learned helplessness
- Acceptability
- Remaining in control
- Involuntary conditioning
- Voluntary conditioning
- Conflicts of interest
- Double standards

TWO WOMEN DIE

Imagine two women, A and B, both of whom are noted for their contribution to others.

A's entire life has been devoted to serving others. Her possessions are few, having sacrificed the most basic of comforts to live in the manner of the desperate, forsaken poor whom she has served with distinction for 50 years. Her philosophy is that to serve these people with integrity, she must become one of them.

B, by virtue of marriage and title, holds a lofty position in society. She is enlisted by several charities to spearhead fundraising for worthy causes, at which she has become extremely adept. Intense media coverage of her activities ensures immense public awareness of her good deeds. Between campaigns she lives a high society lifestyle.

These women die within a few days of each other. Which of them, do you believe, deserves the greater adoration? Your answer to this question is neither right nor wrong, and is dependent upon your values.

A, Mother Teresa, was an elderly Catholic nun. Her life, though full, was particularly unglamorous. B, a beautiful British Princess, Diana, was extremely glamorous and somewhat controversial. She was the only person in decades to effectively raise a question mark in the minds of the British public about the role and value of the monarchy.

For a while in Britain, post-death interest in Diana was a politically and financially viable proposition for corporations, institutions and individuals. The same cannot be said of Mother Teresa.

What do you believe affects your feelings toward one compared to the other? What, if anything, has this question and your answer contributed to your understanding of your values and where they come from?

In the rest of this chapter, we shall look at understanding values, where they come from, and how they affect our living successful lives.

WHAT VALUES ARE

Values are most often defined as a laundry list of items:

Love

Courage

Safety

Faith

Honor

Risk

Security

I do not believe that these "ideas" are values *per se*. The ideas only become values when we prescribe a meaning to them. And so, Love, for example, may be quite a different value for one person compared to another. The moment we become aware of any of these ideas we own it and cannot get rid of it. It literally becomes part of our very being in a physical as well as emotional sense. The meaning ascribed to each idea is formed through personal and third-party exposure to them. Various encounters with each idea continue to form and reform each one in our minds. As the idea changes in the mind, so too does our emotional and physical embodiment of it. Thus, Love may begin in the mind, emotions and body of a child as a pleasant idea, only to be reformed in the now abused child as a painful idea. And yet, this same child may see other (third-party) persons holding Love as a pleasant idea for which they are prepared to risk a great deal, even their very lives.

We have more control over the meanings we ascribe to the ideas and, therefore, how we value them than we give ourselves credit for. To gain and exercise that control requires a great deal of maturity, which is not to be confused with age. As the aforementioned child grows older, he can become more adept at choosing his personal world by exercising his spiritual faculties of imagination, will and so on. While he may require professional help to value the idea differently, it is absolutely possible to do so; otherwise, we definitely live in a deterministic universe in which we cannot shape our own destinies, but are victors or victims at the whim of chance. I have never met a truly successful person who pays any credence to such an idea, even for a nanosecond.

To successfully transmute Love from a painful to a pleasurable value will usually require reliance on other values being held positively. In particular, courage, patience and self-determination. The "bundle of ideas" held by the successful individual is ascribed values that align with the Positive Mental Attitude (PMA) common in such individuals. Success absolutely requires that our values are pointing North, if that is the direction in which we intend to walk.

Values are a set of guiding principles or rules by which an individual interprets events. They are his map of the world. His reality filters through them to him. Though values may be similar between individuals, there are as many Value Systems (bundle of values held by an individual) as there are individuals. Therefore, each of us has a different reality; a different interpretation of what the world is. This awareness clearly has major implications in our understanding of what is required for success. Indeed, success may be defined as the continued adjustment to the meanings we ascribe to ideas, such that those ideas serve to enhance our personal growth. The way we hold these ideas may be changed through coaching, counseling, education, practical experience and sheer willpower, to name a few means.

The individual once paralyzed by the idea of taking a financial risk and who, through education, coaching and a burning desire to succeed, overcomes the fear of doing so, will be observed to have also gained in confidence, courage and willpower, the propensity to delay gratification and so on. Thus, a change in how we hold (value) one idea will automatically change how we hold other values. A change in one value to align with the direction in which we are going will have others following suit; a change in one value to align against the direction in which we are going will have others following suit in that undesirable direction also. A rising tide will lift all boats and a falling tide will lower all boats. The laws governing the alignment of values are spiritual, the laws governing boats rising and falling on tides, are physical.

We must resist the temptation to regard how we value any particular idea as Good or Bad. It is best to consider our values in the light that Rumi encourages in his quotation at the beginning of this chapter. Let us not determine them to be right or wrong, but to be helping or hindering in any given situation when pursuing our goal. Thus, when the goal is to climb to the summit of Mount Everest, we do not regard Fear as good or bad. A fear of falling off the side of one of its peaks will encourage us to pay keen attention to our safety protocols, whereas a fear to release one's grip and transition to another may stop our progress entirely and render the goal unachieved.

The more firmly we hold our values, the likelier we are to stand for something rather than fall for anything. We will be more likely to say what we mean and mean what we say. Those with strongly held values and who remain open to learning and growth are able to experience another's worldview without that worldview threatening their own. Where appropriate, such individuals will adopt something from another's worldview because it adds another road to their own map of the world and, thereby, increases their understanding of it. However, if inflexible and bound by dogma, an individual with strongly held values is often unable to adopt new ideas, even when those new ideas would enhance his understanding of the world and thereby improve his life. Conversely, those whose values are weakly held will fall for anything. They are so tepid that they are absent in their own presence.

Our values reside in our minds, emotions and bodies. In this context, therefore, it would be wrong to say that one's family is a value, albeit one may value one's family. Similarly, while perceiving value in a career or a home, they are not values within correct terms of reference.

Since we interpret the world through our own value systems, one person may react differently to another concerning the same occurrence. On being made redundant from a position held for 20 years, a person holding self-determination as a value may be more inclined to quickly find alternative employment than a person similarly employed but holding the contrasting value of fatalism.

WHY WE HAVE VALUES

The first reason is that we have no choice – we are human! To say, "I have no values" is in itself a value. Most of us have heard someone say of another that he has no values. Not so, it is merely that the two individuals' values are particularly diverse.

Another reason for having values is that they enable us to weigh decisions and guide us through the obstacles that life presents us with. How do we know when we have found Love, if we don't know what Love means for us?

In order that they serve us optimally, we tend to rank our values in order of importance. This is mostly an unconscious ranking which might surface only when we are forced into deciding a course of action. The decision that each person makes in the following values case study is dependent upon each one's value system, how each value is ranked therein, and how each value interacts with the others.

SITUATIONAL ETHICS

Imagine that you are one of only four survivors of a plane crash. You, the other survivors, the dead and the wreckage of the plane are strewn across a rocky, inaccessible, below zero degrees centigrade, arid, mountainous region. None of you has any notion of where you are. You have no means of contacting the outside world. By the grace of God all survivors suffered only superficial injuries. By the end of the third day, all food and water supplies retrieved from the wreckage are exhausted. By the seventh day, the survivors, a middle-aged corporate executive, a vegetarian philosophy student, a devout Catholic nun and you are starving toward certain death. The executive has spent his entire career solving problems. His worsening predicament helps him to recover from the depression which overcame him in his considering what might have been had fate not dealt him this cruel blow. Focusing on his situation, he quickly decides that help is further away than he had hoped. There is only one option open to him and his new colleagues – cannibalism. It is the only way he can imagine to survive long enough for the rescue attempt. There is no means by which to cook the "meat" but it has been preserved in the sub-zero temperatures. The student agrees, thereby renouncing his vegetarianism. The nun, acknowledging their desire to live, understands but abstains nevertheless. What inter-play of values drove each to their decision?

The executive, very ambitious with a high self-esteem has a material achievement orientation. His meaning of life is expressed in worldly things. His values include being pro-active, decisive, courageous and problem solving. Their material manifestation are career progression and financial success. The only way to preserve his life's meaning is to eat the flesh of the dead.

The student, aged 18, has only recently left the parental home. He believes in animal rights and is an environmentalist. He values Love, Peace, Freedom and Morality. In his current crisis, Love – for him, the sentiment of strong attachment – heavily outweighs all other values. Psychologists say that we are incapable of loving another more than we love ourselves. In the circumstances, the student's love is manifest in self-preservation.

The nun, aged 69, has devoted 45 years to the Catholic church and the will of God. Her values include faith, hope, selflessness and courage. The purpose of her life has been to do God's work so that she may avail of everlasting life after death. To her, cannibalism, under any circumstances, is a sure way of losing the sacred key to the Pearly Gates.

What decision do you make; life or death, and why? In truth you may not know until confronted with the circumstances. The extremity of a situation may add such weight to one or more of your values that you are forced into reacting differently than you would under "normal" circumstances. What would it take for you to steal food, someone's wallet, rob a bank at gunpoint, or to even kill another human being?

This is all rather dramatic, but we really don't have to contemplate such extreme circumstances to realize how significant a role situational ethics may play in our lives at the most mundane level. The concept of situational ethics allows us to understand that an individual will account for the context within which his decision to do or not is framed, rather than weighing the decision according to absolute moral standards encased in a vacuum, unaffected by external circumstances that create the context.

One winter a neighbor of mine ordered a cord of firewood for his cabin, which he paid for in advance of its delivery. On inspecting the delivery, he reckoned there to be closer to two cords than one. He called the merchant who agreed to come by and retrieve the overage, if necessary. A week went by, and then two. There was no sign of the merchant. My neighbor called again. The merchant admitted to forgetting and promised to be there within the week. Another two went by. My neighbor called again. This time the merchant curtly informed my neighbor that he was busy and would be over within the week. Another two weeks passed. My neighbor sheepishly called again. He told the merchant, "Sir, I really don't mind that your firewood is on my property; it isn't in anyone's way. I just don't want to cheat you out of your cord of firewood."

Would you believe, the merchant retorted, "If you don't mind it being on your property and it's my wood, stop bothering me. I'll pick it up when I can."

When the merchant came by that week, the wood was no longer laying in a pile in the open. It was neatly packed away under cover of my neighbor's deck. "So where is this extra cord, then?" asked the merchant nonchalantly.

"Sorry, I guess I was mistaken. Once I measured it all up, it really was just one cord." My neighbor was lying through his teeth, and the merchant knew it, but could prove nothing. While there are several lessons to be observed here, let's stick to that of situational ethics. Rather than retaining his integrity around the value of honesty, my neighbor allowed the behavior of the merchant (an external circumstance that created a new context) to influence his own behavior and thus to compromise himself. "Yeah, but the merchant was rude," has no part to play in the mindset of someone earnestly pursuing success.

CONFLICTS OF INTEREST

Conflicts of interest arise when we weigh the short term gains of one course of action with the long term benefits of another. If asked, most people would agree that stealing is wrong, insofar as it is contrary to their value of honesty. We readily condemn the bank robber. And, rightly so. However, we'd also do well to remember that often the most pertinent difference between him and another may be that had had the courage to face the risk inherent in robbing the bank while the other did not. How many would rob the very same bank if we knew with complete certainty that no one would be hurt, that they would get away with it, being financially set for life?

The foregoing example is more extreme than most of us will ever encounter. However, every day of our lives we face subtler conflicts of interest through which our values are tested to the limit and, just like with situational ethics, external factors play a significant role in how we will behave under the pressure.

It is common practice for commercial enterprises to partially compensate its executives with share options. The purpose of this, at the very base level, is to buy loyalty. The term of office of an executive within a company is by and large significantly less than the life of the company. In such circumstances, it is not inconceivable for a share option holding executive, tasked with the direction of the business, to pursue a business plan which maximizes the company's value in the short term and, therefore, the value of his share options, to the detriment of the company's shareholders in the long run. The rapid growth he elects places demands on resources, which are unsustainable in the longer term. The strain on resources is seen in the poor selection, training, and retention of staff struggling to keep pace with growth, a consequential reduction in customer service, the increasing burden of debt, the pressure on space to adequately house the operation, and the delay in upgrading technology to pay for short term growth. In time, it becomes essential for the rate of growth to be sustained since the high share price is a reflection of future growth (expectations) rather than present-day reality. Should it not be possible to sustain a rate of growth sufficient to buoy the share price, the company's valuation is re-assessed, possibly triggering a spiral of downward revaluation as the market loses confidence. In the meantime, the executive has purchased his share options and moved on.

An inexperienced data entry clerk may, each day, receive a batch of work to be completed within a given timeframe. Some of the work will be complex and time consuming while some will be simple, taking very little time. Daily batches with a bias of the complex time consuming tasks will develop the clerk more quickly than those with a bias of the simple tasks, and will, thereby, render the clerk a self-sufficient, fully functioning member of the team in the shortest time. The clerk benefits and the team benefits. If the clerk could choose which pieces of work make up the batch, would he select a bias of complex or simple tasks? Assuming that the clerk is aware of the full extent of both short gains and long term benefits, the answer is obtained by his weighing the short term gains (of, say, looking good in the eyes of his boss and others by finishing quickly) against the long term benefit to self and team (of, say, developing more quickly in his ability to handle more complex tasks).

According to data released in September, 2015 by StateofObesity.org, between 2011 and 2012, 34.9% of U.S. adults were considered to be obese, with sixty-eight percent being overweight or obese. As well, 17% of U.S. children were obese, with 31.8% considered overweight or obese. A further breakdown shows that 28% of men and 13% of women were overweight.

The overweight and obese are generally unwilling or unable to change their eating habits, resorting to binge eating of the foods detrimental to good health. The eating habits of dieters rarely change, making most dieters habitual or at least regular dieters and, therefore, weight loss is usually short term. Clearly, as a society we enjoy eating. In fact, so much so that we are prepared to risk our health for the pleasure derived from eating excessively and eating nutritionally inferior, though delicious foods. This, despite the wealth of information available on health, nutrition and the importance of a balanced diet. It is a conflict of interest whereby we choose the short term gain of pleasure from eating excessively and/or incorrectly in preference to the long term benefits of eating a proper, nutritionally balanced diet. Later, in Chapter 10, we will look at the reason we tend to select the short term option.

DOUBLE STANDARDS

An appreciation of the double standards we keep provides one of the greatest insights into the values that we hold. If we are honest in our examination of them, we will undoubtedly feel an emotional discomfort from the double standards we hold onto since they contravene the demands of our conscience. By releasing them we create the right emotional environment for peace of mind.

Acceptable fraud

I have met numerous managers of cash-based businesses who are prepared to wax lyrical about the sometimes crude but more often intricate theft they get up to in order to supplement the incomes they receive from their employers. These can amount to thousands of dollars annually despite the (adequate to generous) basic salaries and bonuses these managers receive. They justify their actions by seeing such theft as a perk of their position or recompense for the compensation package they convince themselves is less than they deserve. Few ever reflect on the fact that they chose their trade and their employer, thereby knowing the terms and conditions of their employment.

These same managers would not hesitate to dismiss a member of staff who is caught stealing $5 from the cash register. More so, if their views on stealing per se are canvassed, we find that they are all too willing to condemn the unemployed pauper who snatches old ladies' handbags for a living. Their justification: stealing is a crime; the old lady relies on her meager Social Security check to survive; such criminals should not prey on the defenseless; and so on.

I agree. My values tell me that taking what is not mine without permission is morally wrong. There is one question that is the ultimate test of whether the actions of the thieving manager or those of the stealing pauper are consistent with the values they believe they honor: "IF THE SHOE WERE ON THE OTHER FOOT, HOW THEN WOULD I FEEL ABOUT IT?"

It is difficult for me to envisage a manager-turned-business-owner accepting as okay, stealing from the business by the person whom he has entrusted to manage it, having mutually agreed upon a compensation package. He may see stealing, per se, as an acceptable business cost which is different from accepting it as morally okay. Like other business costs, he may seek to control the stealing which could involve the exposure, dismissal and prosecution of the manager.

It is difficult for me to envisage the pauper who steals handbags for a living, and who loves his elderly mother, accepting as okay the same crime being perpetrated on her by another, or that she should have to live with the fear of such a crime.

I'm all right, Jack

A characteristic I find particularly unsavory is that which was originally coined by Sir David Bone in Chapter 3 of The Brassbounder: "Its 'Damn you, Jack – I'm all right!' with you chaps."

Some of the attitudes I'm discussing in this section of the book are so subtly engrained in our way of being that unless they are exposed by someone else, they continue to go unnoticed, forever sabotaging our efforts to break free into the success we believe we richly deserve. So, let me expose a couple of "I'm alright, Jack" scenarios for you.

The U.S. Medicaid and Medicare programs are falling headlong into unsustainable deficits. Some generation at some time will have to bite the bullet and bring them under control. Beyond borrowing to sustain the unsustainable, measures to regain fiscal control of the programs fall into just two categories: a reduction in benefits; and an increase in contributions, be that through payroll or other means of raising (non-debt) revenues. When I ask individuals whether we, as a nation, ought to do something about better managing Medicare and Medicaid finances, 100% of people say, "Yes". When I ask the subsequent question, "Are you willing to pay more taxes to correct the deficit?" I get a significantly lower positive response. I have never had a positive response when asking a recipient of the benefits whether they'd be prepared to accept fewer benefits to help ease the deficit. "It's not my problem, don't ask me to fix it" is what "I'm alright, Jack" is all about. It is doing only what is best for ourselves, and to hell with everyone else.

There is a counter argument that the economist in me could proffer, and that is that, "In the real world, Economic Agents (that's you and me and each individual firm and agency, etc. out there) seek to maximize their personal utility and, therefore, it is naïve to expect them to behave in a manner contrary to 'I'm alright, Jack.'" That is a valid argument when your paradigm is limited to recognizing the universe as solely material and each person within it as separate from all else. In Chapter 7, I expose this myopia for what it is: misguided direction from the blind leading the blind.

If I were to tell you that the Boy Scouts were cleaning up litter in a nature reserve, it would probably not seem that noteworthy. That's what Boy Scouts do, right? There are places of natural beauty far and wide. Those places will be littered and even vandalized. Whose responsibility is it to clean up? There is no right or wrong answer, other than, it depends on who you are. Is the Boy or Girl Scout spirit still in you? The Law of Reciprocity which encourages us to give so that we may receive extends far beyond putting your $5 on the collection plate every Sunday morning.

One last example of "I'm all right, Jack" is the case of a colleague who constantly complains about her property taxes being too high, adding that local authorities should not be able to charge so much. The property taxes in a neighboring borough are significantly less, despite it housing residents that are generally wealthier than those in my colleague's borough. I asked her if she would complain so much if she lived in the neighboring borough. Her reply: "Of course not. The property taxes over there is reasonable." I then asked, what of the people she would be leaving behind to continue paying what she considered to be an unreasonable amount of property tax? She coldly replied: "That would be their problem, not mine." The truth, then, is not that the property tax in her borough is too high, but that she has to pay it. This may be a subtle distinction, which if you do not fully understand, I would implore you to study and discuss, if necessary, with others until you do.

> "There is only one problem, and that is ignorance."
>
> – Bob Proctor

By that, Bob is not referring to rudeness, that is confused for ignorance; he is referring to being uninformed, unaware, lacking knowledge of the way things really are.

Selective discrimination

Many prejudiced people walk about the planet convinced they do not discriminate on the grounds of physical characteristics or beliefs. They are able to convince themselves that their lie is truth because the challenge of their discrimination is too distant for it to be truthfully confronted. These are the people who think that all ethnic peoples are fine until such a family with habits and values alien to their own moves next door, or their daughter brings home a different colored boyfriend, or their new boss is twenty-five years their junior, or the bar they drink in is now frequented by persons who openly display a sexuality different from their own, or the school their child goes to has decided to observe another culture's beliefs by including their religion on the syllabus in recognition of the high concentration of children from that culture attending the school.

WHERE VALUES COME FROM

The foundation of values is beliefs; beliefs about yourself and about the world you live in. The stronger the beliefs underpinning the value, the more firmly that value is held. Our beliefs propel us into our future. If we believe that in the long run crime does not pay economically, spiritually or emotionally, we will develop a value founded on that belief – honesty, perhaps. The more beliefs we have underpinning that value honesty, the more rooted and stable it becomes. So, believing also that to do unto others as you'd have them do unto you is a just way to live and that lawbreaking is unacceptable, will cause the value integrity to be more firmly held and more consistently evident in the individual's behavior.

The understanding of the relationship between values and beliefs may be enhanced by imagining a "Value Tree". The value tree has roots (beliefs). The thicker and deeper the roots (or the stronger the beliefs), the more life is brought to the value tree:

Long held, very established value with many broad, well developed beliefs

Neophutos value fed by shallow beliefs

Beliefs "feed" values with their only source of food – experience. Sometimes we hold values that keep us from progressing in our preferred direction. We may not be aware that it is our values and their underlying beliefs that are holding us back. So let us get underneath the top soil and take a closer look.

We expect a calf to grow from feeding on cow's milk, or a lamb to grow by feeding on ewe's milk. Similarly, we would expect an apple tree to bear apples and an orange tree to bear oranges. After all, these occurrences are ordained by nature – they are natural. Values, we know, feed on experience that is gathered by their supporting beliefs but, like the calf, the value is programmed to receive only a certain type of food to reach its ordained full maturity. The calf is programmed by the ultimate programmer – nature. But your values are programed by YOU. "So what?" you might question. Well, nature has blessed humanity with the ability to think and, therefore, to create. This ability is so developed that we are essentially co-creators with the Creator. "So what?" you still cry. This gives you CHOICE. You can decide. For example, let us assume that Joe, who is 50 years of age, holds the belief that, "You can't teach an old dog new tricks". Joe has never invested in his personal development because of his beliefs. Self-determination is not a value that he favors. But wait, Joe has not always been 50 years of age, so the old dog's new tricks malarkey does not hold true for Joe's lack of investment in himself over the entire course of his life to date. Why did Joe not invest when he was say, 20? Well, Joe's belief then was different. Then, you see, he believed that he was too young to be taken seriously, which then was an excellent source of rich nourishment for his value, which is, "I, Joe, lack self-determination". His value is no different from the calf which started out on cow's milk and then progressed to grass to sustain its momentum toward full maturity. Nature ordained that the cow should change its diet and eat grass to successfully achieve this. The difference is Joe ordained (chose) to feed this value (which stunts his personal growth), the right food at the right time for its maturation. From a young age, Joe sought experiences (food) for his value, which nourished it well. It became a self-fulfilling prophecy. Because nature was controlling the calf's development, it was always going to be a cow. But Joe, the controller, Joe, the co-creator with the Creator, could have chosen to change the value he held by changing its feeding roots (beliefs). Maybe the substitution of the belief, "I, Joe, am totally responsible for all that happens to me" for, "You can't teach an old dog new tricks" would have changed the value to, "I, Joe, am self-determining". We all need to heed the maxim "Seek and ye shall find". What we look for is truly what we shall find.

WHERE BELIEFS COME FROM

Our beliefs are shaped from the moment we are born and possibly even sometime between conception and birth. As they feed our values with the values' sole source of nourishment, experience, so they themselves are affected by experiences. It is not what happens to us that charts the course of our lives, but how we react to what happens. Two brothers are raised by a brutal, unloving father. One grows up and treats his family in the same brutal, unloving way. His reason: "That's how I was brought up. It's the only way I know. How else would you expect me to turn out?" His brother grows up to be a kind and loving husband and father. His reason: "I could never stand the pain of treating my family the way my father treated us. How else would you expect me to turn out?"

Our beliefs will determine how we react to our circumstances. If you believe that all clouds, no matter how seemingly malevolent, have a silver lining, on learning that your house had just burned down, you may react by saying: "Thank you God! I've been meaning to move and it was time anyway for me to get rid of all that unwanted clutter in the spare room!"

The source of our beliefs is varied: family, friends, the media, religion, politics, education, gender, ethnicity, domicile, fashion, art, sport, the workplace and so on. Whatever the source, beliefs are the result of conditioning. Before we examine the ways by which we can be conditioned, we will first explore some of the research that established the significance of conditioning on the minds and consequent behavior.

EXPERIMENTS IN CONDITIONING

It is natural for an animal to react in a certain way when exposed to a given stimulus. For instance, the sound of an unfamiliar loud noise will cause a bird to take flight, triggered by its instinct for survival. Similarly, the stimulus of food in a dog's mouth will elicit the response of salivation necessary to digest the food.

By now, this oft repeated first piece of research will be familiar to many. However, because of its significance and, more importantly, because you and I right now in our lives are likely succumbing to the conditioning circumstances it describes, I am certain it is worth repeating again. In the 1920s, the Russian Nobel Scientific prize winner, Ivan Petrovich Pavlov conducted some breakthrough research in the field of behavioral conditioning. His subjects were dogs. Pavlov, while introducing the unconditional stimuli of the touch, taste and smell of food, introduced the conditional stimulus of ringing a bell at the time of feeding (Conditional, because the bell was rung on condition that it was feeding time). Pavlov recognized that after some time, exposure to the conditional stimulus alone was sufficient to produce the response of salivation in the dogs. They had learned to salivate when hearing the sound of the bell despite there being no food to digest. Pavlov concluded that a conditioned response was acquired based upon past experience and newly formed connections in the brain. What makes the research even more interesting is its application to human behavior. Continuing with the theme of bells, it is quite clear to me that at drinking-up time in pubs throughout the UK, where I grew up, customers have become conditioned to respond to the conditional stimulus of a bell ringing to signal "Last orders – No more drinks". A simple test of this would be to take all timepieces away and to ring the bell at differing times. When I lived in England, licensing law decreed that drinks should not be served past 11:00 p.m. (the unconditional stimulus) and not when a bell had been rung. But I'm sure, in the absence of timepieces, customers would not go to the bar to order more drinks once they heard the conditional stimulus of the bell.

The same is true of when we eat our meals. The unconditional stimulus is hunger. We build up a lifestyle which means we get hungry at a certain time of the day and so we eat. If that lifestyle changes so hunger sets in later in the day, we still eat at say 1:00 p.m. (the conditional stimulus) because our mind says it's 1:00 p.m. and therefore, "I am hungry".

Another classical experiment in conditioning reveals a condition known as Learned Helplessness. Three dogs, A, B, and C, are placed in an enclosed area which is equally divided in two by a barrier. On day one, all three dogs are placed on one side of the barrier. Dog A is given shocks. On each occasion that it is shocked, it is lifted and placed on the other side of the barrier, where it receives no shocks. It soon learns that to escape the pain of shocks it has to jump to the other side of the barrier.

Dog B is given shocks on both sides of the barrier within the enclosure and soon learns that it is powerless. There is nothing it can do to change its circumstances. Dog C received no shocks within the enclosure.

On the second day, the dogs are moved to a different though similar environment with a smaller barrier. This time all three dogs receive shocks. Dog A immediately leaps the barrier to safety. Dog B, "knowing" that it is powerless, does nothing. Dog C eventually learns how to escape the shocks. Dogs A and B were conditioned. Dog C was conditioned neither way. Driven by its survival instincts, it found a way to succeed. Fortunately, as humans we can overcome our conditioning shocks (failures) by employing the faculty of Reason. However, in order to do so, we must first realize we have been conditioned.

Finally, a similar experiment was conducted on students. On the first day, the three groups of students were asked to study in a room at different times. Each group was subjected to a noxious noise. The students in Group A were shown how to stop the noise whenever it sounded by pressing a series of buttons. Group B were not shown, but learned how to stop the noise through trial and error. Whatever combination of buttons was pressed by Group C did not stop the noise.

On the second day, the three groups were asked to study in a different though similar room. On the onset of the noise, Group A duly pressed the correct combination of buttons to succeed in stopping the noise. Group B again found a way. Group C did not even attempt to stop the noise.

These experiments reveal a two-sided coin. On the one side, we can be conditioned to accept a set of "truths" that are true only to the extent to which we believe them to be true, and conversely, that the conditioned "truths" are false to the extent to which we believe them to be false.

"Whether you think you can, or think you can't, you're right."

– Henry Ford

IMPLICATIONS OF LEARNED HELPLESSNESS

Human beings like control; control being the ability to make things happen. Even a two month old infant wants to be master of his own fate. This was one conclusion of a study which took two groups of such infants and placed them in cots above which were fixed mobiles with colorful shapes. Whenever the infants in Group A moved their heads, they triggered a switch which caused the mobile to turn for a while. They soon learned to shake their heads to make their mobiles turn. In doing so they cooed and smiled, delighted in seeing them moving. Group B were given no control over their mobiles which, however, turned about the same amount as those for Group A. After a few days, the infants in Group B, unlike those in Group A, no longer cooed and smiled at their mobiles. In fact, they became disinterested in the mobiles turning or not. This suggests that the infants were not interested in whether their mobiles moved, but that they made them move.

So, what happens to us as adults when we decide to believe that we have lost the ability to make things happen in one or more areas of our life? Martin Seligman, one of the discoverers of the effects of Learned Helplessness in animals, believes that a similar process causes the development of certain types of depression in humans. He asserts that the behavior of the Learned Helpless animal and the depressed human bares similarities. Both choose not to initiate actions; both are slow to recognize successful actions; both lose weight and have little interest in others.

The lack of a coping mechanism or strategy to regain control of our lives in the face of difficulties goes beyond our mental wellbeing, impacting directly on our physical wellbeing. Many studies have proven that patients who give up hope have a poorer chance of survival than those who persist, and that the difference between one and the other is that the former have a poor coping strategy whereas the latter have an effective one. Similarly, if you believe, as is commonplace in some cultures, that the death of a loved one should be celebrated as they have passed to a better life, your chances of continuing to enjoy a long life on this side of the divide would be greater than those who grieve and allow the event to overwhelm them to the extent that they renounce self-control and plunge into helplessness.

Diagnoses were performed on over 100 patients whose X-rays showed a lesion in the lungs. Some of those patients had suffered serious psychological losses in the previous five years: loss of spouse, parent or sibling; loss of prestige; loss of job; or retirement. Others had not suffered any such losses. The development of malignancy was much higher in patients who had suffered one of the losses listed above. Why? It has been suggested that Learned Helplessness impairs the immune system by inhibiting its ability to produce "killer cells" which deal with tumors. While several studies support this suggestion, it remains a matter for debate as to exactly why Learned Helplessness affects the immune system in this way. Nevertheless, what is clear is the necessity to adopt coping mechanisms or strategies to remain in control when confronted by the most frightful adversity. Our beliefs and values have a direct bearing on the level of control we choose to exhibit.

So, let me conclude this section by saying that, as a human being, you have been endowed with the gift of choice – the power to decide – which (if you choose) will condition you wish to eradicate from your life. Use it or lose it!

ACCEPTABILITY

In my campaign to be elected president of the Students' Union at Salford University in England, I was canvassing a good friend who asked whether I was more concerned than my fellow candidates about a particular issue current in student politics at the time. My answer was: "More concerned, less concerned, still concerned". Sufficient non-committed waffle, you may say, to lead me to a successful political career! The point is that being concerned about an issue over which one is unable to exert influence can be disempowering, regardless of the level of intensity of that concern, and, therefore, counter-productive. I am not suggesting that we all adopt an ostrich stance over such issues as the depletion of the rain forests, man's inhumanity to man, atrocious animal experimentation for developing vanity products, and so on. What I am suggesting is that concern without responsibility – the ability to make things happen – can induce anxiety and a general feeling of helplessness. This can pervade other areas of our lives and so become debilitating, causing us to accept that we are powerless and without control in this game of life, and so deciding not to fully participate. In other words, pursuing concerns without responsibility or control conditions us to a state of helplessness. It can be witnessed about us every day; in the family where decisions are arrived at autocratically, in the workplace where decisions are increasingly centralized, and in society where governments increasingly decide issues for us. This helplessness is manifest in the phrase: "Well, there's nothing I can do about it anyway." Is this something that you say and, if so, how often do you say it? It is an admission of no control in some area of your life and, like the two month old babies we studied earlier, you lose interest in that area of your life. Are you fed up at work, at home, in a relationship? How much control do you have over what you do in the area that you are fed up in?

Former British Prime Minister John Major's wife, Norma, when asked by David Frost (a former popular TV presenter and political analyst), "What do you believe to be your greatest quality?" replied almost immediately "Acceptability". By that she meant the ability to accept what is. Night follows day. So be it. She went on to say that she accepts the conditions that life presents her with and makes the best of them that she can. The quality of acceptability renders all excuses void. If life deals you a three, two sixes, a nine and a ten, you get on and make the best that you can of that hand.

To emphasize the point on acceptability, let us consider a situation that most of us can relate to – the traffic jam. The next time you are stuck in traffic with no option but to sit it out, observe your behavior. You may at first feel anxious, then annoyed and even angry, depending on how important the expedient conclusion of your journey is. Ask yourself: "Is there anything I can do right now to positively alter my circumstances?" If yes, take action. If no, ACCEPT the circumstances that you are in. Loosen your tie, undo the top button of your blouse, release your tight grip of the steering wheel, relax your tense neck muscles, and play some relaxing music on your in-car entertainment system. Now that you are relaxed and accepting of your circumstances, you are back in control. The only things any of us ever had and ever will have control over are our minds, emotions and behavior. How did you regain control? By using your ability to respond, rather than your tendency to react.

You can now begin to enjoy yourself. Look around you. Observe the behaviors of others. Are they victims of their circumstances? Someone just ahead of you is honking on his car horn with the futility of a pet gerbil running around and around and around on a carousel wheel in his cage, getting absolutely nowhere fast. Someone in the lane next to you is frantically trying to restrain the playful enthusiasm of children in the back seat. What about the person ranting and raving at no one in particular? All of these behaviors are the means by which the individuals exhibiting them have chosen to cope with their situation. Generally, they tend to be a habitual reaction to a recurring event. These people have learned that they are helpless – no control, no responsibility – and have conditioned themselves to behave the way they do in order to cope with that state of being. These are poor coping strategies because control is not regained and, like our patients with lesions who had suffered serious loss in the previous five years, the psychological torture they are inflicting on themselves can have harmful effects on their physical wellbeing.

Oh yes, while you're observing, you're bound to see that one person in control of his situation. You know, the one with the cell phone rescheduling his appointments. You smile inside as you too are in control of your situation. Your empathy with this individual is unforced. You are at one with the world. Isn't life great?

REMAINING IN CONTROL

I was once gifted a little prayer card, the words of which I later understood to be the beginning of what is known as The Serenity Prayer, and which perfectly summarize this section:

> "God, grant me the serenity to accept the things I cannot change, the courage to change the things I can, and the wisdom to know the difference."
>
> – Attributed to Reinhold Niebuhr

We have concerns over many things we believe we cannot change, which may include:

World Peace

Discovering the ultimate low-cost, infinitely abundant, universally applicable energy source

- Ridding the world of poverty and starvation
- Prudent management of the national economy
- Restructuring the education system
- Improving law and order
- Improving the healthcare system
- The reduction of pollution
- The reversal of global warming
- Establishing communication with extra-terrestrials!

These are all weighty concerns, the resolution of each carrying tremendous responsibility. And, if we are honest with ourselves, we tend to feel overwhelmed by their magnitude to such an extent that a feeling of powerlessness ensues. Nevertheless, they are still concerns. They are still matters which weigh on our minds. As human beings who care, we do feel some shared responsibility for their resolution. We are trapped. We want these concerns resolved but feel powerless to do anything about them. But hope, as ever, springs eternal. Occasionally we remember that we have been responsible. We have taken the trouble to exercise our franchise. We have elected some "fall-guy" to whom, along with similarly elected colleagues, we have transferred our responsibility for resolving these weighty concerns, and so are absolved from them. This, together with the occasional or regular financial contribution to a cause, helps us live with the guilt we can feel around our concerns. The truth is that we are not powerless. We either choose to get involved or choose not to get involved. Either way, it's okay. We are guilt-free. The passionate adoption of every cause may not be possible for you. Rest assured, someone somewhere is doing something to resolve the concerns about which we feel powerless, even communicating with extra-terrestrials! But remember, this does not give us the right to blame them for any concern's non-resolution. For instance, blaming the state of the economy on a government that we the people elected is like blaming a child for taking sweets out of a jar left open and in his reach – pointless. The transfer of responsibility to government does not completely absolve us from all responsibility about managing the economy. Recognizing that responsibility is the ability to respond, we can choose to respond to our own microeconomic circumstances all of which together are the national or macro-economy. We can choose to be responsible about our wage demands, we can choose to be responsible about raising our prices, about how much credit we seek and so on. And, ultimately, we can respond by transferring our responsibility to another government.

While we may feel powerless over many concerns, we are in control and able to exercise influence over many others. These may include your:

Family

Personal finances

Health and fitness

Job

Home

Business

Personal development

Education

World view

Leisure activities

Involvement in the community

Charitable deeds

Let us take one of these areas – community involvement. Imagine that you are a member of a locally-based action group passionately in favor of cleaning up your town or village, ridding it of the litter so carelessly discarded by your fellow citizens despite the liberal availability of well-positioned disposal facilities. You determine that awakening the community's awareness to the consequences of littering the locality will allow its citizens to make an informed decision to litter or not. You campaign using posters, leaflet drops, and a town/village center rally, advertising the main points you want to communicate. Within a month there is dramatic improvement. You estimate that littering has reduced by 80%. Your success is overwhelming and has not gone unnoticed by the district council for which your town/village is one of three the district council is responsible for. You and two of your colleagues are asked to assist the district council in a wider campaign to reduce litter in the entire district. The campaign is a major success. Overall littering in the borough is reduced by 70%. At a national meeting of district councils, the Chief

Health and Safety Officer and the Finance Director of your district council jointly present the health and safety benefits and financial savings directly attributable to the campaign. The people at the meeting are so impressed that every district council in the county implements its own similar campaign. Within 18 months, littering nationally is reduced by 50%.

By influencing an issue in your personal life you have ultimately influenced a national concern which you may previously have regarded as a concern over which you were powerless. So, whenever you feel overwhelmed by one of life's weighty issues, act according to your own values. It may make just a small impression on the entire issue but it is an impression over which you are in control, thereby enabling you to feel good about your contribution.

INVOLUNTARY CONDITIONING

Involuntary conditioning is always an attempt by someone else to get you to do what they want you to do for their reasons and benefits, regardless of any benefit you may derive. This does not mean that the conditioner does not want you to benefit as, clearly, often they do. Nevertheless, they are controlling you.

Advertising

Do you ever ask for a Q-Tip when you want a cotton bud, or automatically search for a Kleenex when you need a tissue? These are classic examples of conditioning through the medium of advertising. Conditioning through this medium can be extremely subtle. It plays on our emotions; our desires to be, do or have. It's associative. Often, the message is that if we use a certain brand of, say, perfume or aftershave, then we will be associated, by others and ourselves, with the glamorous or macho images portrayed by visual, auditory, suggestive and maybe even subliminal means.

Music

Have you ever found yourself humming to a tune and wondered how and why it popped into your head? Annoyingly, it is usually a tune that you detest!

A song's lyrics can affect us more than we recognize. I am especially alert to so-called love songs, which, in many cases, are no more than hurt songs. They can play a significant role in shaping our beliefs about how relationships are. We fall for some songs because they have a catchy tune, rather than for their meaningful lyrics. It is especially these catchy tunes that we play over and over again in our minds, conditioning ourselves to the message of their lyrics in the process, regardless of whether we agree with them.

School

Like many children in England, I attended a school that engaged in a practice called streaming. Basically, streaming is the categorizing of children into groups according to the school's beliefs about those children's intelligence and ability to succeed beyond their school years. The streaming process occurs at a very young age when many children, who later show above average intelligence and even brilliance, are less developed than their peers or are simply, at that time, focused elsewhere. Einstein and Edison, two of the most frequently referred to genii, were regarded by school and loved ones as being academically poor in their school years. The inequity of streaming is to give one child a better chance at life than another based on the opinions of the school who, at the point of streaming, cannot know the child sufficiently well to make a sensible decision, notwithstanding the further complication of latent ability. Do not tolerate this kind of conditioning. Einstein and Edison did not.

It was not until my third or fourth year of junior school that I realized that my class, Class C, was ranked third of four classes in my year. I can still remember the surprise and anger I felt to know that my school had such a low opinion of my ability. I remember being further angered by having to sit Certificate of Secondary Education (CSE) examinations rather than the more accepted and advanced General Certificate of Education (GCE) examinations because of my lowly stream and not because of my ability. Typically, the former exams were offered to students believed to be best suited to the trades, and the latter to those believed to be more clerically inclined. I never believed the guff about CSEs being just as acceptable as O levels to employers. If so, why have them at all?

There were children in my class who were far brighter than most of those at the school streamed A, yet looking at how their lives developed into adulthood, you would never know it. They were conditioned to accept a lot less than they deserved, and their teachers conditioned to give a lot less than they could give.

Family

Most of my bright peers who streamed C along with me, had the school's conditioning reinforced at home. Their parents wanted them to get out into the workplace and contribute to the family income regardless of what job they got. Further education and a career were out of the question. Fortunately for me, my parents believed that if given the chance, my siblings and I could be among the greatest human beings on the planet and be, do and have whatever we chose to. This conditioning was far more potent than that I received at school. It helped me to break free of the limited and limiting expectations the school had of me. When the negative emotional charges of learning about my lowly stream and of having to sit CSE's wore off, my conditioning from home enabled me to put these lessons into a more empowering perspective. In the great scheme of things, they meant very little unless I chose for them to. I went on to get eight O levels and three A levels, gaining entrance to university, the whole purpose of going to school in the first place (my mother conditioned me to believe). At the time, I was one of literally a handful of students in the entire history of the school ever to have achieved a place at university, which was to play a significant role in who I have become.

Peer Group

When I first heard the expression, "If you want to fly like an eagle, don't hang around with the turkeys!" it meant so much to me. When I attended university, it dawned on me that, with all due respect and love, what I had been doing all my life, until that point, was hanging around with turkeys. Turkeys who would not venture to fly. University placed me into an arena with very bright people and very stupid people; very ambitious people and very unambitious people; very rich people and very poor people; people who cared passionately about life alongside people who did not seem to give a damn about life; people with a passion for politics and people with no enthusiasm for it at all; people who had an opinion about everything and people who had no opinion at all; people who were eagles and people who were turkeys; people from all over the world. And the best thing of all, I could choose exactly with whom I would associate. Wow! What a playground. A microcosm of society perhaps. The difference being that your local space-time continuum – the neighborhood – tends, with few exceptions, to be stereotypical; rich or poor; rural or urban; conservative or liberal. The space-time continuum of the university campus has no exceptions, there are no rules. All is acceptable while nothing is accepted.

Associating with people who share similar beliefs and values somehow stimulates and reinforces our own beliefs and values, propelling us in the achievement of our life purpose. One word of caution, however; do not allow the commonality of your peer group to develop into xenophobia.

VOLUNTARY CONDITIONING

Voluntary conditioning is always an attempt by you to get yourself to do what you want to do for your reasons and benefit, regardless of any benefit anyone else may derive. This does not mean that you do not want anyone else to benefit as, clearly, often you do. Nevertheless, you are in control of yourself.

Goal Setting

Goal setting is possibly the most powerful self-conditioning habit available to us. When we set goals that we accept as being possible, regardless of knowing how we are going to achieve them, we effectively <u>decide</u> that no other course of action, no other outcome will do. A goal sought with integrity, persistence and certainty becomes a self-fulfilling prophecy. I have had this confirmed to me over and over again through the interviews and biographies of successful people and, more importantly, I have had it confirmed for myself by myself. This book is a good example.

Affirmations

In simple terms, an affirmation is a statement you make about yourself. One which, when repeated, can produce powerful results. As with a goal, an affirmation must be personal, present tense and positive. That is, it should focus on what you want rather than on what you do not want. I have found that affirmations become more pervasive and potent when a melody is made of them. Three affirmations I have put to my own tunes are:

1. Every day in every way, I'm getting better and stronger;
2. I can do all things in life which strengthen me, with God on my side I am all I can be; and
3. I am fit, healthy, wealthy and successful.

I really like to recite these during exercise, because my mind seems open to suggestion during physical exertion. I also use them when I find an unwanted tune or negative thought rattling around my mind. I simply start singing one of my affirmations which automatically replaces the unwanted tune or negative thought. This brings me to a really important point: nature abhors a vacuum, at least according to the philosophical theory of plenism and Matthew 12:43-45:

> "When an impure spirit comes out of a person, it goes through arid places seeking rest and does not find it. Then it says, 'I will return to the house I left.' When it arrives, it finds the house unoccupied, swept clean and put in order. Then it goes and takes with it seven other spirits more wicked than itself, and they go in and live there. And the final condition of that person is worse than the first."

And, Buckminster Fuller:

> "You never change things [like your thoughts] by fighting the existing reality. To change something, build a new model that makes the existing model [or idea] obsolete."

Visualization

Visualization is the process of using the third eye to see now what you want to be, do or have in the future. It allows you to bring and keep whatever you want into the present, which is the only place you can possibly have a use for it. To visualize, choose a quiet place, free from distractions. Close your eyes and relax. Now, just imagine that what you want to be, do or have is in your present circumstances.

Sensualization

Do not stop at visualization; use every sense available to you. See it, feel it, smell it, taste it, and hear it. Using all the senses makes it much more powerful, pervading and real compared to just seeing it.

Prayer

My definition of prayer is to ask of God (the universe, nature, your higher self, infinite intelligence, source or whatever term you prefer) with integrity and earnestness for what you <u>truly</u> want. What you truly want will be congruent with your conscience. Larry Dossey's *Healing Words* is an excellent treatise on the power of prayer.

Each one of these methods of self-conditioning is powerful in its own right. When practiced together they are a formidable success mechanism. At first, you may find the practice of one or more of these difficult but, like riding a bike, the more you practice, the better you get and the easier it becomes.

In summary, we may define mental conditioning as the creation of a belief, leading to programmed responses, lodged in the subconscious, which comes from the acceptance by the conscious mind of an especially repeated message (stimulus) from a given source. The given source may be self (voluntary conditioning) or another person, place or thing (involuntary conditioning).

CHAPTER 3

EMBRACING FAILURE

"If you realize that all things change,
there is nothing you will try to hold on to.
If you are not afraid of dying,
there is nothing you cannot achieve."

– Lao Tzu

C'EST LA VIE

So you've fallen from grace

Welcome to the human race.

That dream you chased with so much haste

Ended in your loss of face.

So what now, is that it?

Will you remain in the pit?

Your bottom sore from all the grit

Your ego hurt a little bit.

Will you rise above it all?

Searching for another call

Yet again to give your all

Risking still another fall.

– LAC

EMBRACING FAILURE

- Failure in perspective
- Declarations of defeat
- Expectations
- The necessity for change
- He who dares fails
- They failed their way to success

FAILURE IN PERSPECTIVE

The principal reason for mediocrity in human life is the fear of failure. We would do almost anything not to face the prospect of failure.

The fear of failure is conditioned into us at a very young age. We are praised for being right and winning, while chastised for being wrong and losing. We are sometimes chastised even when we are right. I remember an episode in art class at school when I was about 15 years of age. The art teacher asked the class what proportion is the head of the entire body. After a longish pause, I answered, one-sixth. To everyone's amazement, including my own, this answer was correct. I arrived at it by observing the physique of my classmates and the teacher. One-sixth seemed about right. The teacher, not expecting any child of 15 who had not undergone the training and study that she had, accused me of cheating. How could I possibly have cheated? Whether I got the right answer from measuring every person I came across, through casual observation, complete guess work, reading it in a book or being told by someone who knew, does not constitute cheating. By answering correctly, I took away her power to appear learned in front of her captivated, forever grateful for being imparted with her superior knowledge, pupils. From my perspective, she needed to make me to look stupid to preserve her aura of authority, even though I was right.

When we fail, it means our outcome is not as we predicted. Our conditioning tells us and everyone else equally so conditioned, that we are wrong, that we are losers. The next thing we do is to invest in looking good and being right. In order to always look good and be right, we cannot fail. Therefore, we do not even attempt anything at which there is the slightest possibility of our failing. So, we settle into our comfort zone entitled mediocrity in which we live lives of quiet desperation, always wanting more but fearful of endeavoring to get it.

Our commitment to looking great, rather than being great, is strengthened by the belief that the perceived discomfort involved in pursuing success is so much greater than the actual discomfort experienced in our daily lives of quiet desperation, which, in turn, strengthens our psychological inertia. Our commitment to looking great drives so many of us to live beyond our financial means, driving expensive financed cars, living in ninety-five percent mortgaged luxury homes, and wearing credit card financed elegant clothes. At Christmas, we convince ourselves that we must have this trinket or that gadget and that we must buy the same for others lest we are seen as mean and – God forbid – are not bought something in return. This habit is so pervasive that retailers once planned their sales, staffing levels and so on, knowing that our post-Christmas spending in January and February would be significantly lower than at other times of the year while we repaid our credit card debts. Now that they understand consumer psychology even more, they contrive post-Christmas sales to stretch the elasticity of those credit cards even further.

In summer, we convince ourselves that we deserve an expensive vacation because we have worked so hard all year. So, out comes Mr. Plastic who fixes it. We return from our vacation stressed at the prospect of going back to the humdrum job we endure and of facing up to the next two to six months of scrimping to our excesses while away. And living this just-over-broke, put-up-with-it lifestyle, is deemed to be less painful than pursuing the success which is our birthright, providing we choose it. Before you dub me Mr. Scrooge, please understand that I do not begrudge anyone the finer things in life. What I'm counseling against is the undisciplined, unsustainable acquisition of stuff. To repeat the words of a wise carpenter, acquiring stuff in this way:

> "…is like a foolish man who built his house on sand. The rain came down, the streams rose, and the winds blew and beat against that house, and it fell with a great crash."
> – Matthew 7:26-27

The falling rain, rising streams and blowing winds are metaphors for the external forces, often unseen until they are upon us, like illness, redundancy and divorce, to name but three.

Our commitment to looking good leads us to believe that more money is the answer. But how much money is enough? Do we reduce our burden of debt when we get more money, thereby relieving the mental stress it creates? No, with each increment in our income, we choose to service higher levels of consumer debt. Why? So that we may look better still. Surely the pursuit of success must be less painful than this perpetual charade. The Jones' of the world ought to unite in a mutual pact of simultaneous cessation of this absurd pretense. In doing so, they may not look better, but they will certainly be happier. In choosing to do what we believe is right, we cannot also choose what people think about us, but if we choose what people think about us we must behave in strict accordance with their every dictate. The former choice brings freedom, the latter slavery. The cycle is broken, not by more stuff, but by a shift in our thinking. The outward appearance of true prosperity can only manifest when one becomes prosperous, and that is a state of being rather than where the decimal point lies on one's net asset statement.

Because our emotional responses to failure are conditioned, it means we can change them. This is the greatest news of all time since, as will become apparent, in order to succeed, we have to fail. Scientific experimentation is a process of trial and error in search of scientific truths. In this search, a failed hypothesis can be as positive a step as one proven to be correct. If we choose to accept that our lives are lived in search of truths, our own truths, then we can also recognize that our failures are positive steps along the road to success. They reveal more information to us by way of questions answered, questions posed, redirected effort and so on.

Failure in perspective, then, is no more than a:

>	**F**ruitful
>
>	**A**nd
>
>	**I**nformative
>
>	**L**esson
>
>	**U**rging
>
>	**R**enewed
>
>	**E**ffort

If at first you don't succeed, try and try again. You will be ridiculed by those who, unlike you, do not understand what failure really is. Imagine a world without incandescent light. Thomas Edison undertook over 3,000 attempts to perfect the incandescent electric light bulb. What if he gave up after five attempts, or fifty, or five hundred? Was he ridiculed? Yes, he was. How did he cope with it? By understanding the truth and value of failure. After many attempts at perfecting incandescent electric light, eminent scientists of the time were writing scathing attacks on Edison in their scientific journals, even to the extent of questioning his sanity. When interviewed by a reporter on the hopelessness of his quest, he was asked, "Do you not see the futility of your quest? Do not your many failed attempts to perfect the incandescent light bulb tell you that such a venture is not possible?" to which Edison replied, "Son, these attempts do not prove the invalidity of incandescent electric light. Each failed attempt is evidence of what does not work. I have successfully identified many ways that will not work, which brings me closer to what will work." He went on to fail over 10,000 times in his quest to perfect the storage battery.

Julian Richer is the founder and Managing Director of Richer Sounds, the largest and most profitable Home Entertainment retailer in the UK. For twenty consecutive years the inaugural store near London Bridge was featured in the *Guinness Book of Records* for having the highest sales per square foot of any retailer in the world. His retailing exploits supported by his book, *The Richer Way*, elevated Julian Richer to somewhat superstar status in UK business consultancy, particularly in the area of customer service. Note what Richer says about failure:

"My business career has had its ups and downs, and I've twice been on the brink of financial disaster… I think the difficult times have taught me the most valuable lessons of all, and that I'm a better businessman for having made mistakes but pulled through… I would say that it was valuable experience. You learn very fast in a crisis… You also become stronger. I knew we would survive our second period of trouble because we had come through the first. I learned what could be achieved and my determination and self-belief increased."

Pardon the pun, but it is clear even to the blind who would elect to lead the blind that these "negative" experiences made Julian a richer person in every sense one can conjure for the word. Failure is not a punishment for what went wrong. It is a reward for the things we get right. When things do not go according to plan, seldom is everything completely wrong. If we pay attention to the details of the situation, we will discover what we did get right. Failure (the lesson in what went wrong) is our reward for what we got right. Accept the reward and move on.

DECLARATIONS OF DEFEAT

There are three phrases we use that amount to an abdication of responsibility for our destiny: "I have to", "I must" and "I cannot". There is nothing that we have to, must or cannot do. Nothing at all.

> "According to your faith, be it done to you."
>
> – Matthew 9:29

Everything we do is done because we want to do it. We choose to do it. Doing it confers a benefit in pleasure gained, pain avoided or meaning added to our lives. Those who use declarations of defeat choose not to distinguish between what is incontrovertible reason and what is absolute excuse. There is a price to pay for every decision that we make, every course of action we pursue. In deciding for or against, in doing or not doing, we are determining whether the price is right or not. What we choose to do will depend on our beliefs and values. If we fear death, we will have a propensity to choose risk-averse actions that apparently reduce the risk of dying. However, the operative word in the sentence is apparently, since by living life cautiously—existing—we experience less of Life and become a zombie among the ranks of the Living Dead. And, as if that's not enough, we're going to die anyway. Conversely, the person who does not fear death will rise to the challenge presented by journalist, Frank Scully (1892 – 1964) when he asked:

"Why not go out on a limb? Isn't that where all the fruit is?"

This person is one who realizes that Life's abundance is both granted to us and measured by Life's longing for itself, not in years, but in what we put into those years.

As soon as we use "I have to," "I must" or "I cannot," we place a constraint on our lives. "I have to because my boss told me to." The constraint here is that we are controlled by our boss and, therefore, do not have freedom of choice. We have given that right away. "I cannot because I am frightened." The constraint here is that we are controlled by our fear, and cannot experience peace of mind.

We use declarations of defeat to avoid confronting our fears. If we replace "I cannot because I am frightened" with "I will not because I am frightened," the context is completely changed. The latter statement suggests that we have control. We are able to face the fear but choose not to pay the required price for doing so. Retaining control allows us, at any time, to reassess the magnitude of the price in relation to conquering the fear. The former denies any control and, therefore, renounces any ability to conquer the fear. We are enslaved by it. We are defeated before the attempt is ever made. If there is something we want to be, do or have that is fully congruent with our conscience but we find ourselves saying we cannot be, do or have, then, for peace of mind, we absolutely must be, do or have that thing. Abraham Maslow said that, "For a human being to be happy, what he can become, he must become."

We also use declarations of defeat to reinforce our psychological inertia, to allow us to continue to do what we have been conditioned to do. Millions of people do not like getting out of bed early in the morning. They have conditioned themselves to feel overly tired for the whole week. Years ago, a work colleague of mine was particularly strapped for cash. He'd work all the overtime he was allowed to. He'd be at work at 9:00 a.m. and work through to whatever time he could. One day, he was asked to work eight hours on Good Friday for triple pay. He could not believe his luck until he was told he'd have to be in an hour earlier than usual. Knowing his dire financial position, I was amazed when he said he could not do it. Not on any high principled grounds but on the basis that he could not get up that early. I offered to give him a wakeup call, which he refused saying that to get up that early would disrupt his biological clock for at least a week. I have no doubt that he was right. Because he believed this would happen, it would become a self-fulfilling prophecy.

By changing his thinking, my colleague could have changed the outcome of getting up one hour early. However, he may not have been sufficiently motivated to change his thinking in time to take advantage of the Good Friday overtime. So, what if I gave him a little assistance? If I were to have booby-trapped his alarm clock to explode at 6:30 a.m. on the dot and injected him with a poison that became effective only when it detected the body declining into fatigue, I reckon that he would have bounced out of bed no later than 6:29 a.m., turning the alarm clock off and remaining as bright as a button for however many days these conditional stimuli were present.

We can all recall moments in our lives when we committed to being somewhere early – our wedding, a job interview, to catch a plane to go on vacation, only to get up in good time before the alarm clock sounded and feeling as fresh and alive as the proverbial Daisy. The mere action of setting the alarm clock programs the subconscious to wake us up at the required time. Furthermore, our thinking about what time we have to wake up and the importance of why, often programs the subconscious before we get to the stage of setting the alarm clock.

There is another true story, this time of a woman who ordinarily could not get out of bed before midday without the assistance of three alarm clocks and vigorous prodding by her husband. After several years of marriage, her burning desire for children remained unfulfilled. Consultation with their physician brought to light that this couple would require the assistance of Intrauterine Insemination (IUI) to have a child. Part of the treatment in preparation for IUI was for the woman to inhale a spray preparation twice a day at 8:00 a.m. and 8:00 p.m. She was made aware of the importance of adopting a positive frame of mind for the best possible results. Well, of course, during the near two weeks of this treatment, she bounced out of bed every morning at precisely 7:35 a.m. without the aid of alarm clocks or a prodding husband, in a positive mood without the slightest hint of tiredness. Her burning desire for a child was the best cure for her early morning lethargy. Once the treatment was over, it was business as usual – three alarm clocks and prodding – despite her having to be up for 8:00 a.m. to start work at 9:30. The moral of this story is if you are unable to get yourself out of bed without the assistance of alarm clocks et al, your reason(s) for getting out of bed are not sufficiently compelling. You may wish, therefore, to reassess who you see yourself as, what it is that you are doing to serve others, and what it is that you expect from this adventure we call Life.

EXPECTATIONS

Failure occurs when an outcome differs from our expectations. The only place that can happen is in the mind and, thus, failure is not a phenomenon we find in the natural world. It has been said that failure occurs only when we stop the pursuit short of achieving our objective. This becomes patently obvious when we consider what happens in the natural world. After how many "failed" attempts will a lioness stop trying to take down a gazelle? Two? Three? Answer: until she does, or until she dies from trying. How many times will a colony of termites rebuild its destroyed mound? From personal experience of destroying termite mounds as a child, I know the answer to this question is countless times. How many humans fail to dream the life and live the dream? 95%!

Our expectations form our attitudes. If we are disposed to positive expectations, we have a positive attitude. If we are disposed to negative expectations, we have a negative attitude. As we saw in the section on Learned Helplessness in Chapter 2, the conditions over which we dwell are attracted to us. In other words, our expectations are a self-fulfilling prophecy: positive thoughts bring positive outcomes and negative thoughts bring negative outcomes.

While expecting good things to happen, we must not beat ourselves up if things don't go according to plan. It helps to view all experiences as a combination of actions, outcomes and lessons. Every action has a reaction or outcome from which we can always learn something to help further our pursuit of success.

We are able to control actions, but not outcomes. However, as outcomes are a function of actions, actions will determine outcomes. Our focus of attention must always be on actions and not on outcomes. Set the desired outcome with a sense of certainty, then expect the desired outcome, while controlling the required actions to achieve that outcome.

We are one hundred percent responsible for our actions. Outcomes, however, will be influenced not only by our actions but also by external factors. In business, the effects of governmental legislation may impact your plans; in parenthood, the influence of others on your child will help determine how the child turns out; in your job, your boss' values and attitudes will influence your prospects. For some, these unknown quantities will be their excuse for not attempting to succeed, the phenomenon to which they transfer their responsibility. For others, embracing the F.A.I.L.U.R.E. induced by these free-radicals will be their key to success.

Success is a spiraling vortex of actions, yielding outcomes which provide lessons, which in turn initiate corrective actions, and so on. It may be graphically depicted thus:

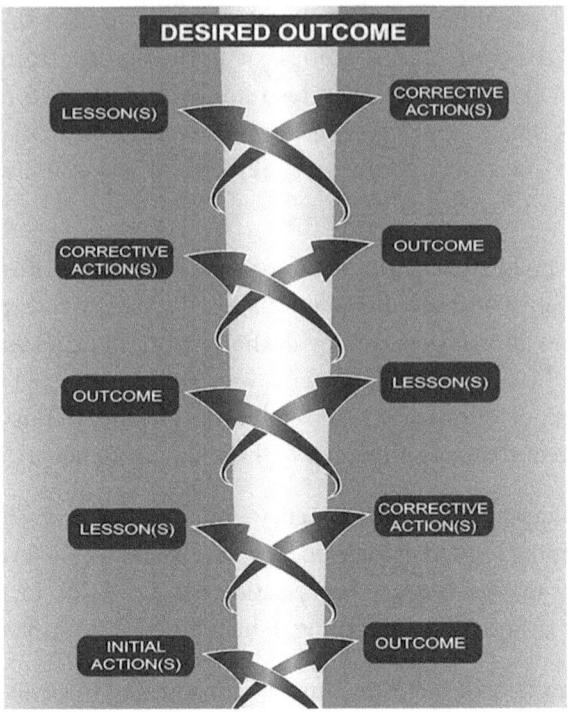

Success has been likened to well-balanced scales, with what you want on one side being equally matched by what you don't want on the other. So, to get a lot you must endure a lot. I have conditioned myself so that the tougher the going gets, the broader I smile, since I know that the Law of the Scales dictates that my success must match the difficulties I encounter, providing I continue seeking to improve.

THE NECESSITY FOR CHANGE

The most prevalent kind of insanity in mankind is that of people who continue to do what they have always done, hoping for things to change for the better. By this definition, there are a lot of insane people out there! For things to change, we have to change. If a current action is producing an outcome that is inconsistent with our expectations, we need to change the action to elicit the outcome we desire.

The necessity for change in success embraces personal change and circumstantial change.

Personal Change

If we want things to change for the better, we have to change for the better. Herein lies the truth that personal growth is a pre-requisite for success. Here we refer, of course, to the growth of our metaphysical, or incorporeal selves, the stuff that does not easily measure into a glass jar. It is improving mastery over our minds and our emotions. It is improving our capacity to love others as we love ourselves and to see the unity of mankind. It is creating an aura whose tendency is to attract and manifest positive outcomes. It is the development of faith sufficient to trust in a higher self and, thereby, surrendering to the purpose of life. It is coming to good (God). We come to know this change, this personal growth, through stretching the boundaries of our comfort zone.

Circumstantial Change

When we stretch the boundaries of our comfort zone, we may become like fish out of water, uncertain of our next step. We are undertaking tasks that may be new and different from whatever we have done before. Change means doing something different. Herein lies the truth that failure, far from being the opposite of success, is, in fact, an integral part of it. When doing something new or different, you will, at first, probably not be very good at it, and so will fail your way to succeeding at it. An inexperienced tennis player's back-hand will probably fail him more often than that of an experienced tennis player.

Fear of Change

Our dilemma is that we want things to change while harboring a fear of the unknown. We fear it because we cannot exercise control over that which we do not know. So we are trapped by the conundrum of wanting change but doing nothing about it because we fear it. So we choose to do what we have always done, hoping for things to change. Shakespeare said, "Our fears, they are traitors. They make us lose the good we oft might gain by failing to attempt." Once we accept that change is inevitable and that it is the only constant we know (other than Truth, that is), and that uncertainty is the only certainty there is, our paralysis is eased. Because of its inevitability, we may as well *affect* it ourselves in our preferred direction instead of allowing it to *happen* to us. By this, we exercise a degree of control over change, so reducing the element of unknown, and thus the fear inherent in it.

HE WHO DARES FAILS

In this section, I am going to review the path which led me to the writing of this book. It is in no way a remarkable story. In fact, it is reviewed specifically for its unremarkable nature. In other words, if I can do what I want to do, you too can do what you want to do.

I left the International Division of National Westminster Bank in 1983 to take up the position of Personal Assistant to the Managing Director of a small property-based bank. My job description was verbal and related to me at the second interview: "Either make the bank money or save the bank money, but preferably do both. Do neither and you're out of a job." After telling me this, the MD said that the job was mine if I wanted it. It was this very job description that encouraged me to accept the job. It meant I had a carte blanche, the freedom to take action, so long as I lived up to the job description; and, that I did. I was successful enough to have many varied tasks from finalizing the negotiations for the bank's purchase of a commercial real estate brokerage, to being one of the key players in setting up a vehicle lease hire subsidiary with the executive directors who had been head hunted from a major competitor to the new business, developing and marketing new deposit products, to establishing and running a new lending function. This latter success proved to be a major turning point in my career.

The bank had a large Arab customer base. What then seemed peculiar to me was our Arab clientele's penchant for lodging millions of dollars in deposit accounts with the bank and then borrowing smaller amounts of money for business ventures. The bank would advance the money using the borrower's cash deposits and whatever assets were purchased with the advanced money as its collateral. The rate of interest charged was 1% over the deposit interest the customer received on his cash. So the bank, in effect, earned 1% for lending them their own money! I thought this was the deal of the century. Earning 1% with zero risk. Naturally, it seemed a good idea to capitalize further on this. I was sent over to the Park Lane (West End of London) branch which, unlike the City of London branch, focused on developing a relationship-style banking philosophy in an environment that exuded opulence and encouraged customers to come in and have coffee and a chat. They would be softly sold, particularly deposit products, so the coffee was not free!

My role was to develop the business of customers effectively paying us to borrow their own money. Things went quite well. I had a system in place whereby I would interview the customer, appraise his project and recommend (or not) that the bank advance the money. The application with my recommendation would be couriered to the City branch where it would be analyzed and approved or declined.

One day, I was taken for a walk in Hyde Park by one of the Bank's senior managers. He praised me for a job well done. He even bought me an ice cream, and then he broke the news. "This thing is bigger than we thought. We are sending Steve over to help you."

"Great, I could do with some help. With Steve on board, I will be freed to market this product more aggressively whilst Steve processes the loan applications."

"Not quite. You report to him on Monday!"

The proverbial rug was well and truly pulled from beneath me. I had set everything up. It was working well. It was expanding beyond the bank's expectations. So, in return, I get walked around Hyde Park (admittedly it was a beautifully sunny day), bought an ice cream (which I did enjoy enormously) and then told that I was no longer in charge of this success. My ego, expressed as pride, could not take this laying down. But, what could I do? I excused myself. As soon as I got out of sight, I cried loud and I cried hard, like the biggest, wide-mouthed baby you ever saw. With my pride sewn into my sleeve (both sleeves, actually), I channeled my anger into achieving something which had long been a goal – to start my own business before the age of thirty.

One of the people I met during my stay at Park Lane became a friend. In my office, very late one evening, I decided, for no apparent reason, to call Phillip and tell him that I was leaving the bank, why I was leaving and, though I had no idea exactly what I was going to do, I intended setting up my own business. Phillip seemed quite calm and very understanding. At the end of the conversation, he invited me over to his flat-cum-office later in the week and lunch would be on him.

On the appointed day, I took the short taxi ride from Park Lane over to Lauderdale Mansions in Maida Vale. Phillip welcomed me in. At first, we made polite general conversation, which later developed into polite conversation specifically about business. After forty-five minutes, the conversation, though not rude, was anything but polite. Phillip was now very excited. He talked of his plans – very, very grand plans – for the future in a strong, positive tone, punctuated only by the rumblings of my empty stomach as Phillip paused, not once, for breath. Just as I was about to say "Phil, let's discuss this over lunch. I have to get back to the office reasonably soon because there is a lot I need to clear before I finally leave," he jumped out of his seat, grabbed a bright red marker pen and hurriedly began to draw diagrams and boxes and circles and lines on a white board. "…and I see you here!" Bam! The tip of his pen met the board in a very specific place (in the midst of the muddle he had created) which read "Director of Corporate Finance."

Phillip was essentially a financial advisor, hungry, very hungry, to achieve greater business and financial success. His idea was to create a business that was a 'one-stop' financial center catering for every personal and corporate financial need. He had already been discussing his plans with David, a Lloyds broker whom I was destined to meet.

The bam of pen on board, coupled with the sudden realization that I had been duped into attending a pitch for my services as part of Phillip's dream team (with dream being the operative word) quieted my expectant stomach. I rose from my seat, smiled pleasantly, reached for Phillip's right hand with my two. I shook his hand and said, "Thanks, Phil, but I do not want another job."

"I'm not offering you a job. It's a partnership."

"Well, I don't really want that either."

"Don't be so hasty. Come and meet David before you say no."

"Look, I'll tell you what. Let me put together some figures for you which will at least give you some idea of what this division you want me to head up might do. It will help you recruit someone who wants to do it. Now, I really must get back to the office." Phillip agreed and we were back to polite general conversation. The only certainty, as I waved good-bye from my taxi, was that I was a lot hungrier now than when I arrived at Phillip's.

When I compiled basic profit and loss and cash flow projections for Phillip's Corporate Finance Division, I was astonished at how viable it all seemed. In fact, the figures looked so good, I scaled down my assumptions and did them all over again. It was still a very viable proposition. I began to get very excited. I called Phillip and said I needed to see him to discuss what I had. I was now more eager to see him than he was to see me, and this considering the electricity he had generated in our first meeting. I did not sleep at all well on the three nights running up to our next meeting.

At the meeting, I was introduced to David, who had produced some figures for what was to be the General Division, which would transact commercial and personal general insurance business. We discussed all the figures, plans, contacts, finance and so on. It was clear that we were all completely consumed by the idea and that there was a magical chemistry between us. Over lunch, we made verbal commitments to go ahead and form a business together. I was brimming with optimism. It was toward the end of the Thatcherite '80s boom and I was a fan of the TV program *Only Fools and Horses* – the main character of which had a motto he'd oft repeat: "Who dares wins." I desperately wanted to go for it.

Our eagerness to succeed and force the business into existence caused us to ignore several areas of difference between us. Effectively, the business was founded on shaky ground. Nevertheless, we achieved some success. We did everything lavishly. It was a key element in our corporate image. However, such corporate exuberance and the differences we overlooked were coming home to roost. Internal bickering ensued and our overheads began to outstrip our income. Result – insolvency. The Official Receiver wound us up, the bank called in its guarantees, I lost my house, a spouse, my dignity and my pride. I had no business, no job, no income, nowhere to live. The impending inquest into the directors' responsibility – or lack thereof – for the failed business weighed heavily on me, particularly so as I was also Finance Director and Company Secretary. Reality Street was under my feet. Never before or since have I read any text with the same verve and hope with which I then read the King James version of The Bible.

From having a lot of money, I had none. What's more, I became used to having none. Not that I didn't want more – absence makes the heart grow fonder. Only, I developed different emotions about money. It no longer controlled me. Its importance was re-evaluated. I asked myself, "Why did I want a lot of money?" Answer: "It allows me the freedom to do what I want, when I want." Second question: "If this is true, how is it that I have spent my working life slaving from dawn to dusk?" I was working so hard to earn the darn stuff, I had no freedom. No time to enjoy spending my lovely money. Answer: "I'm a slave to money." Third question: "So what, then, is freedom?" Answer: "It has to be a state of mind. Freedom is a state of mind."

And with that my whole perception of who I am, what life is all about, how to conduct business and earn money and the meaning of other BIG Life questions began to change dramatically for me. I still wanted a lot of money, but became less anxious about getting it. Somehow, I just knew that getting money was not going to be difficult. Find something that other people want and focus hard on delivering it to them COME WHAT MAY. The difficulty was to find something I really liked doing which others saw sufficient value in to part with *their* hard earned cash to put bread on *my* table. I figured that if I did not enjoy doing it, I would only be doing it for the money, a situation I was not eagerly prepared to tolerate, since I would yet again be a slave to money.

A free man, I was stuck. I made two lists. One of everything I enjoyed doing (including having sex and drinking beer) and one of all my attributes (including having a cute bum!). If I could find something I liked doing from list one that matched an attribute from list two, surely I had the raw material to succeed at the highest level. I would have my answer. At the top of my list of attributes was my cute bum, which I paired with what I enjoyed doing most – having sex. For a nanosecond, I considered a career as a gigolo, then decided Richard Gere had a lot more to offer in that department than I, and look at the crap he had to contend with in the movie *American Gigolo*! Next on my Enjoy Doing list was sport, especially soccer. And, on my Attributes list, communication skills. I could not quite see that all-important relationship between the two and, besides, while I believe <u>all</u> things are possible, the risk-reward ratio of becoming a professional footballer at the age of 31 did not seem the most attractive I could conjure. I was still stuck. I had a problem – NO INCOME – which I needed to resolve presently. It seemed there were three options available to me:

1. Find a J.O.B (Just Over Broke!) now;

2. Commit suicide now; or

3. Work for myself now.

Having had the freedom of self-employment for the previous three years, Option 1 was only marginally preferred to Option 2. I therefore made a firm commitment to work for myself. I got on the phone to clients from the failed business, telling them that I was in business as a sole proprietor and convincing them that I could provide the same quality of service they were used to getting from me. This was not easy. There I was, a business consultant whose own business had failed, seeking to advise successful business people (whose businesses, in some cases, had been on the planet longer than I had) how to improve their businesses. It all seemed so absurd. I felt a gamut of negative emotions: stupid, embarrassed, inferior, insecure, afraid, bemused, confused, and so on. I convinced myself it was okay to be a failed businessman telling others how to succeed since failure was an experience I could use for good. After all, the best doctors I knew were, without exception, the unhealthiest (or so it seemed). By the grace of God, two former clients gave me a chance. I was back in business. This time all alone.

For several years, I carved out no more than a reasonable living, knowing that I had not yet found the answer I was looking for when I made those lists. A slave to money, I became so despondent that I was not performing to the standards that my clients and I demanded. Deja vu. The cycle of the previous business was repeating itself. Overheads, though quite low this time, were outstripping income. I began to wonder if I was engaged in some self-fulfilling, self-sabotage prophecy. I was not doing what I really wanted to do, therefore, I could not succeed at it despite being a damn good business consultant, a role in which my number 1 attribute (excluding my cute bum) – communication skills – was essential. I had failed in business for a second time.

This second failure moved me to take convalescent refuge in a job as a pub manager. Somewhere along this path, I started writing notes to help me understand how I had failed so miserably in business, not once, but twice. Many people I had met in life seemed to have no hope, no dreams, no enthusiasm for anything. A few, like myself, regardless of how successful or not they had become, were always looking for a way. My introspection forced me to contemplate what made some people so positive about their prospects even though they may have nothing to show for years of trying while others, without the scars of many failed attempts, were so negative about their own prospects. When I pondered the question for a while, relating it to my own experience, I soon realized that it was not the success or the failure that mattered but the joy, the personal gratification of going "out there" to carve out a piece of the world, real or metaphorical, that one could call one's own. It was the reason that getting a J.O.B seemed only marginally more appealing than suicide some four years earlier. My thoughts took me to an understanding that every failure I had taught me something and that perhaps, just perhaps, I had to experience them in order to achieve success at something. I adopted the belief that those failures were preparing me for my finest hour. And while I was not totally convinced when that would be or in what arena, I had faith that it simply would be.

As time passed, I began to realize that my time commitment and enthusiasm for understanding was taking me to postulates and conclusions that I couldn't foretell and these were coming at an increasing, and somewhat exponential rate. The changes occurring in me would decree that my position as a pub manager was rapidly becoming untenable. As the manager, a mere twelve-hour day was a luxury, when I got one. More often I'd work my shift and then cover for an absentee member of staff or have to deal with some unexpected challenge.

I needed more time to write. My frustration unconsciously began to affect my performance in the pub. Staff were noticing the lack of spring in my step, customers would notice I was less able or willing to roll with the blows of their sarcasm and wit. Inevitably, business began to suffer. I became more aware of and concerned with the unnecessary red tape, politics and personal injustices that seem to plague large organizations. Rather than concentrating on running the pub, I found myself knowing how best to run the entire company and spent too much time telling the Chairman and the Operations Director the same. They both had big enough shoulders and could take it. But, the very corporate structure that had afforded me convalescent refuge became my rusty shackles of incarceration. I needed out. I rationalized the situation and convinced myself that I was right in concluding that two and half years was enough of this game for any sane individual and that what I had learned would be useful at some future date.

The short term consequences of my decision, financially, emotionally and physically were not easy. Nevertheless, the writing of this book helped to open my heart and my mind. It enabled me to become more aware of the spiritual nature of Life.

Reflecting on the path traversed from successful corporate banker to failed businessman, published author, successful entrepreneur and (patent pending) inventor, I recall the end of a brief but potent speech an aged Sir Winston Churchill gave at a graduating ceremony at Harrow School, which he had attended as a boy:

"Never… never… never give in."

THEY FAILED THEIR WAY TO SUCCESS

> "One has to be grown up enough to realize that life is not fair. You just have to do the best you can in the situation you are in."
>
> – Stephen Hawking

In this final section on embracing failure, we will see how embracing failure was a necessary process in the success of two important and now very public success stories; one business and one scientific.

3M (Post-it Notes)

Founded in 1902 when five businessmen formed the Minnesota Mining and Manufacturing Company, today 3M is one of the largest corporations in the world with over 70,000 employees operating in more than 70 countries.

But how has 3M fostered its success? One of the reasons for its success is that as an organization, 3M understands that F.A.I.L.U.R.E. is a Fruitful And Information Lesson Urging Renewed Effort. As long ago as 1941, one of its founding fathers and then president, William L. McKnight, included the following quote in a letter to his staff:

"As our business grows, it becomes increasingly necessary to delegate responsibility and to encourage men and women to exercise their initiative. This requires considerable tolerance. Those men and women to whom we delegate authority and responsibility, if they are good people, are going to want to do their jobs in their own way. Mistakes will be made but if a person is essentially right, the mistakes he or she makes are not as serious in the long run as the mistakes management will make if it is dictatorial and undertakes to tell those under its authority how they must do their job."

This statement can be regarded as cutting edge management by today's standards and would make any contemporary management guru expounding these views seem a visionary.

It is indicative of an attitude that enabled the Minnesota Mining and Manufacturing Company to survive its early years of failing to apply the mineral it was mining – corundum – to a practical use; and its struggles as a sandpaper company. Today, 3M is a highly diversified Fortune 500 company that has over 100,000 patents with 60,000 products selling in 200 countries.

The spirit of the quote is now inherent in 3M's corporate culture. It is a culture of innovation. One which recognizes that innovation is the creation of positive change; that change necessitates F.A.I.L.U.R.E. and that F.A.I.L.U.R.E. encourages success. Innovation is formally encouraged by:

- The company's rule, whereby researchers are encouraged to spend 15% of their working time pursuing ideas of their own by which the entire company may benefit. Inherent in this is the 'risk' of failure. Some 90% of ideas put forward by researchers will never proceed beyond an idea. Fifty percent of the 10% that reach the formal project stage will fail. So this 5% of successful ideas provide the new products and services that propel the company forward;
- Providing financial support to kick start ideas;
- A corporate objective (one of four) that states 30% of sales should be from products that were not around four years ago. In 2014, one-third of 3M's sales (over $10 billion) came from products introduced within the previous 5 years;
- Holding inter-departmental/inter-disciplinary forums where ideas are shared;
- People working in small supportive groups.

Innovation is informally encouraged by:

- The culture itself, which encourages and challenges people to dream;
- A culture which is not seeking to blame or criticize mistakes, but accepts them as part of the process of success;
- A culture which says if it's new we want to know about it.

One of 3Ms biggest successes and certainly its most proclaimed is the Post-It Note. Post-It is a classic example of a F.A.I.L.U.R.E. to a successful outcome.

Post-It was invented by a researcher, Ray Silver, an adhesive technologist, using his 15% time during the 1970s. Ray developed an adhesive, the molecular structure of which is tiny spheres, rather than the usual stranded structure. The adhesive qualities of the spherical adhesive proved to be comparatively weak compared to that of the stranded structure. Consequently, Ray could see no immediate application for the adhesive, but shared his findings with 3M by recording them in the usual way (F.A.I.L.U.R.E. No 1).

Meanwhile, Art Fry, another 3M researcher, ultimately credited with the Post-It Note success, was looking for an effective way to mark the pages of his hymn book without blemishing it. Recalling Ray Silver's research, he pasted the spherically structured adhesive on one edge of a piece of paper, thereby replacing the old scraps of paper in his hymn book with the adhesive, but importantly, removable new cuttings of paper. This proved to be the optimum solution for him.

Art extended his personal use of the adhesive backed paper to leave notes for himself. Others around him in the office began requesting the adhesive paper to send notes to others. By now Art was beginning to see the commercial value of the spherical adhesive – a means of communicating by notes. Making a pilot run of the Post-It Note, he sent supplies to the secretaries of main board directors, who became reliant on them as a means of inter-office communication. This internal success did not convince the company's business managers of commercial viability (F.A.I.L.U.R.E. No 2).

Art, however, was more convinced than ever and, with strategic brilliance, he cut-off the supply of Post-It Notes to the main board directors' secretaries who were most vociferous about this. So much so that it became an issue at board level, forcing the business managers to thoroughly research the commercial viability of the Post-It Note. The product was marketed and promoted using traditional methods. The company's distributors all agreed it would fail; office stationers were convinced they could not sell it at up to 10 times the price of conventional products – note pads and the like. The doubters were all right, the product simply did not sell in the quantities sufficient for commercial success (F.A.I.L.U.R.E. No 3).

Nevertheless, Art had a champion. One business manager believed the product could achieve commercial success. He, like Art, had seen the reliance that built from habitual use inside 3M. Surely this same reliance would build in the market place if they could get customers using the product. The second piece of strategic brilliance in the Post-It story followed. The key to customer reliance and, therefore, commercial success of the Post-It Notes was to sample the product. By so doing, customers became habitual users and thereby reliant on the product. Sampling has proven to be so successful that it is still widely used by 3M to market Post-It despite its now high profile in the stationery marketplace. From a near still-birth, Post-It Notes are so successful that one cannot go into a stationer's of any repute and not find them; many derivative products using Ray Silver's adhesive have been developed and marketed by 3M; and, today, we even have electronic Post-Its.

Penicillin

The discovery of penicillin, far from being accidental, as is usually the claim, was the consequence of an opportunity created in the manner described in the section Opportunity Knocks in Chapter 7. It arose from Dr. Alexander Fleming's F.A.I.L.U.R.E. to keep an agar plate, cultivating a pathogenic bacterium free from a random micro-organism; in particular, a mold of the penicillium variety. This resulted in the co-existence of the three elements necessary for opportunity to arise:

Serendipity

Fleming, by chance, discovered that the presence of the mold inhibited the growth of the bacterium he was cultivating.

Synchronicity

It was coincidental that Fleming was cultivating the bacterium on a particular agar plate upon which the particular variety of penicillium mold capable of producing a therapeutic penicillin, to which Fleming's mold happened to be susceptible, settled at the same time.

Grace

Four years prior to Fleming's discovery of penicillin, two young research scientists, Andre Gratia and Sara Dath, at the Pasteur Institute in Brussels, found that a mold of the penicillium variety seemed to inhibit the growth of a pathogenic bacteria which they had been cultivating. Their observations were recorded without attracting the attention of the scientific fraternity. Yet, Fleming making the same observation four years later was impelled to look further, recognize the opportunity and, thereby discovering penicillin. Grace also resolved that it would be Dr. Fleming who examined the plate and not one of his assistants who may have simply laid it aside for washing.

So, the discovery of penicillin was ignited by a F.A.I.L.U.R.E., the F.A.I.L.U.R.E. of Dr. Alexander Fleming to keep an agar plate free from foreign agents. The path from its discovery to its widespread use in therapy is further littered by F.A.I.L.U.R.E. Each F.A.I.L.U.R.E. giving rise to another opportunity for success.

With the wisdom of distant hindsight that we call today, Fleming's discovery of penicillin seems the obvious answer to many of the exacting questions being asked of medical science in the first half of the 20th Century. This makes it difficult to understand why it failed to be scientifically accepted immediately; why it lay languishing silently for ten long years as an item of research in the *Lancet*; and why the evidence of its research failed to gain the confidence of the medical profession. The fact is that a "miracle" drug, from a mold similar to a fungus that can turn cheese moldy, was too revolutionary for the conservative minds of the same scientists who daily operate in an environment of innovation and discovery. They were victims of a self-imposed inhibiting oxymoron – scientific myopia.

During the ten years in which his findings lay dormant, Fleming was busy improving and producing penicillin just sufficient for his experiments on animals. Then, together with Dr. Harold Raistrick, he produced sufficient quantities of penicillin for clinical tests. They failed to convince any doctor of note to try it on a few patients. Fleming then failed in an appeal to a meeting of bacteriologists when his report on the discovery was lost in a sea of other papers.

Hope, diminishing with the passing years, was revitalized with the outbreak of the Second World War when the development of antibacterial remedies became a top priority, lest the dismal experience of the First World War recurred, when many a serviceman died from wound infection rather than from the wound itself. Thus, penicillin was rediscovered with the benefit of research and development funding.

A team of medical scientists at Oxford's Sir William Dunn School of Pathology, headed by Dr. Howard Walter Florey, Professor of Pathology, recultivated the penicillium mold. Within a year or so, Florey and his team, with the benefit of excellent funding, developed penicillin from a research project to a practical therapeutic drug capable of curing illnesses which had previously perplexed medical science.

In February 1940, a patient with blood poisoning lay dying in Oxford University's Radcliffe Hospital. All conventional treatments given to the patient did not work. As a last resort Florey and his assistants decided to treat the patient with penicillin. This treatment, hitherto, had not been tested on any human being. Penicillin was injected directly into the patient's blood stream every two to three hours. On the second day, the patient's condition had improved with a slight reduction in body temperature and a diminishing of facial swelling. Despite further improvement over the next few days, the patient died of an acute infection of the lungs. The supply of penicillin had run out, creating a crucial gap in the patient's treatment, allowing the illness to return with renewed vigor. The doctors drew great encouragement from this F.A.I.L.U.R.E. From it, they learned that:

1) Penicillin is not harmful to human beings; and
2) Penicillin must be continuously present in the blood stream and system of the patient, lest the infection returns. Therefore, the drug must be given continuously without interruption until the infection is completely gone, otherwise it will simply leak from the body, losing its maximum therapeutic effect.

With the knowledge provided by their F.A.I.L.U.R.E, the doctors found themselves in another "all else has failed" situation with a second patient, a young boy on the verge of succumbing to blood poisoning. Again, their supply of penicillin was modest. Luckily (no, let's say opportunely), the doctors had collected the urine of their first patient from which they were able to recover penicillin which, together with their modest stock and the little they were able to produce, was sufficient to treat the patient. The complete recovery of the boy seemed nothing short of a miracle. The incredulity of this wonder drug is exemplified by its source, being produced from a mold closely related to the fungus that can cause bread to go moldy and which can turn milk sour. Up until this point, drugs used in Western medical practices had been synthetically based.

In June of 1941, in the midst of war, Florey and his associate, Dr. Heatley, accepted an invitation from the Rockefeller Foundation, instrumental in funding Florey's research at Oxford, to continue their research in the United States. Although their clinical records showed that just five cases of blood poisoning had been treated with penicillin, two of which had failed, they were enthusiastically received by the American scientific and medical communities. Large scale clinical investigations were undertaken and more than 20 American pharmaceutical companies were encouraged, with the aid of government grants, in the mass production of penicillin. This commercial mass production itself encountered many F.A.I.L.U.R.E.s on the way to success. In particular, they involved the need to discover and develop new strains of the original mold which were more chemically stable and higher yield producing than the original strain. Techniques were successfully developed to optimize the extraction and purification of the drug. Penicillin had now come of age.

The original group of penicillins were mainly effective on the group of bacteria classified as gram-positive, but not those which are gram-negative, excepting gonorrhea, meningitis and syphilis. From this F.A.I.L.U.R.E., later penicillins were produced expanding the spectrum of effectiveness to include a greater number of gram-negative bacteria.

The F.A.I.L.U.R.E. to success story of penicillin is such that though many hundreds of antibiotics have been introduced since Fleming discovered penicillin G in September 1928, it remains the drug of choice in treating many severe infections, including those causing meningitis, septicemia, pneumonia, sore throat, scarlet fever and infection following limb amputation.

CHAPTER 4

DISCIPLINE:
The Sovereign Road to Freedom

"Discipline is the bridge between goals and accomplishment."

– Jim Rohn

NO SUBMISSION

I hear you sing your song

That life has turned out wrong

This is but the sum of your efforts all along

It doesn't have to be this way at all for very long

Your effort's not in vain

But you have to bare the pain

Life is just a game of sunshine and rain

If you keep on trying no doubt you will gain

Your next adventure could be filled with splendor

So don't you dare surrender to this sorry misadventure

Summon up your strength to pursue the next venture

It could be the one that is the thirst quencher.

– LAC

DISCIPLINE: THE SOVEREIGN ROAD TO FREEDOM

- The ultimate paradox
- Goal setting
- Planning
- Self-management
- Clutter management
- Self-control
- Health care
- Financial management
- Paradox revisited

THE ULTIMATE PARADOX

Prima facie, the title of this chapter, may seem somewhat paradoxical. After all, we tend to view freedom as doing what we want, when we want, with whom we want, and having the financial substance to do it. If we add to this peace of mind from living in accordance with the demands of our conscience, the absurdity melts away.

Even if we do win the lottery jackpot, we will not obtain peace of mind from lying on a beach in our favored part of the world, sipping cocktails in between the massages and the manicures. Right at the very beginning of the first chapter, we saw, according to Viktor Frankl, that:

> "Man's main concern is not to gain pleasure or to avoid pain, but rather to see a meaning in his life. That is why man is even ready to suffer, on the condition, to be sure, that his suffering has meaning."

And later we heard from Abraham Maslow that:

> "For a man to be happy, what he can become he must become."

A life of perpetual leisure is not consistent with becoming all we can become. Personal growth is a pre-requisite of success. It is achieved through endeavors that provoke the deepest emotional responses, the overcoming of which engenders personal growth. A life of recreational golf is vastly different from a life of professional golf in which the player initially risks all in his faith in his ability to continually improve so that he may put food on the table. The former may be growth enhancing in that it may teach us something about life. In comparison with the latter, however, it is minuscule and cannot be measured on the same scale.

Many people spend the last ten or so years of their working lives looking forward to retirement. Within two years of retirement, they die. They spent the previous ten years doing nothing of any meaning, with their lives on hold, awaiting retirement. On retirement, they have nothing more meaningful to do than what they had previously done for the past ten years. The message to the sub-conscious mind is that life has no meaning, and without a meaning is without purpose, and if there is no purpose, what is the point of it? The subconscious mind helps them age quickly and die – a self-fulfilling euthanasia. Becoming all we can become through meaningful pursuits is a challenge for all of us from birth to death. It does not start or finish at retirement, puberty, middle-age or any other arbitrary point in our lives. It may take us until, say, middle-age or retirement to wake up to this truth, but so be it.

Paradoxically, then, it is in pursuing our life's purpose with discipline and even routine that is the sovereign road to freedom.

The disciplines we need to master include:

GOAL SETTING

Goal setting is a skill. Like all skills, it improves with practice. It is a skill that many of us do not practice enough. There are four reasons why this is so:

Why we do not set goals

1) We do not understand the importance of setting goals;

2) We do not know how to set goals;

3) Fear of failure. If we have goals which are obvious, it is also obvious when they are not achieved; and

4) Fear of rejection. Our goals may not appeal to the Jones', who may tell us we cannot achieve them. They may make our goals the subject of frivolous, jocular chat behind our backs. They may openly ridicule us. So, we fall back into the trap of looking good in quiet desperation.

What is a goal?

A goal is the object of effort or ambition. A destination, which implies one's destiny.

Why should we have goals?

One simple reason is to know where we are going and when we get there. Goals provide a focused meaning and, therefore, purpose to our lives. Writing goals down keeps them at the conscious as well as the subconscious level, drawing things to us that would otherwise not be so drawn. We see opportunities we may otherwise have missed. We become a focused arrow. Without them, we wander about confused in a murky wilderness we call life, not ever really knowing what we want. When we do not know what we want, anything will do. So, we buy into anything that anyone convinces us we should have, without thought of whether it is right for us or not: unsatisfying jobs, unfulfilling relationships, addictions, crime. We would try anything once in the hope that it just might be what we want. Our energies are diffused as we attempt to be all things to all men.

I am aware that it is popular in some quarters to scorn the practice of goal setting on the basis that life is for living, to be enjoyed and not for striving, which goal setting implies. I can only once more draw your attention to the thoughts of Viktor Frankl and Abraham Maslow, and to suggest that you trawl your own experience for the truth. Is it possible to achieve peace of mind without knowing what we want (our goals) or how to get what we want (our plans)? I think not. Worse still, we can never achieve peace of mind if we know what we want, know how to get it but are too lazy, too disorganized, too undisciplined, or too busy doing other things to do anything about it. Psychological turmoil must ensue. This state of affairs is typified by that something we have always wanted in life, but worked at a job (we may have hated) or were equally engrossed in some other activity that seemed to take up so much of our time that we just never got around to it. The truth is we did not get around to it because we had no formal mechanism for getting straight to it, i.e., goals and plans. If everyone were to read this chapter and put its principles into practice, I guarantee that the manufacturers of Round-To-Its would go out of business through a massive decline in demand, leaving the market wide open for those who manufacture Straight-To-Its!

In the previous chapter, we discussed change. We concluded that as it is inevitable, we might as well affect it ourselves in our preferred direction. The most effective means by which we affect change is to have clear, specific goals and precise plans to carry them out. In the wilderness of the unknown our goals provide the only certainty. When we encounter new experiences and uncertainty, we can rely on our goals as our guides; the ultimate reference through the change and uncertainty.

Those who do not have goals may be lost without even knowing they are lost. They want to get somewhere, but where, they do not know. In Lewis Carroll's *Alice's Adventures in Wonderland*, Alice comes to a place in Wonderland where she meets the Cheshire Cat and says:

> "...I just wanted to ask you, which way I ought to go?"

"Well, that depends a great deal on where you want to get to."

"I don't much care where…"

"Then it doesn't matter which way you go."

"So long as I get somewhere."

"Oh, you're sure to do that if you only walk long enough."

Without goals we have no direction. We may walk long enough only to find that when we arrive, we are in a place we do not care much for with little energy, will or know-how to get to somewhere more satisfying.

I became a consistent and avid goal setter when I learned of the research project that found, of the graduating seniors at Yale University in 1953, only 3% had written goals with plans to accomplish them, and that when interviewed twenty years later, the 3% who had goals and plans had more wealth than the other 97% altogether. The object "wealth" could have been replaced by another object, say, mental health or success but the measurement of these is less precise than that of wealth. A gold-leafed copy of this research document should be handed to every child immediately after it shows its first sign of courage by popping out of its mother's womb to engage the challenges ahead of it on this planet earth. The embossed title should read, "ALL YOU NEED TO KNOW ABOUT LIFE, THE UNIVERSE AND EVERYTHING."

Setting the right goals

Each child should be encouraged to bring his copy of *All You Need to Know About Life, The Universe and Everything* to Kindergarten when practical lessons would be given on how to get the best out of the document. Lesson number one would be "Determine what you want." Now, the child may take many years to get to the bottom of what he really wants, but better to start early than late or never.

The ten questions/tasks that follow have been pooled from several sources. These are what I have used to determine how I express the purpose of my life:

1) What are the six most important values in your life?

2) In thirty seconds, write down the three most important goals in your life.

3) If there were no limitations upon you, what would you be, do or have?

4) What would you do if you knew with certainty that you would live a perfectly healthy life for the next six months but would then drop stone cold dead on the one hundred and eightieth day?

5) If you could be present at your own funeral, what kinds of things would you like your family, friends and colleagues to say about you? Are they consistent with what you think they would actually say about you?

6) What would you do if you were not afraid to do it?

7) Reminiscing on your life, what things have given you the greatest feeling of self-importance?

8) Reminiscing on your life, what things have you done which have given the greatest feeling of joy (or other positive emotion) to the largest number of other people?

9) What would you dare to do if you knew with certainty that you could not fail and would not have to go through the pain associated with striving for it?

10) Who and/or what are you prepared to die for?

Answering these with complete honesty and integrity will bring you closer to writing, acting out and producing your own drama, in which you are the main character, rather than an extra. It should be noted that if your answers to 2 and 3 are inconsistent with 4, 5, 6, 9 and 10, you will need to rethink your answers to 2 and 3, since the answers to 4, 5, 6, 9 and 10 are most likely to be congruent with your conscience.

Completing this exercise will help to ensure that what you want is internally inspired and not externally imposed. You will find that what you want is values driven and, so, most likely to be congruent with your conscience. Lifestyle and conscience, therefore, match leading to greater peace of mind.

Goal setting rules

1) Know your starting point. Getting to Paris, France is easy enough. Getting there when we don't know if we are leaving from London, Moscow or New York is more difficult.

2) Write them down. By doing so we unclutter the mind, the importance of which we will discuss later in this chapter under the heading "self-management". Psycho-educational studies have shown that by writing things down we learn more quickly and retain information with greater clarity and longevity. Writing down our goals helps to program them into the subconscious, which works at the metaphysical level in bringing them to pass. The more detailed and precise the description of the goal, the more powerful and meaningful it becomes. Hence: "I can run fast," is more effective when expressed as, "I can run 100 meters in 9.95 seconds."

3) Express the goal in the present tense. The difference between saying "I can run 100 meters in 9.95 seconds" and "I want to be able to run 100 meters in 9.95 seconds" can be the difference that makes the difference. The subconscious mind can only deal with the present. The past and the future do not exist for it. So expressing a goal in anything other than the present tense is of no use to it and to not use the subconscious in goal achieving is akin to leaving your best player on the substitutes bench for the entire game for no other reason than you did not recognize he was your best player. The subconscious is unable to distinguish between reality and imagination. If, therefore, we can convince it that what is imagined is real, it has to bring that which is imagined into reality. Hence, Napoleon Hill's statement, "Whatever the mind of man can conceive and believe it can achieve."

4) Goals should be expressed positively. So we would say, "I am of sober character," rather than "I have given up drinking." The subconscious mind latches onto key words or phrases to work on. The key word in the positively expressed goal is 'sober' and in the negatively expressed goal 'drinking.' We can see even at the conscious level the alternative effects of focusing on one or other of these words.

5) Goals should be personal to the goal setter. Thus, the following do not work because they are one person's expectations for someone else:

"My husband is a fit 170lbs. hunk";

"My wife is a shapely 120 lbs. babe!"

6) Express the goal with passion. If your goals do not arouse powerful positive emotions in you, you will not be inspired to follow through with

them when the going gets tough, which, almost by definition, it will. As important, the subconscious is moved to action by deeply felt emotions.

7) Determine a date by when the goal is to be achieved. If we have done all that we can and our goal is not achieved by the deadline, so be it. Treat it as we know F.A.I.L.U.R.E. is to be treated. The purpose of the deadline is to focus our attention, to provide something to aim at, without which we are back in the wilderness and subject to the caprice of uncertainty.

8) Ensure that you are able to identify measurable progress. If you are unable to measure your progress, you may become despondent in the midst of effort and apparent absence of reward. And, ultimately, if not measurable, how will you know when you have achieved your goal?

Executing your goals

1) The first thing to do is to decide that you are going to pursue the goal. The power of decision is magical. Once we decide, we become a different person, a changed person. Choosing sobriety in favor of alcoholism will change a person's destiny the moment the decision is made – that is magical. Deciding is analogous to pruning the dead wood from a tree. In doing so, we encourage the growth of new shoots in a different direction. They yearn to seek the light, whereas the dead wood no longer had the capacity to do so. We must continually prune to ensure new growth in our chosen direction, providing balance in our lives. To decide means not only to choose but also to exclude all other options. When this state of being exists in us we are compelled to succeed. There is only one way forward with nothing to distract us since nothing else exists. To decide means to continue until you succeed. To make this decision graphic for you, it is like being in a battalion, landing on the enemy's shores and casting your extra rations into the sea. The point being that they are baggage irrelevant to the task ahead. If you succeed you will have all the food you need. If you fail, you will have all the food you need! Does this scare you? It frightens the pants off me, but it also excites them back on. We must feel the fear and do it anyway, as Susan Jeffers tells us in her excellent book of the same title. Success is like a set of scales with equal amounts of what we don't want on one side balancing what we do want on the other.

2) Commit to a successful outcome. The American psychologist and personal development trainer, George Zaluki, defines commitment as,

"Doing the thing you said you would do long after the mood you said it in has left you." This reminds me of the time at a school dance when, under the influence of a modicum of alcohol, I had the courage to ask *the* most desirable girl in school out on a date. Unfortunately, she never turned up at the dance and on the following and subsequent days, the mood in which I was going to ask for the date had well and truly deserted me, along with any chance of that date.

3) The next thing to do is take some action. Start formulating plans. This is the "How to" phase of achieving your goals. But remember, the best plan in the world will not work unless you do. So, consistently do something, large or small – preferably large – toward achieving your goals. Organize your life so that every day you are doing something toward achieving those goals.

4) Always remain flexible. There are more ways than one to skin a cat. If the plan or some aspect of it is not working, it is no reason to abandon the goal, just an indication that the plan or relevant part of it needs to be reviewed. How many times should the plan be reviewed? As many times as it takes to achieve your success. Do not necessarily expect to have to change the plan, but if you do remember that, as far as we know, there are only three natural constants: light speed, Truth and change so don't allow change, if required, to phase you.

5) Believe that your goal is achievable, but do not confuse believable with realistic. It was not realistic to send a rocket to the moon when the idea was first conceived and believed by a mind. It was not realistic for Roger Bannister to run a mile in four minutes. Doctors agreed that to do so was physiologically impossible but Bannister and his coach believed it could be done and so it was. Once he had achieved it, others believed it could be done and that they could do it, and they did. I love the story of the weight lifting world champion who, having tried many times, could not lift a pound over his world record. His coach one day decided to put on an extra pound but tell the world champion that the bar was set at below the world record weight. He lifted it with the relative ease he would lift the actual weight that he believed he was lifting. Sound familiar? Our old friend 'conditioning'. We can often times do that which we tell ourselves we cannot. When we believe that something can be done we create our own reality. There are always two creations of an entity: the physical manifestation which is always preceded by the

mental creation. A chair was only a physical entity after its conception in the mind of its creator. Its creation has nothing to do with reality and everything to do with belief.

If your goal is big enough, you likely won't know how to achieve it no matter how meticulous your plans. Let this encourage rather than deter you. Move into action. Have faith. Answers will come, often from unknown and unexpected sources, so long as you expect to succeed.

6) You will encounter mini-milestone achievements along the way to realizing your ultimate goal. Celebrate these. Pat yourself on the back, treat yourself to a day out, make your favorite meal, open a bottle of wine, whatever. Just make sure that you honor the specific milestones. Doing this will encourage you to look forward to achieving the next step and so on.

7) Take things step-by-step. As the ancient Chinese proverb says, "The journey of a thousand miles begins with the first step." If our goals are established to help us become all that we can become, viewing them as an entire mass can be daunting. It is encouraging to focus only on the next step which in itself will seem eminently possible. Determine, from the outset, what constitutes a step and become dedicated to daily or weekly measurable progress.

8) Use leverage. The principle of leverage is that whereby using the same effort yields a greater return, exactly the same way in which pedaling a bike in third gear with the same effort you would use in first gear gets you farther more quickly. Creating leverage in the goal setting sense would include listing all the benefits that will accrue to you on the achievement of your goal; money, personal development, self-esteem, fame, control… all of which will bring greater peace of mind if your goal and lifestyle (your physical and mental disposition while pursuing these things) is congruent with your conscience. Knowing all the benefits that will accrue to you on achieving a goal will provide greater encouragement to set about achieving it. If there is more encouragement, there will be more enthusiasm and more focused effort. We receive a greater return from focused effort than we do from effort which is dispersed. Further leverage is to be had in utilizing the abilities and resources of other persons and organizations willing and able to aid your success: partners, mastermind groups, coaches, finance, research… this list is limited only by your imagination.

Reinforcing your goals

There are four things you can do to reinforce your goals by driving them deep into the subconscious:

1) Goal reminders. Place pictures, affirmations and statements of your goal in strategic places around your home, office and maybe other frequently occupied places, but not somewhere that will entice ridicule from insensitive minds. For instance, if one of your goals is to be slim, you may put a full color picture of a slim you on the refrigerator door and on food cupboards. Every time you seek access to one of these you will see yourself as you want to be, which will act as a deterrent to breaking your diet. Remember, your subconscious does not distinguish between reality and imagination. The message to it is clear, "This is who I am." Seeing the slim you on the refrigerator may also just dissuade you from snacking out between scheduled meals. Create a dream board of your ideal life. Look at it often, especially when arising from and going to sleep.

2) Create affirmations. Particularly ones which you can set to a melody as we covered under Conditioning in Chapter 2. By doing this, we create an environment of belief about the goal. When recited, the affirmation may help us out of moments of doubt, despair and confusion which are inevitable obstacles along the way. This is particularly true when it is infused with appropriate, heartfelt emotions. Remaining with the goal to be slim, an affirmation may be something like this: "I am so thankful that, right now, I am a fit and healthy, classically shaped woman of 120 lbs."

3) Sensualize the goal. This is a particularly useful exercise when your mind is in alpha – the state between being asleep and awake. Alpha is achieved when going to sleep, when awakening and through meditation. In alpha, the subconscious is particularly susceptible to suggestion. Take pictures and affirmations of your goal to bed with you, looking at the pictures and reciting the affirmation before you go to sleep. If these are the last things on your mind before you go to sleep you will take them into alpha, thereby programming the subconscious in the most potent way there is.

4) Keep a chart of your progress. By doing this, you have a ready reckoner of what you have achieved, where you are now and what you need to do to complete the goal. This can be a source of great encouragement, lifting your spirits and keeping you in a positive mood, which is necessary

in the face of the adversities to be confronted ahead. On the other hand, learning that you're wildly off track will allow you to make course corrections sooner (and while the damage is small) rather than later (when it may be catastrophic).

Obstacles

Obstacles are what we see when we take our eyes off our goals. If we allow them to, they will prevent us from realizing our goals, reason enough to take a look at what they might be:

1) Our emotions are the main obstacle to our realizing our goals. Life is ten percent what happens to us and ninety percent how we react to what happens to us. We are able to choose our emotional and physical responses in all situations. If you find this difficult to believe, I suggest you set about finding ways to believe it. Observe your behavior. Do you have set responses to specific events (stimuli)? Do you allow the mood of your spouse to affect your mood? How do you react when someone criticizes you? How do you feel when your favorite team loses an important game? What about when your boss fails to recognize your efforts? And, what's your reaction to the crazy driver who cuts in front of or tailgates you at 75 miles per hour? Train yourself to divorce your behavior from events. While they may correlate, they are absolutely independent of each other. That we see them otherwise is absolute evidence that we are allowing external circumstances to control our state of being. Is this conditioning easy to change? Well, that's entirely up to you. If your worthy ideal is backed by a burning desire, you will be more apt to clearly determining whether such behaviors are helping you toward goal achievement and, therefore, ultimate success or whether they are keeping you from it. This will aid your cause. Break the pattern of behaviors that are obstacles to your goals. Whenever confronted by the stimulus, resolve to respond in a positive way, in a way that is helping you and which may help the person (if it is a person and not an event) who is the stimulus. Be bold enough to expect to overcome the emotion at the first attempt. If you do, fantastic. But, be prepared to fail your way to success. Practice makes for improvement.

2) Ignoring the right people while listening to the wrong people. If you want plumbing advice do not consult your doctor; if you want medical

advice do not consult your plumber. In doing so you may end up with water on the brain and blood in your drains! This may seem obvious but it is almost a knee-jerk reaction for Fred to consult his best buddy and drinking partner, Bill, whenever some opportunity of which he is unsure presents itself to him. Bill, of course, knows as little about it as Fred, but he has an opinion which Fred must hear.

3) Keeping up appearances is an obstacle since it prevents us from taking the risks we may need to take – being different from the pack, daring to appear ridiculous and so on. Ignore the Jones' at all costs.

4) Becoming side-tracked. Og Mandino said, "Many of us never materialize our greatness because we become side-tracked by secondary activities." Why should this be? Perhaps we do not have clear, specific goals and are, therefore, wandering generalities blown hither and yon by the winds of change or the persuasiveness of others.

5) Fear of the unknown, which by now we know how to manage

6) Procrastination. This is born out of fear, laziness or psychological inertia. It is the great thief of time. It prevents us from giving all that we have to become all that we can. We will look in more detail at procrastination under self-management. The basic principle in combating it is to do first things first and to do them now.

7) Fear of failure, which by now we know how to manage.

8) Learned helplessness, which is overcome by our knowing that, come what may, there is always a solution and that we are responsible for finding it and implementing it.

9) Lack of knowledge. Seldom do we know all we need to know about an endeavor. It is wise to understand what little we know. It is our responsibility to bridge the knowledge gap by learning what we need to know or by hiring the knowledge we need. So, you may be an excellent caterer with poor bookkeeping skills. In order for your catering business to succeed you need to either develop your own bookkeeping skills or hire a bookkeeper.

10) Lack of direction. This becomes probable when our goals are vague, our planning is poor, or we are undisciplined and unorganized.

11) A negative attitude. Belittling ourselves, our project, living in permanent doubt about the outcome we want will bring about an outcome we do not want. "The thing which I have feared most has come upon me." – Marcus Aurelius.

PLANNING

A plan is an organized method by which something is to be done. It is not descriptive, it is active. As I stated earlier, the best plan in the world will not work unless you do. So, plan your work and work your plan. The simpler the plan the more likely we are to want to work it.

The purpose of a plan is to ensure that we have an organized method by which to complete a task or achieve a goal. It makes sure that we do not miss a step that may be fundamental in fulfilling the task and that we take all variables into consideration. By being thorough we achieve the optimum outcome.

In planning, we list the activities necessary to achieve our goal, and give them a significance by prioritizing each in terms of its importance and timing relative to each of the other listed activities. If the goal is to throw an annual staff party we need to decide the relative importance of venue, music, food, drink, attendance and cost, among other things. We may decide that securing a venue big enough to house the expected attendance is more important than finding a DJ or sourcing the booze, since (you may reason) without the venue there is no party. Each activity or variable may impact one or more others. Attendance will vary according to the perceived availability of food, drink and music, for instance. It will also vary according to cost. If the company is to foot the entire cost including transportation to and from the event, more staff will be encouraged to attend which, of course, has an implication on the size of venue required.

Some variables will be completely independent of others. A professional DJ will perform his role independently of how many staff turn up, whether or not food and drink are provided, irrespective of whether the company foots the entire bill and regardless of the venue size.

Our job, as the planner, is to recognize and understand the relationships between the variables so we are optimally placed to achieve our expected outcome. In doing so, we must recognize that there are variables that are beyond our control, but which may affect the outcome we expect. Atrocious weather conditions on the night, a breakdown in the transportation system or a previously unscheduled monumental government announcement concerning the existence of extra-terrestrials in New Jersey just might affect the attendance at the party, resulting in an over-expenditure on food, drink and venue. We have to retain control as best we can. The best we can do in these circumstances is to remind people of the importance of the party – team building, bonding, cost incurred, viability of future parties and so on.

The possibility of change affecting your plan is enormous. Part way through organizing the party you receive strong feedback that the staff would like something different to what you have organized for the last six years. In fact, they want a '60s night with full '60s dress, memorabilia and, of course, music. Well, the verbal agreement you had with last year's DJ to come back this year needs to be reviewed considering he has no '60s tunes. The decorations that you have committed to for the hall will have to be reviewed, and you need to tell your oh-so-conservative CEO to dig out his flared jeans, sandals, flowered shirt and the beaded necklace that he vowed never to don again. At the very least, you will learn that consulting the staff about their party is a good idea as it conveys ownership and allows you to give them what they want, thereby enhancing the probability of a good turnout.

Summary of planning deeds

1) Plan your work and work your plan.

2) Keep it simple.

3) List and prioritize activities in importance and time.

4) Recognize and understand the dependent and independent relationships between each activity, noting that some activities will be dependent on others happening first.

5) Identify variables beyond your control that may affect your expected goal outcome.

6) Concern yourself with the areas within your control.

7) Be prepared for change, altering the plan as necessary.

SELF-MANAGEMENT

There has been a general misconception that we can manage time. I would like to lay that to rest right now. Are you able to speed time up, slow it down, or stop it completely? Can you alter the number of hours in a day, minutes in an hour, or seconds in a minute? If your answer to these questions is no, then you have no ability to manage time. For you, time is a fixed resource. Any attempt to manage it is futile and a waste of your time. Time is the same for you as it is for everyone else who answers no to these questions. What you can manage within time is yourself.

Elements of effective self-management

1) Clear, specific, measurable goals are essential in effective self-management. They focus our attention and provide the direction for our daily effort.

2) Detailed plans are also essential as they provide the "how to" in our daily endeavors, effectively keeping us from being side tracked by unplanned occurrences which would otherwise divert our attention away from our goals.

3) Make a to-do-list every night for the following day. It is more effective to prepare the list the night before, rather than first thing in the morning, because that way the subconscious (our best player) gets to work on the list while we are sleeping. Do not do anything that is not on the list. If an urgent or important issue not on the list arises in the day, put it on the list before tackling it. Your goals should be on the list, otherwise you cannot be making progress toward them.

4) Make a weekly planner. I find Sundays ideal for this simply because it is the last day of the current planner and the day before the new planner begins. Carry forward any items that remain unresolved or works in progress to the following week. In the same way, issues should be carried forward from one to do list to another. The weekly planner gives a good overview of your activities in the coming week. You may identify gaps you can profitably use for activities you had been delaying because of their relative low priority, or leave open for items hitherto unknown.

5) Prioritize. Some things on the list will be more pressing or important than others. There are two ways of determining what tasks should take priority.

a) Ask yourself, "What is the most valuable use of my time right now?" Anything less than the most valuable use of your time is a relative waste of time. Do one thing at a time until it is finished, starting with the most valuable followed by the next valuable and so on.

b) Use Pareto's theorem, otherwise known as the 80-20 rule. Wilfredo Pareto recognized that in any set of tasks, 80% will yield 20% of the value while 20%, 80% of the value, and, therefore, it makes sense to concentrate on the 20% of activities that yield 80% of the value. In sales, one may be able to identify the 20% of customers who provide 80% of one's business; a stock market investor may be able to do the same with his portfolio of stocks; or a senior manager with his team of managers, and so on. A salesperson would be well advised to spend 80% of his time selling and 20% of his time administering his sales; a retail operation with 80% of its staff in head office functions and only 20% in the stores would soon struggle.

6) Do it now. Have a sense of urgency. Do not allow procrastination to be the thief of your time. A good plan that breaks things down into manageable daily chunks guards against procrastination.

PERSONAL ORGANIZATION

Use a personal organizer. Make sure that it is tailored to your personal requirements even to the extent of creating it yourself. The more user friendly you find it, the more inclined you will be to use it. Consider whether you will be more comfortable with an electronic or conventional one.

In the calendar section, I find it useful to be able to see a month at a glance, a week at a glance and a day at a glance as these are the levels at which I do my planning. I tend to use colorful symbols to make my calendar aesthetically appealing. At the back of the organizer I keep a journal to register important events that happen in the day, which I review on a weekly basis, and a notepad to log ideas that come to me during the day. These I review every evening. My to-do list is a prominent feature at the heart of my organizer. It is the section that gets the greatest use. In another section is a list of my goals – monthly, three-monthly (quarterly), annually and five-yearly. Why this particular breakdown? Simply, it is what I am comfortable with after trial and error. The final item in my personal organizer is a record of my personal finances.

CLUTTER MANAGEMENT

The ancient and traditional Chinese art of Feng Shui is now quite familiar in the West. Hitherto seen in the West as yet another Chinese superstition, Feng Shui is now being openly used by large Western corporations and individuals alike. The essence of Feng Shui is the harmonization of Chi energy (that which passes through all things in the cosmos, giving them life) to maximize the opportunity for success. A key underlying principle of Feng Shui is that the flow of Chi energy can become blocked by natural or artificial barriers; perhaps a tree in front of one's house or clutter in the bedroom. For the purposes of this book we shall focus on clutter. It is easier to manage than uprooting a two-hundred-year old oak tree from the front of your house, or bulldozing three neighbors' properties to enhance the flow of Chi energy in your favor. We need to address three questions:

1) What is clutter?

2) Why do we have it?

3) How can we manage it?

What is clutter?

My personal definition is that clutter is anything that one has that has not been used for at least one year. It is usually found in attics, garden sheds, vehicles, garages and spare rooms, but can also be found in rooms that are frequently used or even in storage. Are you paying to keep possessions in storage that you have not used for a considerable time or will not use for a considerable time, if ever? Do you have the wreck of an old classic car in the driveway? Have you ever been able to use your garage for the car? Can you list everything of use in the attic? Do you complain of space shortages in the house, yet have a cluttered spare room? We know from the art of Feng Shui that this clutter is inhibiting to the flow of Chi energy throughout your home (or office) and, thereby, limits your ability to succeed.

Each property or room has a bagua, or map, relating to specific areas of your life. The bagua is mapped out from the front of the house, i.e., where the entrance is and contains nine areas:

4	9	2
3	5	7
8	1	6

Entrance to House

1. Career/life purpose
2. Relationships (especially romantic)
3. Elders/Ancestors/Family
4. Blessings and wealth/abundance
5. Health
6. Helpful friends/beneficial coincidences/travel/cash flow/bills
7. Offspring/children/creativity
8. Inner reflection/contemplation
9. Fame and success/self-confidence

These numbered areas will relate to rooms in the property, with one or more rooms being covered by an area. Identify which rooms relate to which numbered areas. Clutter in area 1 will adversely affect your career or journey through life, clutter in area 5 will adversely affect your health and so on. Draw a bagua of your home and/or business right now. If, say, you live in an apartment or your business premises are in a complex, use the entrance to the apartment or business and not to the property or complex at large to construct your bagua. Where is your clutter? Are these areas in which you feel held back? If so, get rid of the clutter and review after one week, one month and three months, the progress that you have made in that area. Incidentally, do not put your life on hold waiting for something to happen. Continue to do all the things you know you need to do toward the achievement of your goals.

Why do we have clutter?

1) Fear of loss and a scarcity mentality. We believe that one day those 24-inch flair-bottom pants will come back into fashion and/or we do not like the thought of having spent so much money on the item and getting so little use out of it. We hoard items of food that we will never eat for the same reason. Do the world and yourself a favor – give them away!

2) Living in the past. We cling to possessions for nostalgia, sentiment or to remind us of who we once were. Your wedding dress that your daughter did not want to wear at her wedding and that her daughter did not want to wear at her wedding, you somehow convince yourself that your great, great, great, great, great grand-daughter will want to wear. The truth is that it represents one of the greatest moments in your life, one that would be painful to relegate to the back waters of your memory for good. You may even convince yourself that to get rid of it may be bad luck, or disrespectful to the union it represents.

Years after any useful service to me, I finally got rid of a tuxedo I bought while president of the students' union at university. At that time I had much use for it, continually attending official engagements and giving speeches. It was reminiscent of a time of much joy in my life; a time when I began to shape my style of public speaking, something which I enjoy doing more than most things; a time when many people had respect for me, which boosted my ego and self-esteem to no end; a time when I would rub shoulders with the Chancellor, Prince Phillip, the Mayors of Salford and Manchester, the Bishop of Manchester, et al. I bought into the mistaken idea that the tuxedo represented who I once was. Anyway, from a practical point of view, I must have worn it twice in the 15 years since leaving university and finally getting rid of it. Just think of how much more dashing I'd have looked in a more modern, hired one!

Other examples of nostalgia, sentiment and reminiscence in accumulating clutter are: keeping clothes we know in our heart we'll never fit into again; keeping the children's toys, clothes etc., which become relics of memorabilia, freezing them at a young age when they depended so much on us, listened to what we had to say and did what we told them to do; and keeping relics of memorabilia from our own childhood which reminds us of a time when we could rely on mommy and daddy to be responsible for us. A time when, if the going got tough, we got mommy and daddy to sort things out.

How can we manage it?

The first thing to do is to define what is clutter and be ruthlessly honest. Then, go around and make an inventory of your clutter. Thirdly, get rid of it! Step three will probably prove to be the most difficult. However, if you have defined everything on your clutter inventory as such, then by definition you do not need it. Sell it, give it away, throw it away. Just get rid of it. When you do, you allow the Chi energy to flow freely around and through you and your home/office. In ridding yourself of it you create a space for something positive to come into your life.

Once you are happy with the level of clutter in your life, carry out a monthly audit to ensure it is kept to within a level satisfactory to you. In doing this, make a list of the geographical areas in which clutter accumulates and a list of the type of clutter – paperwork, clothes, food, toys, furniture, etc. Work through both lists until you are satisfied that you are as clutter-free as you can be. Schedule your monthly audit on your calendar and make sure it is on your to-do-list.

When we get rid of our clutter, something else important happens. We unclutter our minds. "To each well ordered mind comes a thought each day," was the valuable insight from Ralph Waldo Emerson. Clarity of thought is a most important facet of success. Without it, our thoughts and judgments are clouded, leading us to less than optimum solutions.

SELF-CONTROL

We noted earlier in Chapter 2 that we humans want to exercise control over our environment and that it is healthy to do so. The challenge that we face is knowing how best to gain that control. We know of people who seek to gain control through their domineering of others, and of those who believe that money or high office is the answer and, therefore, seek to gain a lot of either or both. Yet others believe that knowledge is power and from their position of knowledge-based power seek to control their environment. The problem with all of these means of controlling our respective environments is that when things go wrong, as they sometimes will, we are prone to react in an out of control way. The only means by which lasting control is gained is the effective management of one's mind and emotions. By doing this we control ourselves and not our environment. However, our environment is entirely the projection of our internal world into the realms of our physical surrounds. Therefore, by managing the internal – mind and emotions – we are tackling causes rather than symptoms.

The three most important areas that we should seek to control are our:

1) Thoughts;

2) Personal chatter; and

3) Emotional responses.

Thoughts

You will recall that there are two creations: the physical preceded by the mental. This truism is such that each of us today is the manifestation of what we have thought about ourselves all our lives to this point. It follows then that what we think about ourselves now will determine who we are tomorrow, and that our history does not determine our future. Therefore, in conjunction with acting appropriately to become all we want to become, we should only ever think about ourselves in terms that are consistent with who we want to be. The mind holds one thought at a time so substitute a positive thought for a negative one.

Personal Chatter

Again, you will recall that the subconscious mind does not distinguish between reality and imagination. Therefore, be careful what you ask for as you may get it. Refrain from saying things like: "I'm dead hurt"; "I'm pig sick"; "I'm feeling ugly"; "I'm gasping for a cigarette". If you feel a certain way, so be it. Get yourself out of negativity. Moderate your language. For instance, substitute "I could use more energy right now" for "I'm dead tired".

Emotional responses

When something happens to us, we interpret what it means before we respond. The chain of events are:

Stimulus > thought > emotional response > physical reaction

So, someone calls you a nasty name > you think and interpret what it means > you choose to feel an emotion you decide is appropriate > you react according to your interpretation and emotional response.

Imagine yourself sitting on a park bench eating a bag of chips. A stranger walks by and calls you "Piggy." You think this is a derogatory term and choose to feel upset by this unprovoked outrage. You leap off of the bench and retort, "Piggy yourself," at which point you recognize that the person is not a stranger but an old flame who used to call you Piggy as a term of endearment because that person used to adore your beautiful hair which curled like cute little pigtails. Now, to the same word you give a completely new interpretation, your emotional response is that of tenderness and your reaction is openly receptive.

What if every time you are confronted with a negative stimulus you choose to respond in a manner which empowers you? How fantastic would you feel all of the time? This is a skill that can be mastered. The key is to pause once the stimulus has been experienced, interpret what it means, pause again and select an emotional response that will make you feel good, and respond accordingly. You may not always find it easy to do, but practice makes for improvement. Imagine, you never have to be upset by anyone ever again. No circumstance can ever get you down again. You are in complete control over your environment. Not by pulling others down to make yourself appear relatively good, but by controlling the inner you; the You that matters most, and the only You that can manifest the success you want. The degree to which you want that success will determine the diligence with which you practice this restraint.

HEALTH CARE

You may be wondering what health care has to do with the general subject matter: successful living or, more specifically, the role of discipline in living successfully. Its importance is embodied in the joke about the man who lives to be a centenarian. He is asked, "If you knew you were going to live this long would you have done anything differently?" to which he replies, "Yes, I'd have taken better care of myself!" It is better to be an active, vital one hundred than an inactive, dependent one hundred. Life goes on and so too does the quest to satisfy the purpose of Life.

Good health has little to do with trying to live forever and much to do with living with more vitality every day. It is about having sufficient energy and drive to achieve the things we want to achieve. I don't know exactly, but I would guess that 95 of every 100 people who come home from work have no energy to do the things they want to do for themselves. Their day ends when they arrive home from work. All of their energy is spent in making a living. In fact, they are not working for the sake of a living, they are living for the sake of work.

Health care is one of the more obvious areas of our lives in which we transfer responsibility. We lead unhealthy lifestyles and then check-in to be fixed by our local physician who, most of the time, will prescribe a pill to fix the ailment. We do not consider at a deep enough level the cost of this lifestyle on our being – spiritual, mental and physical – otherwise we would not live this way.

We are going to look at health in a way you may have never before considered. The first thing to recognize is that health and fitness are not the same thing. Fitness is a measure of explosive power that we may witness in any sporting arena. It is an element of health. While an important element, for our purposes, it is one beyond the scope of what I want to convey here. We are going to look at health at the micro-organic level, the cellular level. We are going to define health in terms of the requirements of a cell for optimal efficiency. This is not unreasonable since the building block of the human organism is the cell. If we can keep every cell healthy, it must follow that our bodies will be healthy. The requirements of a cell for healthy growth and life are:

1) Aerobic exercise;

2) A proper diet; and

3) Stress management.

Aerobic exercise

I stress aerobic as opposed to other forms of exercise – anaerobic, isotonic and isometric – because aerobic exercise is the only form that does not create an oxygen deficiency during the period of exercise. Oxygen deficiencies are inconsistent with the requirements for a cell's healthy growth and life. The conditions that aerobic exercises induce are:

a) Greater lung capacity whereby our lungs process more air with less effort;

b) A stronger heart, capable of pumping more blood in fewer beats, thereby transporting oxygen to the cells more efficiently; and

c) Increased oxygen consumption giving increased endurance and, therefore, reduced fatigue (allowing us to live our day with more vitality).

Exercise generally helps to stimulate the lymphatic system that eliminates waste from the body through the skin and, thereby helps to create a clean environment for cells. It has no pump mechanism so it relies on muscular movement to do its job. Deep diaphragmatic breathing is said to be the best stimulant for the lymphatic system.

A proper diet

There are many ways of determining what a good diet is. However, the acid test has to be whether your diet is producing a clean, non-toxic environment for healthy cell growth and life. The primary consideration for this is efficient digestion. The most important elements for efficient digestion are:

a) A healthy body, which is gained through exercise, adequate rest and abstinence from (or moderate intake of) toxic substances – caffeine, nicotine, alcohol and so on;

b) The consumption of high water content foods – principally fruits and vegetables. Our bodies consist of 70% water. High water content foods cleanse rather than clog the system. Our bodies need water for many of the functions they perform;

c) A high fiber, low saturated fat diet. Fiber aids digestion and protects the veins, intestines and arteries (the vascular system). It is found in unrefined foods. The best sources being fruit, vegetables and especially cereals. Fats are an important part of any diet. They provide energy, heat and assist in the absorption of fat soluble vitamins and calcium. However, the type and amount of fat we consume is important. Excessive fat consumption encourages obesity as it has more than twice the number of calories per gram of either proteins or carbohydrates. Saturated fats are associated with heart and circulatory diseases; and

d) The elimination (or moderate consumption) of refined and processed foods. Such foods tend to be high in harmful additives, preservatives and colorings which have no nutritional value and are toxic to the body, i.e., they do not promote a clean environment for cells. Additionally, the "empty" calories promote obesity.

Stress Management

That stress management has an impact on healthy cell growth and life suggests a connection between mind and body since stress is an emotional (mind) response and where it impacts (cell) is a physical phenomenon. Dr. Deepak Chopra has made the understanding of this mind-body connection the center of his life's work. He says, in his book, *Quantum Healing*:

> "...The immune system secretes certain anti-cancer agents called interleukins, a class of proteins that resemble hormones... This means that when our emotions join up with our molecules, like riders on a horse, the mounts they choose are almost identical to interleukins. For all intents and purposes, to feel happy and to fight cancer are much the same thing at the molecular level. We could call both of them healing messages."

> "At the very instant you think, 'I am happy,' a chemical messenger translates your emotion, which has no solid existence whatever in the material world, into a bit of matter so perfectly attuned to your desire that literally every cell in your body learns of your happiness and joins in."

There is a direct and positive correlation between our ability to cope with the daily hassles of life or specific stressful events, and the state of our health. The more control we are able to exert over our lives the better able we are to cope with stress. If our worldview is of life as hopeless and fateful, we relinquish control of ourselves (mind and emotions) and, therefore, over the circumstances of our lives, thence being prone to the debilitating effects of stress. If, on the other hand, our worldview is of life as full of boundless possibilities of which we are the sole selector, we accept control of ourselves and respond to stress as a challenge to be met along the road to success, being encouraged every time it is overcome, so handing a healing message to that chemical messenger in our bodies.

FINANCIAL MANAGEMENT

Here I want to provide some simple principals.

Be open

If you're in a relationship or have a family, be completely honest and open about finances. Do not keep a secret bank account. Do not secretly obtain debt. Do not secretly mortgage your commonly owned property. Do not have credit cards that only you know about. The psychic energy wasted on covering these up, and that are wasted on your guilt or hiding it is not worth it. Above all, without honesty a relationship will never be fulfilling. The anger and resentment caused by the discovery of such clandestine acts is deep and can be difficult to overcome.

Pay yourself first

This is money you are going to set aside for savings and investment. As to what instruments and vehicles to invest in… that is beyond the scope of this book. Observing this practice has several physical and psychological benefits. The physical benefits tend to be obvious and include building a nest egg to hedge against unforeseen financial crises, building significant financial wealth by the power of compounding, and being able to take advantage of great deals when most others are running for cover in economic downturns. Psychological benefits include developing discipline and persistence, building self-esteem, demonstrating belief in yourself and in your future. You decide what portion of your income to set aside; most suggest 10%. The more you can set aside for saving and investing, the better. But, start where you are. If where you are is 1%, so be it. Build from there. The best book on this subject is also the simplest and most fun to read: *The Richest Man in Babylon*.

Give as much as you dare

In one of his many excellent presentations, Earl Nightingale shared the story of the person who wanted heat from a stove, but refused to light it until first it gave out the heat. Put in these terms, the folly of expecting to receive before we give is patent. In the rest of our lives, it may not be so obvious. However, I would suggest most strongly that each of us takes literally the various expressions of the sentiment that we must give before expecting to receive: what you sow, you shall reap; what goes around, comes around; the law of cause and effect; give and it shall be given unto you; it is more blessed to give than to receive; and on and on and on. Give not just your money, but your love, your time, your respect… The more ways you find to give, the more of like kind will be given unto you. A word of caution. Intention is a spiritual phenomenon that few who speak and coach on spiritual growth mention. Intention is, however, of the utmost importance. Do not give with the intention of receiving. Give because it is the right thing to do. Do not give begrudgingly. Give because it is the right thing to do. Do not give because you read that you should do so, no matter how great the book. Give because it is the right thing to do. Do not give because you feel guilt-tripped into doing so by spiritual leaders. Give because it is the right thing to do. The abundance awaiting you will remain elusive if the spirit in which you give is unsavory. How much should you give? Again, that is up to you. But, the more you give in the right spirit of giving the more you are open to receiving. And, you are receiving, not because God has marked you down as "one of the good guys," but instead, because of who you become when giving in the right spirit.

Give to Caesar what is Caesar's

Do not shirk from paying your taxes. The time and energy some people spend on evading taxes would be better employed creating more financial wealth, rendering the tax they seek to evade insignificant. Knowing that you are square with Caesar will afford you a more relaxed persona, not to mention that paying your taxes in the right spirit, like giving in the right spirit, opens up the channels of receiving for you.

Budget

One of the reasons we choose not to bring our finances under control is denial. Subconsciously reasoning that if we don't see it, it cannot exist, or otherwise believing that some fantastic chance event – a lottery win, an inheritance, a 50% pay raise – will favor us some time in the future. Isn't it amazing how the future never comes? We go to bed, wake up and find it is still NOW. The only consistently reliable way to keep your finances under control is to budget. Your budget can be as simple or as complex as you choose. It can be computerized or paper based. The important point is that you use it.

The budget can be for any period you choose. Most of us are paid weekly, bi-weekly or monthly. It is sensible to budget according to the frequency with which you receive your income, although not all expenditures will coincide with this frequency. For instance, property taxes typically have an annual periodicity or a car repair bill may arise unexpectedly. What we must do with these types of expenditure is to accrue them – put money aside in the certainty of or potential for them. The frequency of such accruals should coincide with that of your income. So, if your property taxes are $1,200 annually, you would accrue for them, thus:

Weekly $23.08 x 52 = $1,200.16

Bi-weekly $46.16 x 26 = $1,200.16

Monthly $100.00 x 12 = $1,200.00

Furthermore, we know that many expenses are subject to inflation. It would be wise, therefore, to account for this inflation. We may, then, forecast the cost of our next property tax bill to be $1,300, in which case our accruals will be:

Weekly $25.00 x 52 = $1,300.00

Bi-weekly $50.00 x 26 = $1,300.00

Monthly $108.34 x 12 = $1,300.08

I don't want to overcomplicate this, but the next point is important. If your property taxes are due in, say, six months from now, it is pointless to accrue over a twelve-month period. You will have to accrue over six months unless you are allowed to pay it by instalments over a longer period.

The real value of a budget is that it tells you the truth, and from the information it provides, you can make decisions based on that truth.

Why budgets fail

Budgets fail because we do. Four areas in which we most frequently fail are:

Impulse Buying

If an item of expenditure is not in the budget, you perhaps shouldn't incur it. Adhering to a budget requires discipline, courage and commitment. Do not convince yourself that the sound system with a 50% discount is too good to be missed, or the refrigerator on "buy now, pay later" terms does not affect your budget now because payments commence 18 months hence. The former will wreck your budget today, the latter provides a false sense of security since your future budgets will suffer.

The Jones Effect

We are extremely adept at convincing ourselves that luxury items are basic necessities. I know of one family of three children, each one year apart from the other, whose parents HAD to buy a brand new stroller for each while the old ones remained in excellent condition cluttering the garage. This family was hugely in debt. I have known people to buy bigger houses and brand new cars when in dire financial straits so that they may appear better off and upwardly mobile, when in truth the purchases made them very much worse off and steeply downwardly mobile.

The Feel Good Factor

There is no doubt that adhering to your budget will help you out of financial difficulties. When you start seeing the forest instead of just trees, you will inevitably feel better about your situation and yourself. It is at this time you need to guard against becoming careless. Guard against your welcome relief duping you into making unbudgeted purchases. If there is something you want, then build it into your budget.

Inadequate Accounting

It is easy to issue a check or obtain cash from an ATM and forget to account for it. As soon as you complete such a transaction, account for it. Checkbooks and other accounting aids, freely available, are adequately endowed to cater for this.

Beware of unexpected bank charges and penalties. They should not be unexpected. If you don't know, find out when in the month the bank takes its interest and other charges. Avoid exceeding your agreed credit limit. Doing so will result in your being charged a hefty penalty for the privilege of receiving an impersonal, computerized, form letter telling you that your check or direct withdrawal has been dishonored. Keep a schedule of the automatic from your account. Note the day of the month they are due to be debited. If necessary, change the dates to suit your cash flow.

Debt

If you have unmanageable debt, make a list of all of your debts. Rank them in order of magnitude: the highest monthly, or soonest to be paid off. Getting rid of the debts will improve your cash flow. You may not be able to do so all at once so, given the opportunity, which should you get rid of first? The largest? The one which charges the highest rate of interest? My personal preference would be the soonest to be paid off, even if it's the lowest monthly payment. Any monies no longer outgoing may be used for other purposes, including paying down other debt more quickly.

Credit Cards

Credit cards are a safe and most convenient means of payment for a whole variety of goods and services. As such, their use should be encouraged. Consider this, however. Would you be okay with your local grocery store charging you an additional payment of, say, 20-30% of the price of your groceries whenever you bought from them? Of course not! But this is what you pay every time you buy groceries using your credit card if you don't settle your credit card charges within the interest free grace period. It is fantastic business for credit card companies, and there is nothing wrong with that. For your part ask, "Is this the highest and best use of debt for me?" Think of your credit cards not as credit cards, but as convenience cards. Resolve to pay them off within the grace period.

PARADOX REVISITED

Freedom is everlasting. It is not readily explained, but our thoughts of it can be likened to those of an astronaut preparing for his first space flight. What is it like? The astronaut has trained and prepared and dreamed and spoken of his impending flight so much that he gains a vivid image of what it is like. This image, to him, is as real as anything he has actually experienced.

The icon of freedom in Christendom is Jesus, the Christ. In him, freedom is exhibited as a state of being in which there is no strife. It is a state in which there is nothing left to lose; and there is nothing left to lose because all has been lost or given away. "It is easier for a camel to go through the eye of a needle, than for a rich man to enter into the kingdom of God" – Mark 10:25. How, then, does this vision of freedom correspond with the principle of disciplined effort being solely responsible for the attainment of the state of freedom?

To lose presumes that one had first gained something that could, indeed, be lost. To gain something, we have to strive. It is my contention that it is only through striving that we come to know the purpose, value and necessity of

SURRENDER to enter the kingdom of God; that is, to achieve everlasting freedom. Our striving is not necessarily in the direction of wealth creation. Personal growth, a prerequisite for freedom, is the reward for an individual's striving to master his emotions and to overcome ego in order for spirit to triumph. Whatever is lost is that which appeals to and motivates ego. The one who responds to the demands of ego is the rich man who cannot achieve everlasting freedom.

The conditions for freedom have already been set. They are articles of universal law. We are playing the game of Life according to God's rules, over which we have no power to change. God has set things up so that freedom is a place on the other side of town, to get to which we have to drive through a traffic light permanently set on red. We know that to do so is contrary to the law. Those who want to reach freedom have to distinguish between the practicalities of the law and common sense. So to strive (go through the red light) is the only way of getting to the place, freedom, where strife is no longer required, since in that place all the lights are green. Those who never endeavor to travel to the other side of town are stuck at the red light, afraid to risk what might happen if they drive through it. They content themselves with the notion that going through red lights, even stuck ones with no traffic to control, is against the law and that those who have succeeded must have done something wrong to have all that success. They convince themselves that they are morally better off doing nothing wrong at the cost of remaining spiritually poor at best and spiritually bankrupt at worst. They never get to the awareness that what is 'wrong' is their fear to risk. They could learn from the ant who gives all that he has to become all that he can, or the tree which grows as tall as it can, or the wind that will continue to blow so long as it has energy to expend, or the star that will shine as bright as it can for as long as it can. These elements of nature do not have to think about it, they just do it as they are programmed to. The spiritually poor have taken God's greatest gift to us – our ability to think and co-create – and made a prison of it, the bars to which are chronic procrastination and indecision. They are the meek who shall inherit the dust of the earth while those humbled by the strife toward an ultimate surrender to their purpose shall enter the kingdom of God.

What about you – dust or kingdom?

CHAPTER 5

WORK:
The Ethic of Success

"The only place success comes before work is in a dictionary."

– Vidal Sassoon

SUCCESS

I must confess I like success
It's more to me than just a test
For me it's life's most earnest quest
Which until I have I cannot rest

I always want to do my best
So live my life with love and zest
This way I ride the highest crest
Which helps me fortify my nest

I am on fire with desire
Driving me on to aspire
From deep in the mire to somewhere higher
Leaving me no time to tire

Success is not a matter financial
It's something rather more substantial
These views I know are existential
But success is more about potential

Success is in the mind of the beholder
It's a burden that we each must shoulder
My strides forever must be bolder
So marching onward I must soldier

– LAC

WORK: THE ETHIC OF SUCCESS

- Become self-centered

- Work ethic

- Work at your relationships

- God knows best

- Contribution

- Work beyond your comfort zone

It would seem that to some, work is the most abusive four letter word in the English language. A great idea will always remain just a great idea unless it is worked on to become reality.

Work is an ethic, the ethic of success. Successful people have mastered work. They know how to work. They concentrate their work where it will achieve the greatest return for their efforts.

BECOME SELF-CENTERED

I am reminded of a story I was once told of a French naturalist who was fond of experimenting with processionary caterpillars, so called because of their tendency to blindly follow each other around. In one experiment, several of these creatures were placed around the rim of a flower pot end-to-end. Pine kernels, a food source for this species of caterpillar, were scattered in the middle of the flower pot. For seven days and seven nights, the caterpillars proceeded around and around the flower pot, not one leading, but all following, until one by one they dropped dead, despite there being ample food a mere six inches away. Their demise may be attributed to their confusing activity with achievement, and so too it is with us. We proceed to work hard all our lives, blindly following what someone else has done or told us to do, yet so many of us die with stomachs empty of success. The focus of our work is what is important, and not just that we work hard.

We have seen that for success to develop we have to develop. Our work, then, is to find ways of applying the continually improved self to add value to the areas of our lives, of which there are but three we need to consider. All else is subject to these areas, which are God, relationships and career/purpose. These are inextricably linked so that whatever is done in one area automatically affects the other two. The sea in which they bathe is love. It permeates throughout, so that everything done with love and for love's sake in any area will enhance that area and the other two.

Become self-centered. Operate from the center of your world. This self-centeredness is not to be confused with that to which we attribute the meaning selfishness. Far from it. It is the only way that we can give all that we have to become all that we can while retaining balance in our lives. Too many of us make our career or relationships the center of our world only to find that the effort we put into that area burns us out and detrimentally affects all that we do.

When we are self-centered, we recognize that our key responsibility is personal development. We invest in ourselves, spending the necessary time and money on learning new skills to improve our effectiveness in each of the areas of our lives. We are forever reading books, listening to CDs, attending seminars, workshops and tutorials. We are not afraid to risk exposing ourselves to new ideas; ideas that often mainstream thinking seriously doubts or ridicules. And, because we are centered in self, we have the confidence and awareness to decide correctly whether the new idea is beneficial or harmful. We understand that our employer or the government is not responsible to develop us, unless we choose like others have, to transfer our responsibility and, in so doing, accept whatever development happens to come our way.

WORK ETHIC

The first thing we need to develop is a good, healthy work ethic. We have to sow in order that we may reap, and what we sow is what we will reap. To plant a single tomato plant and expect a full crop is to try God's patience a little. The laws of the universe conspire against this ever being possible. We must also remember that not all of our efforts will bear fruit, but each time we will learn from them.

> "Listen! Behold, a sower went out to sow. And it happened, as he sowed, that some seed fell by the wayside; and the birds of the air came and devoured it. Some fell on stony ground, where it did not have much earth; and immediately it sprang up because it had no depth of earth. But when the sun was up it was scorched, and because it had no root, it withered away. And some seed fell among thorns, and the thorns grew up and choked it, and yielded no crop. But other seed fell on ground and yielded a crop that sprang up, increased and produced: some thirty fold, some sixty, and some a hundred." – Mark 4: 3-8

Our happiness will depend upon the seed that we sow. If we enjoy cultivating a particular seed, but choose through fear, conditioning or some misguided notion of security to sow some other seed, we may find that we are very good at cultivating that other seed, which may return us a good financial harvest. If, however, our enjoyment of its cultivation is lacking, we may find our unhappiness in this work detrimentally affecting our relationships, including that with God. The price we have to pay for our decision based on fear, ignorance or perceived safety is misery. If we fully appreciated the price at the time of deciding, we would decide differently. The problem is that the price is not paid upfront and, like all credit purchases, it seems most attractive and affordable at the time. The reality of the burden of repayment – misery – comes well after the purchase is made. At this time, our purchase is well sown, and so to return it will result in our having to continue making credit repayments long after we have relinquished it. For this reason, many will not. They will persevere with it, hoping that things will get better, that the burden of repayments will become lighter as time goes by. Their investment has created a psychological inertia, imprisoning them in a jail fashioned from polystyrene, the strength of which derives solely from the inertia itself. And so we have doctors who don't want to be doctors, carpenters who don't want to be carpenters and butchers who don't want to be butchers.

Remove the inertia and the prison is seen for what it is. When we become self-centered the reality of the prison is obvious. The price we have been paying is understood. From this awareness we are able to relinquish our unwanted crop and invest in the seed we enjoy cultivating.

Regardless of the complexity of the seed we choose, it is important to recognize that to be successful our work will be 90% sweat and 10% savvy. This is one reason why it is so important to enjoy our work. When we work hard and enjoy it, the load is lightened, we feel satisfied that we have done it. In fact, the level of satisfaction derived from hard work enjoyed is among the highest there is. Arsene Wenger, the exceptionally successful French coach of London-based Arsenal Football Club has said, "I try to work harder than everyone else. I never stop to breathe. I have not taken a holiday for 15 years, because when others rest, I try to go to see other players and to recruit. It is so exciting." Now, as someone who loves breathing and taking vacations, I am not advocating that we all abstain from these. However, it is clear that the man's passion and enjoyment of his work enables him to carry what is a heavy burden of responsibility in a highly stressful profession.

While savvy may be just 10% of what brings success, it is an important 10%. Savvy truly is the difference that makes the difference. Savvy includes thinking and, as Henry Ford once said:

> "Thinking is the hardest work there is, which is probably the reason that so few engage in it."

Being among the few gives you a great advantage. When savvy is used wisely, it provides the right focus, ensuring that we do not confuse activity with achievement. Savvy is recognizing the talents you have and applying them to maximum effect in everything that you do. After a thorough personal audit, you may discover that your best assets are intelligence and vision or communication and kindness. If you look back over your career and relationships, you will find these qualities prominent in all you have done.

Few could doubt the adroit political prowess of Golda Meir, Prime Minister of Israel for five years from 1969-1974, during one of the most turbulent periods of one of the most politically volatile regions on earth. Reading her autobiography, *My Life*, it is clear that her abundant skills in diplomacy, organizing and public speaking, which were to serve her so well as Prime Minister, were innate from a tender age. The following excerpts refer:

> "...I did my childish and not very effective best to cheer up both Sheyna and Shamai [her sister and future brother-in-law] and to intervene on their behalf with my mother and father whenever the tension seemed about to explode into a crisis." – Aged 10

> "One important event (to me) took place when I was in the fourth grade. I got involved in my first 'public work'. Although school in Milwaukee was free, a nominal sum was charged for textbooks, which many of the children in my class could not afford. Obviously someone had to do something to solve the problem, so I decided to launch a fund. It was to be my very first experience as a fund-raiser but hardly the last!"

> "Regina [a friend] and I collected a group of girls from the school, explained the purpose of the fund, and we all painted posters announcing that the American Young Sisters Society was to hold a public meeting on the subject of textbooks. Then, having appointed myself Chairman

of the Society, I hired a hall and sent invitations out to the entire district... and considering it was my first public address, I think I did rather well. At any rate, with the exception of major policy statements at the United Nations or the Knesset, I never got into the habit of using a written text, and I went on for the next half-century making 'speeches from my head'..." – Age 11

We are sometimes prevented from giving all that we have to become all that we can by comparing ourselves with others, believing that we could never perform to their level of ability. Success is an internal state of being. Being the best you can has nothing to do with the performance or ability of anyone else. Even if we were to make such comparisons we would find that often best does not mean most successful. A basic analysis of the winning-most horse racing jockeys in Britain for the six years between 1992 and 1997 amply illustrates the point.

YEAR	JOCKEY	WINS	RIDES	WINS/RIDES %
1992	M ROBERTS	206	1068	19.3
	P EDDERY	168	729	24.4
	W CARSON	125	856	14.6
	S CAUTHEN	107	557	19.2
1993	P EDDERY	169	813	20.8
	K DARLEY	137	799	17.1
	L DETTORI	135	845	16.0
	W CARSON	115	837	13.7
1994	L DETTORI	183	1087	16.8
	J WEAVER	162	909	17.8
	P EDDERY	154	802	19.2
	K DARLEY	138	875	15.8
1995	L DETTORI	176	815	21.6
	K DARLEY	142	897	15.8
	W CARSON	139	715	19.4
	P EDDERY	125	646	19.3
1996	P EDDERY	186	882	21.1
	T QUINN	149	882	16.9
	K FALLON	135	900	15.0
	L DETTORI	114	536	21.3
1997	K FALLON	196	909	21.6
	L DETTORI	173	767	22.6
	K DARLEY	128	841	15.2
	P EDDERY	114	630	18.4

The most successful jockey is based on who has ridden the most winners in a season. The best jockey, however, we could claim is the one with the highest percentage of wins from rides in a season. Analyzing the statistics for the most successful against the best we get:

Year	Most Successful	Best
1992	M Roberts	P Eddery
1993	P Eddery	P Eddery
1994	L Dettori	P Eddery
1995	L Dettori	L Dettori
1996	P Eddery	L Dettori
1997	K Fallon	L Dettori

The best jockey was the most successful only twice in six years – 1993 and 1995. Sixty-seven percent of the time the best jockey was not the most successful. So, if you must compare yourself with others, do not allow it to be your excuse for not giving all you have got. To succeed more, do more, fail more.

> "And to one he gave five talents, to another two, and to another, one, to each according to his own ability; and immediately he went on a journey. Then he who received the five talents went and traded with them, and made another five talents. And likewise he who had received two gained two more also. But he who had received one went and dug in the ground, and hid his lord's money."

> "After a long time, the lord of those servants came and settled accounts with them. So he who had received five talents came and brought five other talents, saying, 'Lord, you delivered to me five talents; look, I have gained five more talents besides them.' His lord said to him, 'Well done, good and faithful servant; you were faithful over a few things, I will make you ruler over many things. Enter into the joy of your lord.'"

> "He also who had received two talents came and said, 'Lord, you delivered to me two talents; look, I have gained two more talents besides them.' His lord said to him, 'Well done, good and faithful servant; you have been faithful over a few things, I will make you ruler over many things. Enter into the joy of your lord.'"

"Then he who had received the one talent came and said, 'Lord, I knew you to be a hard man, reaping where you have not sown, and gathering where you have not scattered seed. And I was afraid, and went and hid your talent in the ground. Look, there you have what is yours.' But his lord answered and said to him, 'You wicked and lazy servant, you knew that I reap where I have not sown, and gather where I have not scattered seed. So you ought to have deposited my money with the bankers, and at my coming I would have received back my own with interest. Therefore, take the talent from him, and give it to him who has ten talents. For to everyone who has, more will be given, and he will have abundance; but from him who does not have, even what he has will be taken away.'" – Matthew 25: 15-29

WORK AT YOUR RELATIONSHIPS

Many of us enter relationships with an unwitting will to fail. Openly we express our desire for our partner to accept us as we are with our own hidden agenda to change who they are. We are exposing ourselves to great disappointment and pain on both counts. "Accept me as I am," suggests this is who I am and I will not change, like it or not. We are who we are and should not have to create a facade to please another, yet to be so dogmatic about one's unwillingness to change is to ignore the inevitability of change. If the relationship is to succeed, each partner has to commit to shaping change for the benefit of the relationship. On the other hand, seeking to change our partner into that ideal person is telling them quite plainly that they are not good enough as they are. How would you respond if you were told that you are not good enough for me as you are? Enough said! Let us, then, accept that change is going to be an element in all our relationships and that we can use it for their betterment or to their detriment. The only foundation for a successful relationship is love. To love another is to allow them the freedom to do as they would please, even if that means the freedom to leave you. In a mutually beneficial relationship we need to work at allowing our partner this freedom and having them choose to be free within rather than without the relationship. What, then, can we do to encourage our partner to choose freedom within the confines of the relationship?

Be Honest

When we share our lives with another, we create a psychic bond between ourselves. We know when our partner is not at his best or is troubled in some way. We also know when he is lying, although we may choose to ignore it. How often on the break-up of a relationship due to infidelity do we hear, "I knew there was something going on, I just could not face the truth."?

> "For nothing is secret that will not be revealed, nor anything hidden that will not be known and come to light." – Mark 2:17

Cease doing whatever it is that you are unable to be honest with your partner about. To continue doing it is simply building a psychological barrier between you and your partner, through which one day you realize you are unable to communicate with each other. At this point you have to go through the pain of working to recover the relationship with the honest communication you should have started out with, reconciliation and forgiveness. Otherwise, you may decide to break up or continue to live the lie while expecting to be accepted for who you are while harboring the desire to change the other. Prevention is better than cure, so get it right at the beginning. Be honest.

Share your goals and plans

When you did the exercise in the previous chapter to determine your major goals, the chances are that your family featured highly on the list. If you are not awake to the possibility, you may allow your personal goals to conflict with the demands of your family. Share your goals and plans with them. Let them know how important they are to you. Ensure that your family is a central feature in your personal organizer. Quality time is a function of quantity time. When you treat yourself for achieving a milestone in your progress toward success, include your family. Allow them to experience the pleasure as well as the pain of your success. When the going gets tough, the number of shoulders available to cry on tends to dwindle. By allowing your family to experience this part of your life, you at least ensure that they are there for you. If it helps, let them read this part of the book.

Accept that change will affect your relationships

Change will affect your relationships, but – if you choose – it can be for the better. Doing what you want to do rather than what is expected of you will be challenging and often stressful. Under stress you may allow petty differences to completely phase you. As the relationship grows you will notice things about your partner that, maybe you did not hitherto. He leaves the toilet seat up, she leaves it down; he sees belching as masculine, she as crude; he just opens the curtains, she takes care to tie them back; he is engrossed in sport, she in soap operas; she wants to live in the perfect show home, he creates conditions akin to a poorly kept pigsty; he leaves later than he intended to leave, she leaves earlier than she is ready to leave; being late is her prerogative, coming early is his! If we are not awake to the possibility, we can allow what, in the great scheme of things, are petty differences to destroy a relationship. As each individual grows within the relationship, the scope for differences widens. We are changing. We are not the same person the other first met. It is not that we stop caring, but that we value things differently. It is not enough to expect each other to understand simply because you have each other, any more than it is to expect success just because you want it. You have to work at it. The rule is 90% sweat, 10% savvy.

Commit to developing your understanding

At one end of the scale, opposites attract; at the other end, like minds attract, and in between are a whole host of various attractions. Whatever may be the reason for the initial attraction, the glue that keeps a relationship together is understanding. No matter how much someone loves you, they can never believe in your project as much as you do. If you suffer doubt and fear (which you will), then surely they must also. There may be times when things get tough and all your partner wants you to do is to give up on your crusade and come back to a "normal" existence. Nothing may be said, but you know. If you accept this as a lack of faith in you on their part, you may allow it to sour the relationship. An understanding that it is born of the same doubts and fears that you have, multiplied by ten because they do not have the same control over outcome that you do, and out of love – they do not want you to be hurt – will create a different environment, one in which the relationship can be enriched regardless of the outcome of your pursuit.

Understand that while their fears and doubts will be greater than yours, those of their parents and family may be greater still. And from that place of mega doubt and fear, your partner's family may pressure him or her to encourage you to come back to what they regard as normalcy, but for you is imprisonment. All of this is fine providing you remember why you are doing whatever you are doing in the first place, and providing you are honest with and involve your partner in your goals.

As much as some people wish to deny it, there are emotional and temperamental differences between men and women; not better or worse, just different. Do all that you can to understand your own makeup and that of your partner. Being honest with each other and communicating well with each other will help enormously. There are also some excellent books you may refer to. Such books have helped me to understand some of my wife's peculiar (from my perspective) behavior, and also helped me to understand that my completely rational behavior (again from my perspective) is, to my wife, utterly peculiar. No longer do we fret about the toilet seat being up or down!

Incidentally, if you have children, be certain that you work at your relationships with them by being honest, sharing your goals and plans, accepting the effects of change, and committing to develop your understanding of them just as you would with your partner.

GOD KNOWS BEST

Before I lose those of you who do not believe in God, and since I do not have to convince those of you who do of God's existence, let us approach the God phenomenon from a scientific perspective. I am not attempting to prove the existence of God using scientific principles, I simply want to apply some common sense to what is nonsense within the confines of our physical reality, experienced through our nervous system and expressed by our five senses.

When exploring the question of creation and the reality of the cosmos, there are so many concepts that we are unable to embrace using our relatively crude apparatus for measurement and observation – the nervous system. This does not make them invalid. Technology has enabled us to extend the range of measurement and observation – microscopes, telescopes, particle accelerators and the like. Prior to the development of this technology we were unable to embrace the concepts of microscopic lifeforms crawling all over our bodies, distant galaxies and sub-atomic particles. That we were unable to measure and observe these did not render them non-existent. We believe in radio waves because we can tune-in a box with a transistor to receive them, but they existed long before we were able to harness them.

The level of awareness required to embrace the existence of God goes far beyond the reach of our five senses or the apparatus we use to enhance their range. Whatever phenomenon (which we shall call Source) lit the match to start the big bang and thereby create the universe some 13.7 billion years ago has been around awhile. That Source was the catalyst for the big bang suggests that it must precede the big bang and, therefore, the big bang is not the beginning of time, since it is preexisted by Source. A further extrapolation of thought leads us to the possibility that there is no beginning of time, since whatever created Source may itself have been created and so on.

At some point in time, this universe is going to expire. The nothingness (if it is that) that will ensue at that time will exist in time. Thus, as well as no beginning, time has no end.

The universe is expanding, but into what? The edges of the universe cannot be the edges of space-time.

We rightly get so excited on the discovery of something new to us about the universe. Big deal: Newton's laws of gravity; Einstein's theories of relativity; Hawking-Penrose black hole singularity. There are two things that interest me greatly about these. First, they are all discoveries born from an awareness which goes beyond the five senses of the discoverer. They began in the imagination. The proof of the discoveries occurs when they are brought from the imagination into the realm of our five sense physical reality, using mathematical formulae, measurement and observation. Hence, the hypothesis (hunch, intuition, awareness) is proven so that it may be accepted by all. It is this acceptance which renders the finding "true" for humankind.

Second, these discoveries are not new. They were already in existence. Source knew about them before we tripped over them. We are like a child who discovers words and walking; we have a distorted view of our independence from our guardian until we cannot make ourselves understood or until we fall over and hurt ourselves.

There are many more phenomena in the universe and beyond which will be discovered. It is by the grace of Source that they are. And it is through a higher awareness than this waking reality that they come to us. Our prime responsibility is to work with Source to bring about our own reality. We have discovered through quantum mechanics that, at the sub-atomic level, matter is manifest in either wave or particle form. Further, we know from the work of Stephen Wolinsky and others that quantum matter is manifest in particle form only when observed by a conscious mind. In other words, our decision to see the matter as physical, changes it from wave. Hence our directed attention creates a physical reality, our physical reality. This is of significant importance as it substantiates the belief that we have free will. We create our own reality. Nothing is pre-destined. In fact, what we think is 'pre-destined' is exactly that: our thoughts NOW creating our destiny TOMORROW. Therefore, in hindsight, the outcome, "circumstances of my life," are in a sense pre-destined – completely self-created. You and I are in control of what is manifest in our lives. This level of awareness comes from a surrender to Source. Knowledge that there are universal laws, some of which we, as yet, may not understand, but which, if we are willing to relinquish our distorted view of our importance (ego), we can harness in conjunction with Source to create the destiny we want. The expression of our surrender to Source is faith.

> "… For assuredly, I say to you, if you have faith as small as a mustard seed, you will say to this mountain, 'move from here to there.' and it will move; and nothing will be impossible for you." – Matthew 17:20.

Successful people know that their conscience is a product of Source and that to live in accordance with the demands of their conscience is to live according to the universal laws laid down by Source. They continually work on their faith so that they may surrender to Source. Surrendering to purpose is a fundamental part of this process.

CONTRIBUTION

Our worldly existence is dominated by materialism – the preoccupation with satisfying physical wants. It is not surprising, then, that man's preoccupation throughout the ages has been how best to make a living, wrapped up in the concept of survival and security.

"How best" has changed with the ages. In the Hunter-Gatherer and Herder eras, essentially, just enough was done to feed self, family, tribe or clan. Agriculturalists were able to produce more than they needed for themselves, and so surplus and exchange were developed. During the Industrial era, we sold our labor for money which gave rise to greater choice. The surpluses we were now capable of creating and exploiting led to greater demand for non-essential material desires. Man's concern about survival became more a concern about how best to survive more comfortably than his neighbors – the Jones'.

Throughout all of these ages runs an underlying principle: in order to get, one has to give. Some contribution has to be made. Some understand this more than others. In fact, they realize that the more they give, the more they get. They become rich being able to enjoy all the material wealth they desire. But still, their paradigm is founded on scarcity, survival and security. Success, happiness, freedom and peace of mind are sought in the possession of things, which is all they know. They are the owners of property and yet are possessed by it. Their emotional attachment to their things prevents them from exploring realities beyond that which their nervous system allows them to experience. Because they believe that happiness is to do what they want, with whom they want and when they want, they seek it in more of everything material: more goods, more services and more relationships, until they awaken to the truth that more of their everything is unable to fill a void of despair somewhere deep inside. Satisfying the demands of the body and mind have reached a threshold beyond which more money, more power, more status, more property, more trips abroad and more shallow relationships can take them. Some eventually grasp that the purpose of life is the pursuit of happiness beyond that which the nervous system is capable of perceiving, and when they become self-centered, the old paradigm is overlaid with the new of spiritual wisdom.

In some sense we have a duality of purpose: the pursuit of happiness (returning to Source), and in that pursuit, to serve other people. When we are self-centered, in touch with our core being, the unchanging silent self, our inwardly inspired goals are not materially based. We do not focus the attention of our work on the acquisition of things. When you answered the question, "If you could be present at your own funeral, what kinds of things would you like your family, friends and colleagues to say about you?" in the goal setting exercise of the previous chapter, I doubt you will have visualized a loved one saying something akin to, "He always promised to get a 7-series BMW, but never did. What a loser!"

The irony is that in the pursuit of everlasting success the things that are pursued by most come along as a by-product of success. It is rather analogous to the bee's production of honey. Bees make honey as a food source for themselves. Nectar, the base material for honey production, is sucked from the center of flowers. In the process of obtaining the nectar, pollen collects on parts of the bee's body. As it flies from one flower to the next, the pollen seeds from the male part of the first flower are deposited in the female part of the second flower, and so we have cross-pollination, allowing the second flower to grow new flowers, which in turn are able to support a larger bee population. So, the bees' material wealth, honey, is a by-product of, and dependent upon, its contribution to the flower population through cross-pollination.

You can choose to express your purpose selfishly or self-centeredly. The first is founded on a win-lose philosophy, the paradigm of which is steeped in scarcity, survival and security. It is analogous to a bee extracting nectar from a flower and washing its body of the pollen it has collected before it moves on to the next flower. The bee with this philosophy does not understand that it is a part of something bigger than itself, that it is an actor with a specific role in the successful outcome of the play and not the play itself, so it cuts off its nose to spite its face. A wiser bee might say, "Forgive him Lord for he knows not what he does."

You can choose to express the purpose of your life in the most financially competitive market available to you without compromising your conscience. We are taught in business schools around the world that the principal object of being in business is to maximize profits. This assumes that the prime motive for going into business is to earn as much money as one can. It does not account for an individual's emotions, conscience or spirituality. What is more, we can be conditioned into accepting this philosophy, especially since the learned agents of business – bankers, accountants, corporate lawyers and financial advisers – confirm the philosophy to be incontrovertible. This overwhelming paradigm prevents many from starting their own business, unable to associate themselves with the stereotype or, alternatively, it creates unhappiness for some who do, for they end up operating in their career endeavoring to maximize financial profits while neglecting the demands of a broader life. The reasoning of this paragraph would equally apply to a job in which we are ruthlessly pursuing money, promotions or status.

In Chapter 1, under the heading "Live and let live," we looked at replacing the attitude "What's in it for me?" with that of "How can I serve you?" This is wholly consistent with our duality of purpose. If we embark on a career or business venture with this attitude at the heart of our mission, we are self-centered and living congruently with our conscience. We are that wiser bee who understands the connectedness of all things, who sees that contribution is seeking to give and having faith that in doing so we shall receive in accordance with the universal law of reciprocity.

When we earnestly adopt the attitude 'How can I serve you?' we are using love as our medium of exchange. Trading in love enhances our spiritual growth. It brings us closer to Source, closer to happiness which is success. This spiritual success is real. It is an energy that the nervous system detects, only after transmutation by the brain, in the body or mind as wellbeing. In accordance with the findings of quantum mechanics, our focused attention on this energy manifests its physical being. Hence, Richard Bach's insight that:

> "When we come to the last moment of this lifetime, and we look back across it, the only thing that's going to matter is 'What was the quality of our love?'"

It will determine the quality of everything else that we have.

Material wealth can result as a byproduct of service in the spirit of love. Now, though, we have a different appreciation of it. From our self-centeredness, we enjoy material wealth not through attachment but through association; an association with us as custodians of it. We see it as providing a stream of services over a period of time, which, depending on the asset, may or may not outlive our physical being. Either way, we respect it and ensure that if it is to be passed on by gift or sale, it is done so in the best condition for the benefit of its next custodian. We do not seek our happiness in assets, though they are the physical evidence of our spiritual wellbeing.

Some of you will read this and want to verify its validity with your spiritual advisor, priest, analyst or guru. Others of you will take responsibility and search within where you will find the truth.

> "The conclusion is always the same: love is the most powerful and still the most unknown energy in the world."
>
> – Pierre Teilhard de Chardin

Many of us do set out intending to serve others. We recognize the immense pleasure that satisfying others brings to us. Unfortunately, we may allow our three-dimensional existence to corrupt our intentions. Lord knows, school teachers do not enter the profession for the money. Most genuinely see their purpose as being to bring out the best in the young minds they have responsibility for. Is it not true that in some, those intentions fall by the wayside in the wake of school politics, finances, and some of their students' poor attitudes toward learning? Compounded over several years, it becomes easy to go through the motions. The reward, though, for those strong enough to withstand these corruptions, is the joy that that one student in 30 or 100 who, at that early age, truly seeks to become all he can become, who relishes the knowledge that the teacher can impart. The mutual reliance of such a relationship transcends our physical reality and is seated in love. The pupil carries the memory of that teacher with him for a lifetime.

My empathy, respect and love for the many people who day in, day out serve that seething mass of emotional puss, The General Public (of which I am a fully paid up member), is complete. They are subject to physical and verbal abuse, condescension, arrogance and servitude. We all know that their role is to provide service, but what does that really mean? It goes beyond the nurse changing a patient's dressing, the bank teller crediting a payee's check to the right account, the bar person serving a perfect pint, the crew member in a burger joint remembering to offer the customer a choice of dressings, or the customer service operative at the end of a phone listening and responding well to a customer's complaint. Customer service includes:

1. Subjugating one's ego to that of the customer;

2. Being belittled;

3. Being the butt of the customer's blame;

4. Always being wrong;

5. Being defenseless;

6. Providing psycho-analysis;

7. Surrendering to the customer's demands; and

8. Smiling in the process.

The best of those who serve the general public know that they too are the general public. They are the ones who endure the ordeal of customer service with a genuine smile and sense of wellbeing. They understand that a confrontational interaction with a customer is not reflective of themselves but of that customer's lifestyle. They continue to ask 'How can I serve you?'

Making the best contribution you can is, again, a product of 90% sweat and 10% savvy. We know what to do. The key is to do it come what may, regardless of how we feel, what other people think or how they choose to behave. Service with integrity is born of love which shows no favors.

The focus of your work in this area should be on:

1. Giving people what they want. It is the only way to get what you want;

2. Giving without expecting to receive, but having faith that you will receive when Source knows that the time is right for you to receive. This kind of faith is known as PATIENCE;

3. Seeking to add value to the lives of others; and

4. Seeking to involve others in your endeavors to the mutual benefit of all. To paraphrase J. Paul Getty, the sum of 1% of 100 people's efforts is greater than the sum of 100% of your own efforts.

WORK BEYOND YOUR COMFORT ZONE

The comfort zone is the chosen habitat of most people. Prima facie, its characteristics are neutrality, satisfaction and physical ease. Beyond the boundaries at the head of the comfort zone is Territory A, fraught with progressive change; the catalysts of which shape their own destiny. Beyond the boundaries at the rear of the comfort zone is Territory B, fraught with regressive change. Those who reside here are swept along in the wake of change created by those in Territory A.

The comfort zone appears to cocoon its inhabitants from the harsh effects of change. It is like a bubble in a torrent of water. Inside the bubble all seems calm, but in reality it is being tossed and turned and dragged wherever the flow takes it.

Its contents are as susceptible to change as if they were exposed in Territory B, only the walls of the bubble, while truly ineffectual, create the illusion of comfort and security.

A more profound study of the comfort zone exposes its true nature. The conditions inside are not such that the inhabitants are in comfort, rather they are such that the inhabitants are in need of comfort – the relief of despair. They do enough to remain clear of Territory B, in which people are on the streets begging for a living or perpetually unemployed and being assisted in a living. Their self-image does not allow them to play in this Territory. Some would like to play in Territory A but fear they are not good enough, or fear the prospect of failing and falling from grace into Territory B when they do. The net result is that the inhabitants of the comfort zone remain just over broke; financially, emotionally and spiritually.

To live life successfully we must break the habit of *surviving* in this way. We cannot grow in neutral, so we must come out of the cocoon into the Territory of risk – A. In doing so it helps to:

1. Have a vision of what we want;

2. Embrace change;

3. Go the extra mile; and

4. Understand that there are no extraordinary people, only ordinary people, some of whom achieve extraordinary things.

My personal list of history's most successful people include Jesus Christ, Mother Teresa and Mahatma Gandhi. With the possible exception of Jesus Christ, these are ordinary people. If you choose to believe that Jesus is the only begotten son of God, the product of a virgin birth, then he is most extraordinary. If you choose to believe that he was just the son of a carpenter, then he is quite ordinary.

What makes them extraordinary is the magnitude of their purpose and their determination to see it through, which took them beyond their respective comfort zones. Each purpose is internally inspired and focused on serving others.

Mother Teresa

Ordinary

Mother Teresa was born in Skopje, Macedonia, in what was Yugoslavia. Named Agnes Gonxha Bojaxhiu, she was the youngest of three children whose father was a merchant tradesman, sometimes builder, who died when she was 9 years old. On becoming a nun, Agnes began teaching geography and catechism at St. Mary's School in Calcutta, and remained there for 17 years.

Purpose

Mother Teresa's purpose was to bring help to those in distress, to the poorest of the poor, the sick, the starving, the dying, the neglected, the homeless and the unloved. She saw, in St. Francis of Assisi's prayer, the ultimate expression of her role in this mission:

> "Lord, make me a channel of Thy peace, that,
>
> Where there is hatred, I may bring love;
>
> Where there is wrong, I may bring the spirit of forgiveness;
>
> Where there is discord, I may bring harmony;
>
> Where there is error, I may bring truth;
>
> Where there is doubt, I may bring faith;
>
> Where there is despair, I may bring hope;
>
> Where there are shadows, I may bring light;
>
> Where there is sadness, I may bring joy.
>
> Lord, grant that I may seek rather to comfort than to be comforted;
>
> To understand than to be understood;
>
> To love than to be loved;
>
> For it is by forgetting self that one finds;
>
> It is by forgiving that one is forgiven;
>
> It is by dying that one awakens to eternal life."

Legacy

Mother Teresa's purpose continues to flourish beyond her physical presence through the more than 400,000 strong International Association of Co-Workers of Mother Teresa.

Mahatma Gandhi

Ordinary

An apparently model child, as an adolescent Gandhi rebelled not unlike any other adolescent. He surreptitiously smoked, saw girls other than his wife (whom he was arranged to marry at age 14), and he ate meat, forbidden to Hindus, to become big and strong like his British oppressors. Later, Gandhi traveled to England to study law, which he was to practice in South Africa, a shy and insecure young professional.

> "Gandhi's mistakes, his imperfections, were perhaps the most moving thing about him, a reminder that he was just an ordinary mortal."

Catherine Clement and Ruth Sharman, Gandhi: Father of a Nation.

Purpose

His purpose for over 20 years in South Africa, was the pursuit of equality for an oppressed people. Later in his native India, his purpose became the liberation of a nation from imperial rule through Satyagraha – firmness in truth – a means of passive resistance.

The essence of Gandhi's purpose, the means by which it was to be achieved and the commitment its successful outcome required are inherent in the following excerpt from an address he gave to a rally in Johannesburg in 1906:

> "Everyone must search only his own heart, and if the inner voice assures him that he has the requisite strength to carry him through, then only should he pledge himself and then only will his pledge bear fruit… Therefore, I want to give you an idea of the worst that might happen to us in the present struggle… We may have to go to jail, where we may be insulted. We may have to go hungry and suffer extreme heat or cold. Hard labor may be imposed upon us. We may be flogged by rude warders. We may be fined heavily and our property may be attached and held up to auction if there are only a few resisters left. Opulent today, we may be reduced to abject poverty tomorrow. We may be deported. Suffering from starvation and similar hardships in jail, some of us may fall ill and even die. In short, therefore, it is not at all impossible that we may have to endure every hardship that we can imagine… Even then there is only one course open to someone like

me, to die but not to submit to the law. It is quite unlikely but even if everyone else flinches leaving me alone to face the music, I am confident that I would never violate my pledge."

Legacy

Gandhi's ideas and actions were so far reaching that they spread beyond South Africa and India to the world at large where they endure, still today, in the philosophies and lifestyles of many different peoples who seek social reform or their own path back to Source.

Sir Stafford Cripps said of Gandhi:

> "I know no other man of any time or indeed in recent history who so forcefully and convincingly demonstrated the power of spirit over material things."

Jesus Christ

Ordinary

Jesus was born in a trough in a stable while his parents were en-route to his father's birthplace in accordance with Emperor Caesar Augustus' decree. He grew up in a small, unimportant city, Nazareth, in the hills of Galilee, where he played with his brothers, sisters and cousins. His parents were deeply religious and family life was very much centered on the scriptures of the Old Testament and spiritual instruction. Joseph, his father, taught him to be a carpenter and he became known as "The Carpenter".

Purpose

To forsake his own life so that mankind may live.

> "The hour has come that the son of man should be glorified. Most assuredly, I say to you, unless a grain of wheat falls into the ground and dies, it remains alone; but if it dies, it produces much grain. He who loves his life will lose it, and he who hates his life in this world will keep it for eternal life. If anyone serves me, let him follow me; and where I am, there my servant will be also. If anyone serves me, him my Father will honor. Now my soul is troubled, and what shall I say? 'Father, save me from this hour'? But for this purpose I came to this hour."
> – John 12: 23-27

"I have come as a light into the world, that whoever believes in me should not abide in darkness. And if anyone hears my words and does not believe, I do not judge him; for I did not come to judge the world but to save the world." – John 12: 46-47

<u>Legacy</u>

Christianity. Over 2000 years after his death, one-third of the world follow or seek to follow a lifestyle that he bequeathed, believing still that he is the Savior and the sovereign road to God. According to the *Global Religious Landscape*, based on 2010 data and issued by the Pew Forum on Religion and Public Life, 2.2 billion (32%) of the world population professed to be Christian at that time.

CHAPTER 6

RISE TO THE CHALLENGE

"Whether or not our efforts are favored by life, let us be able to say, when we come near the great goal – I have done what I could."

– Louis Pasteur

TRIUMPHANT SPIRIT

A brash and focused bright young man

Always taking what I can

before I walked I nearly ran

Of course I was my biggest fan

But then I heard what wise men said

It matters not how well you're read

Much will depend on your good stead

For by your deeds you make your bed

This is wisdom truly known

From which a little seed was sown

And now a great ideal has grown

I'm so at peace while others moan

Oh what a day it is today

I've let my spirit out to play

And now I know it's here to stay

I shed the tear that washed my ego away.

– LAC

RISE TO THE CHALLENGE

- About the challenge

- Communicate effectively

- Confront your problems

- Emotional mastery

- Deal with blame

ABOUT THE CHALLENGE

It is mid-morning on Tuesday, May 19, 1998. Sitting in an expansive tree-filled park, I reflect on the death, a few days earlier, of Frank Sinatra, whose bequeathed are reportedly squabbling over the divvy of his personal fortune.

The weather is already gorgeous. The British summer is having one of its going days. The park, devoid of people, is alive with a plethora of color, sweet smells and melodious tunes. A haven in the midst of what, in the moment, is difficult to accept as a busy district of South East London. My attention is taken from my sun-trapped wooden bench, bleached of its original hue by many days just like this one. A parent and their child are approaching. The boy's mother opens a gate for them to pass through but her son, aged about five, is insistent on climbing over the gate which, to him, is head high. I ask myself, "Why? Why do kids have to do that?" The moment I ask is the moment I receive an answer. Simply, like the mountain, it is there. It is a challenge. We thrive on a challenge. To accept a challenge satisfies ego. To overcome a challenge lifts our spirits. We gain a greater sense of appreciation for that which is overcome, and by this, ego is subordinated to spirit. Old Blue Eyes was right all along. We have to do it our own way.

This chapter is about overcoming the challenges presented to you by your own ego. You may have been taught that ego is bad and must be suppressed. I believe that ego is good, but must be overcome if we are to be successful. Part of our existence is physical. Your ego is that part of you which reacts to your physical world and gives you a sense of individuality; self-esteem. To suppress ego is to suppress your natural being. The effect may be likened to the docility endured by a castrated bull. Suppressing ego, then, leads to low self-esteem, shyness, timidity and a reluctance to accept responsibility to create one's own desirable reality. You do not have to be the most observant of people to notice, as a general rule, that it is those with the biggest egos that achieve the most, doing as they choose to do. The smallest egos are most susceptible to conditioning and do as they are told to do. Once the ego has been used to achieve a certain level of growth, measured by spiritual awareness, it renders itself obsolete. To cling onto it prevents progression to higher levels of awareness which success demands of us. What we are about to do, then, is to focus on specific things we can do to enable us to rise to the challenge of overcoming ego

COMMUNICATE EFFECTIVELY

Success depends upon positively affecting other people. To do so we must understand what it is they want. A famous businessman, when asked how he became so successful, replied, "I simply find out what other people want and then I give it to them. That way, I get what I want."

How often have you heard, or indeed, yourself said, "I've done all I can for those kids and look how they've turned out." How they've turned out is as much a measure of their parents as it is the kids. As parents, politicians, business people, caregivers, ecclesiastics, authors and so on, we have to understand what our public wants and then deliver it. Only by so doing can we achieve success. Anything else will be a short term triumph – the battle is won but the war rages on. The key to understanding what people want is effective communication. And, to communicate effectively we must overcome ego. My purpose here is to prescribe several principles which enable effective communication.

Listen

During a debate some years ago a colleague said to me, "God has given us two ears and one mouth, which is the ratio in which we should use these gifts." In the heat of the moment I took this as a slight, but it has increasingly proved a valuable pearl of wisdom. We can all recall meetings, formal or informal, in which the participants have competed fiercely for airtime to get the next word in. A real battle of egos: each knowing that his contribution is the most important; each concentrating so hard on what he wants to say and on ensuring that the next available gap in the conversation is his to monopolize; and so, he hears what is being said by others, but does not listen to what is being said. There is a vast difference between hearing and listening. It can be the very difference that determines our success. As Sir Winston Churchill said, "Courage is what it takes to stand up and speak; courage is also what it takes to sit down and listen."

Hearing is passive and requires little effort. Someone speaks and your ears pick up the sound vibrations. Your brain will interpret the sounds into an order which is familiar to you. You know what has been said. Listening is active and requires great effort and the subjection of one's ego to that of the speaker. It requires that you know what is being said and that you understand it from the speaker's perspective. It may be simple: establishing eye contact with another person while concentrating on what they are saying in order to correctly interpret its meaning. It may be complex: establishing a customer service department with the facilities to respond to customer complaints, queries and suggestions or empowering customers by establishing working parties and action groups in which they participate to better satisfy their needs. It may be sophisticated: say, using the Internet to take customers' orders. Above all, it must be to earnestly understand what the other person is saying.

Be Honest

Tell the truth. If your spouse asks you how the meal is let him or her know, tactfully but honestly. "It tastes bland" may cause offense. "I can see you've spent a lot of time preparing it for which I am truly grateful. It doesn't quite meet the high standards of the meal you cooked last Thursday. The spices you used made it amazing!" Being honest in a non-offensive way will encourage your spouse to give you what you want.

If your boss asks for your opinion, tell the truth. Tactfully, but assuredly give him your opinion and not his. You will earn greater respect and be taken far more seriously if you are courageous enough to do this.

Be clear and specific

Have you ever paid someone a compliment which they have taken as an insult? I remember a hairdresser saying to someone he wanted to win over as a customer, "The state of your hair does not do justice to your good looks." The volley of abuse the hairdresser received confused and shocked him. Had he said, "You really are an extremely beautiful woman. Give me the chance and I'll make you look stunning", he may have earned the business.

On another occasion, I worked for a company which operated a system of flex-time. The standard working week was 9 to 5, Monday to Friday. A colleague was particularly keen on taking advantage of the system, working late some days, coming in late on others and going home early on yet others. One night he had a blazing row with his wife. Pots and pans were thrown, old emotional scars were ripped wide open, the works. The following morning in the process of making up he said to his wife, "I'll tell you what, why don't you cook a nice meal for two, and I'll bring some wine home to go with it." He kissed her on the cheek and went to work. Two o'clock arrived and his meal was in the oven. Three o'clock and it was drying out in the oven. At four o'clock it was laying burnt in the oven, and at five o'clock it was in the dog! Finally, he arrived home at six o'clock, wine in one hand, flowers in the other.

"Honey, I'm home."

"What time do you call this? I spent the best part of my day preparing your favorite meal and you turn up four hours late as though nothing is wrong."

"I'm not late. I finished work at five."

What he did not explain was that the meal was for two (people) not two o'clock, the time he had been arriving home most days for the past two weeks. What he thought was the end of the argument when he left for work that morning was just the end of round one, with round two about to begin in earnest simply because of an innocently imprecise communication.

Understand how it works

It is extremely helpful to know the components of communication and their relative importance to the whole process of communication. It surprised me greatly to learn that words represent a mere 7% of a spoken communication, intonation 38% and body/non-verbal language 55%. This awareness completely changed my perspective about what communication really is. It certainly reinforced the adage, "Actions speak louder than words." Can you recall a time when someone was telling you something apparently quite plausible, but nevertheless evoking complete doubt in your mind as to its truth? We are able to detect lies because there is little congruency between what is said (7%), the manner in which it is said (38%), and the body language (55%) that accompanies the words. Lie detectors work on this basic principle of non-congruency. No matter how plausible a verbal communication we may be capable of projecting, under duress, the language of our bodies, including heart rate and skin temperature, will more often than not tell the truth. This is the principal upon which the polygraph – lie detector – operates.

Actions also speak louder than words in other ways. Occasional gifts for a loved one can be a more powerful way to say, "I love you," than speaking the words. Supporting a child, come what may, is always more fluent than saying "I love you unconditionally." A company's Executives sharing the same dining and bathroom facilities as their staff is an expressive way of saying, "We are in this, a team, together." So before you say anything, remember that what you DO speaks so loudly, no one can hear what you SAY.

The relative importance of body language in communication is a good reason to lead by example. "Do as I say, not as I do" is rendered obsolete.

Ortega in *The Origin of Philosophy* writes:

> "Hence a word's magical power of enabling a thing to be simultaneously in two extremely remote places – there where it actually is, and there where it is being discussed – should be held in rather low esteem. For what we have of the thing, when we have its name, is a caricature: its concept. And unless we proceed with caution, unless we evince distrust for words and attempt to pursue the things themselves, the names will be transformed into masks, which instead of enabling the thing to be in some way present for us, will conceal the thing from us. While the former is the magical gift of words, their feat, the latter is their disgrace, the thing language constantly verges on – a masquerade, a farce, mere jabber."

I take this to mean that to use words rather than deeds should be a last resort, since the words cannot, however eloquent, convey the fullest meaning of the deeds they seek to replace.

Empathize

We can empathize by understanding not only what the other person wants but also by fully understanding our relationship with that other person. For example, if the chairmen of 50 leading companies were asked to profile their best customers, we would hear a lot about customer loyalty, average spend, purchasing power and frequency. However, a company's best customers are its staff, regardless of whether they ever buy a single product or service for which the company is known. If companies were to treat staff like customers they would want to know of their staff, "How can I serve you?" and would seek to deliver the service required within the bounds of reasonableness.

The challenge is that companies are comprised of individuals in some form of command structure. Ego encourages those higher up in the hierarchy to believe that they ought to embody all of the wisdom required to steer the company through its journey to success. To truly allow the anarchical practices of thought and, especially, speech freedoms within the company is the ULTIMATE challenge to Corporate Man's authority. When the company's values are challenged, so too are his own, and by extension, his ego. It requires great courage, maturity and wisdom to listen to criticism, take it on board, extract the bits that add value to the company's mission and discard the rest without the feeling of personal assault. The company's published official statement of values embodied in one or (usually) several documents will, prima facie, encourage individuals to express views contrary to the cultural norm. Sadly, in many corporations this is disinformation greater in extent only to that witnessed in the arena of political subterfuge. What is more, Corporate Man is often misinformed by his own disinformation – he starts to believe it.

A true communication culture is not one in which only those ideas supporting the status quo or the company's existing values are heard. Rather, it is one in which all recognize that there is no such thing as a bad idea. Ideas are seen as either adding value to the company's mission or not. The question should be asked of an idea: "Does this idea add value to our mission?" Too often the question, "Is this a good idea?" is posed. It is too vague and encourages the decisionmaker to justify whether the idea supports existing values and culture. It serves to protect the ego of the decision maker. Typically, organizations with poor staff communications are characterized by a macho-culture. Their senior executives strut around like Groucho Marks leading with their genitalia. In such organizations, creativity is stifled. There is a fear of being wrong, of making mistakes, of upsetting the boss and of not towing the line. Progression is the reward for he who makes the least mistakes, is most in the image of Corporate Man and has a crude level of competency, lavishly coated with an infinitely abundant ability to say "YES" to his bosses' demands without thought of challenge.

How, as an employee, do you relate to your employer? Is it a relationship in which you do just enough not to be fired, and in return get paid just enough to stop you from leaving or have you fully invested yourself in the organization? After all, you chose to be there. Was it just for what you could get or did you believe you had something to give? Give it all. Be the best that you can be and have faith that your service will be recognized and rewarded accordingly. If you don't have such faith in the organization is it because your ego is expecting more than you deserve or because you need to be elsewhere? If your lack of faith is the outcome of a difference in values between the organization and you for which you do not see a reconciliation, maybe it's time to leave.

As parents, we often fail to see the truth about our relationship with our children. They are not ours to own or direct. It is our role to develop their self-worth and self-esteem through unconditionally loving them whatever they do or may wish to do. This is not an advocacy for abdicating responsibility for their social integration to the winds of chance. The problem here is that ego makes a calculation of the investment we have made in their upbringing and starts to demand a greater return on that investment. We become possessive and expectant of them. We are unwilling to listen to them because we know best. After all, not so long ago, we were wiping their butts and changing their diapers. What could they possibly contribute to our understanding of anything? When ego is overcome we see that we have learned much from our children; all along, they have been our teachers as much as we have been theirs. Without them we would not be who we are today.

If children chose their parents (and some believe they do) how, then, would they relate to them? Maybe their understanding of the parent-child relationship would not be, "You are so different, you don't understand me." Rather, it might be, "I am here to learn from you – the good and the bad – maybe I ought to listen more carefully to what you say." Teenagers' attitudes may not suggest that they are the center of the universe and are here in this living hell because of their dimwitted parents. Rather, they may wonder what they could do for their parents – hardworking or not, loving or not – in return for all the wonderful lessons for which they chose to be in their particular family, so that they may become a better parent and citizen than their parents from observing the latter's behavior under varied conditions.

To empathize through understanding the reality of our relationships we have to communicate from a perspective of equality. Ego will fervently resist this. The thought of others not being less than ourselves – yuk! Also, and just as important, is for us not to regard ourselves as inferior to anyone else. When we communicate from a perspective of equality we listen more intensely to the other person since their views are equal in importance to our own. We can now learn more and serve others more effectively because we truly understand what they want. Empathizing in this way is a very expedient way of overcoming ego.

K.I.S.S.

There is no point in being overly verbose, so Keep It Short and Simple. Ego, nevertheless, will want to impress with its superfluous verbosity.

Feedback

What we do not know cannot help us, therefore, we should provide feedback to check our understanding. For instance, after listening to someone's point of view, we might say, "So what you mean is…" or, "If I understand you correctly…" If it is what they mean or you do understand them correctly, they will affirm. If it is not, they will get the opportunity to let us know exactly what it is that they do mean.

A final word on communication. No matter how good a communicator we become it is important to keep a sense of humor and humility. These help us to overcome the inevitable failures we will encounter in communicating. Communicating effectively is, in part, a function of understanding the person to whom the communication is aimed. We are meeting new people and developing existing relationships all the time so we cannot know enough about everyone to get it right all the time. We have principally examined how the ego of the speaker may get in the way of effective communication, but often it is the ego of the listener that is the hurdle to surmount.

Some time ago, I became acquainted with a very talented, very handsome young man called Stephen. Three weeks into the relationship, Stephen introduced me to his wife, Jane. The following day, I complimented him on his choice of partner, since Jane was not only very attractive but exuded a rare warmth and motherly tenderness. Stephen snapped back, "And why shouldn't she be?" Hearing, but not listening to what I had said, he picked up on the single word attractive. Stephen is one of those men who genuinely believes that he is the greatest gift to women since Adam met Eve. His ego was saying, "Well, of course… she is my woman, she is bound to be attractive." I could have tried to explain and engaged in a minor argument about it, but chose not to. All I said was, "Stephen that was meant as a compliment. No offense intended." I subjugated my ego to his. He felt good about it, I felt good about it knowing that I did not have to engage in a battle of egos to be satisfied or gain self-worth, and the relationship between us was better for it, for in that moment we gained more understanding of each other.

CONFRONT YOUR PROBLEMS

Problems are a feature of our existence even before we have life, assuming that life is created at conception. The sperm's development in the male scrotum is dependent on its host's ability to keep its environment about three degrees centigrade lower than the rest of the body. Its journey from the scrotum into the vagina, through the cervix, up the uterus and along the fallopian tube to unite with an egg is not without problems. The egg's journey from the ovary and into the fallopian tube is no picnic either.

In life, no matter how emotionally snug we choose to be, no matter how risk averse, we are certain to face problems and consequently decisions.

The inevitability of problems and decisions

Problems only occur when things change. They <u>cannot</u> otherwise occur. A problem may arise out of a status quo in which case the change will be in one's attitude toward that status quo. For instance, becoming frustrated at remaining in the same position at work for too long or becoming fed up with the same wallpaper in the living room we once thought was the ultimate statement of who we are. If not our attitude, what has changed about these two situations?

Given that problems arise out of change and that change is inevitable, problems must also be inevitable and so, then, are decisions, especially as to make no decision is in itself a decision. A problem should concern us sufficiently so that we may seek its optimum solutions. I use the word concern and not worry. Worry is counterproductive. Medical science has shown that worrying actually shuts down part of the brain used in problem solving. If you find optimum to be elusive, make a decision anyway. Successful people decide, when necessary, that good enough is good enough.

When once faced with what I believed to be a really difficult problem, I was told that God does not give us problems we cannot deal with. I accepted this wisdom. I have since learned that the more we seek to improve ourselves the greater in number and difficulty are the problems we get. And this we choose. But on the plus side, the more problems we take on, the greater is our personal growth and therefore our ability to succeed. The rules of the game could not be more equitable. So, my advice would be to go out and seek massive problems.

See problems for what they are

How we see and relate to problems is very important.

<u>Modify your language</u>

Recognize the problem for what it is – a CHALLENGE which presents you with an OPPORTUNITY for growth. We know that there is no success without growth. If problems, then, are a source of growth, they are necessary for success. If you want success you must want problems. However, the word problem has its historical baggage. We associate it with hopelessness, helplessness, trouble, pain and stagnation. When confronted with a problem, therefore, speak of a challenge or an opportunity. If you cannot bring yourself to be so positive about your problems, at least begin by calling them situations.

<u>Be detached</u>

Never see yourself as the problem. Isolate it and detach yourself from it. That way you can remain objective about it. You know from your own experience that your emotions can cloud your judgment and, therefore, produce poor decisions.

<u>Confine the problem</u>

See the problem as limited in its scope and effect on you. It is easy to allow the problem to become pervasive. Unconfined, a problem can permeate every aspect of our lives, thereby completely debilitating us in all that we do. For instance, divorce or the end of any profound relationship. Many sufferers of such a severance will carry the baggage from the broken relationship into another, into their working environments, and into their social and family lives to the extent that their beliefs about the broken relationship permeates and taints the good relationships in these other areas. Their personal growth is restricted and they may become a victim of their circumstances, blaming the circumstances, their ex-partner and even God for everything they believe is wrong with their lives, when all that was necessary was to confine the problem in the first place and take responsibility for it. Similarly, we may allow business failure, death of a loved one, problem children, addiction and so on to permeate all that we do.

Keep the right perspective

If you perceive a problem to be large and unmanageable, change your thinking. There are no rules that say you have to think in that way. Tackle the problem in the same way you would tackle dining on the proverbial elephant – one bite at a time. See the problem as a series of smaller challenges. If you want to lose weight, do it one pound at a time, each pound being a mouthful of elephant (or maybe not in the case of a diet!). If you have suffered an emotionally disturbing bereavement, get over it one day at a time, each day being another mouthful of elephant.

Focus on what you want

What is a problem anyway? Crudely speaking, a problem is something that we do not want, that is to say, the opposite of a goal, something that we do want. Therefore, we should not focus on our problem, but on what we want, which is likely to be the opposite of our problem.

If your problem is that you have no money, you may choose to focus on having whatever amount of money you want. Inherent in your situation of being broke is the challenge, a real opportunity, to plan your way to financial freedom. Being broke may have been, for you, the essential stimulus you required to achieve your financial success. Every cloud does have a silver lining but we may have to look and work hard to find it. Herein is the essence of why we need to be positive about our problems. In a mood of despair, it is difficult to see a way forward. In a mood of optimism, we expect to find a way.

Know that a solution exists

Be a possibility thinker. Just accept that there is at least one excellent solution to your problem. IBM's success was founded on the principle of Possibility Thinking. Its slogan once was "We do not sell computers, we sell solutions". Buy into some solutions of your own.

Accept responsibility

Do not blame yourself or anyone else for your problems. They are known as your problems because you own them. However, don't mistake them for yourself. Once you accept responsibility for your problems it opens up the space that already exists within you that holds an enormous reservoir of power to change any situation, and you become the master of change.

Problem solving and decision making

We may take responsibility for our problems, see them in the right perspective, rename them challenges and so on, but they are still there. We need to deal with them. Often we do not know how to. We do not know where to start. What we need is a system which we can apply to all of our problems, and that is what follows.

Do not panic

Remain as calm as you can. Otherwise, you will shut down the problem solving parts of the brain.

Define the problem

Write the problem down clearly and specifically. On doing so you will find that the magnitude of the problem shrinks, sometimes considerably.

Worst case scenario

Determine what would be the worst thing that could happen to you if all goes wrong. Write it down and resolve to deal with it no matter what. Now that you know the worst possible outcome, do all within your power to avoid it.

Determine the cause

Write down all possible causes. Doing so will help you to understand how the problem has arisen and why, and will provide a firm stepping stone for the next step. It may also help you to avoid the problem again.

Determine solutions

Write down all possible solutions. The more you write down the better. The first few may come easily, but often it is those solutions that you drag from deep within that ultimately prove to be the most appropriate.

Share the problem

Share the problem with others who have a vested interest in its solution. A problem aired is a problem shared, is a problem halved, quartered and so on. Do not, however, vomit your problem all over people who have nothing to do with it. They have problems of their own. Not everyone wants to be an advice columnist. If you need professional help, get it. Consult a psychologist, priest, counsellor, coach, psychic or whatever works for you.

Decide

Make a decision. The more you procrastinate, the bigger your problem will get. It has an energy and velocity of its own, which is fueled by your inertia.

Select the most appropriate solution without imposing limitations (reasons it won't work) – lack of courage, patience, knowledge, finances, time, ability and so on. If these are limitations, then do what you have to do to make them resources. If it is truly impractical to do so in the circumstances, then choose the next best solution. But you must make a decision.

If the decision is a weighty one, you may wish to sleep on it. Doing so may elicit help from your subconscious. It will also reduce the risk of a hasty decision. Have you ever bought a blouse, a tie or an insurance policy and the following day (if not hour) regretted your decision? Of course you have. Sleeping on decisions is a good way to avoid "buyer's remorse". Be careful, however, not to procrastinate. It is hardly appropriate to sleep on the decision over what to have for dinner! Some will argue that 80% of decisions should be made more or less immediately when the problem has been correctly evaluated.

Trust in your intuition. If you have used a systematic approach to arrive at a decision and your "gut" says no, trust in the gut reaction. Again, a word of caution. Make sure that the feeling in your gut is inspired by intuition and not brought on by fear of doing what you have assessed and know to be right.

Take action

Remember, the best plan will not work unless you do. Often, people's desire to have things outweighs their desire to do things. This holds true for problems. It takes courage, often a lot, to do what you know to be right, even when you are certain that to do it will cure the problem. If this were not true, many more of our problems would be very transient, indeed.

Deadline

Deadlines reduce procrastination and, therefore, encourage action. If you have an outstanding problem that you have not known how to solve or have been reticent to solve, I strongly encourage you to use this methodology right now. What you do not use cannot help you. Not only is there no time like the present, there is no time but the present, so do it now. Do not procrastinate.

EMOTIONAL MASTERY

One of the unique attributes of humanity is the wealth of emotions we are capable of experiencing. When writing this part of the book, the research I encountered had the number of emotions we experience varying from six to three thousand. I believe six to be sublime and three thousand to be patently ridiculous. Nevertheless, regardless of how many we are capable of experiencing, to succeed we need to be their masters, and not vice versa, as is so often the case.

Imagine that one evening you stay out later than you had intended. Consequently, you sleep through the morning wake-up call shrieking from the alarm clock. A little hungover, you are late for work. You throw on your clothes, rush out the door and hop on the train. It is only then that you notice that your unwashed body is the object of unwelcome attention. At work your boss unexpectedly invites you to present some financial projections for your department to a meeting of senior colleagues. During your presentation, the stench of stale alcohol combined with that of the decaying debris stuck between your teeth is wafted evenly with each word that you utter. The dank odor from your musty armpits is sufficiently potent to sour the unopened bottles of mineral water neatly placed in the center of the small table around which you all sit. This constitutes your worst nightmare. The embarrassment endured in this moment of space-time sufficiently lacerates your emotional being, that in ten years' time you will recall it with an acute sense of dread. You may even use it as the excuse why you didn't get on with that firm and had to leave. Yet, a sparrow will defecate in the face of another while they are both dining AND without either batting an eyelid.

An emotion is a feeling. It is experienced in the mind and transmitted to the body. Positive emotions make us feel good and are health promoting, while negative emotions make us feel bad and, unchecked, can engender disease. I believe, along with many medical professionals, that a lot of diseases are (at least partly) psychosomatic, arising from a "dis-eased" state of mind. I cannot remember the last time I had a cold or flu, and when I used to suffer from them, it was only ever when I was particularly stressed, my stress being the outcome of the negative emotions I held about a situation I was in.

When working hard on an enjoyable task, one may get very tired, but seldom stressed. However, when working hard on a task one doesn't care for, tiredness may be accompanied by symptoms of stress; stress that I am certain is the manifestation of the negative feelings one holds toward the task. Stress may also become evident when one's lifestyle is incongruent with one's conscience. We cannot get rid of our emotions. We can, however, manage them by changing our perception of them. Successful living depends on it. Emotions are our teachers and when we learn from them we grow.

We often use negative emotions as a Coping Strategy. For example, feeling guilty is how most of us live with something we have done wrong. In the complete absence of guilt there would be little restraint on our propensity for wrong doing. We may think, "Okay, I've done wrong, but at least I feel guilty about it." This satisfies the need of the conscience for self-retribution when we commit something we believe to be sinful. When we realize that all negative emotions are a positive stimulus because they are teachers which encourage us to do something positive, we can move on to an enhanced coping strategy by replacing the above thought with, "I've done wrong. I am not perfect. I cannot undo what I have done, but I know the universe is perfectly on purpose. What has happened, therefore, has happened for a reason. I must learn the lesson(s) from my wrong doing and commit to improving myself for the experience. I pray that those against whom I have sinned will learn what they have to learn from the experience so that they too become better for it, and as a result of our respective experiences, we can make a greater contribution to life."

Such self-forgiveness is an essential first step toward growing from the experience, thereby making it a positive phenomenon. However, to forgive oneself in this way and continue to commit the same sins is a convenient strategy for coping with one's sins and resisting the change necessary for one to grow beyond the state of being in which the sins are being committed.

Nevertheless, if we truly view things from the perspective of improving ourselves through learning and moving on from our sins, we will be inclined to make a greater contribution. Whereas stuck in "Okay, I've done wrong but at least I feel guilty about it," there is no impetus for progress. It is a poor coping strategy because it encourages the guilty feeling to perpetuate. Every time we recall the wrong doing, we call on guilt to appease conscience. We are wallowing in our guilt.

Arguably, negative emotions are more difficult to manage than positive emotions, yet most of us tend to experience a wider range of negative emotions than we do positive emotions. We will be examining a range of commonplace negative emotions, define what each means, look at how and/or why each may arise and review the lesson(s) each seeks to teach, as well as learn how to manage each one.

One important point to note is that we are not here trying to suppress emotions. To suppress an emotion is to hold it down, causing it to fester beneath the surface, and so allow it to eat away at us, creating the possibility for dis-ease. Some people, those with the poorest emotion coping strategies, accelerate and accentuate the process of suppression through drug or alcohol abuse, gambling or some other quick fix. It is a strategy which attempts to numb the emotion out of existence. Suppression is even used indirectly against feeling positive emotions, notably love. If someone has been hurt in a relationship they may use suppression to never be hurt again in that way, and, therefore, indirectly deny themselves the joy of being loved by another. However, no amount of avoidance, denial or indulgence will properly release the emotion and, thereby promote growth. Each emotion we feel is a communication. If you whisper to someone and they do not hear you, you will talk louder. If they still do not hear you, you will shout. And so too do emotions. Their intensity will increase until the message is heard and understood. Better, then, that we listen while they are an audible whisper.

All emotions are self-imposed conditions. We decide when it is appropriate to experience them, and we can choose to change how we feel in any moment, under any circumstances.

We decide which emotion is appropriate to be experienced in any situation by adhering to a set of pre-conditioned arbitrary rules. Some examples are:

> "When I meet Mr./Miss Right, then I'll be happy."
>
> "When the kids have grown up and moved away, then I'll be able to relax."

"When this cold spell is over, then I'll cheer up."

"If I could just get that promotion, then I'll be overjoyed."

What if we change the rules? What if we gave ourselves permission to feel happy regardless of a Mr./Miss Right in our lives? What if, when we experience a negative emotion, we learn from it immediately and decide to replace it with a positive emotion? By taking these actions surely we would experience more of what we want in life. An excellent reference for changing your attitude in this way is Chapter 6 of Anthony Robbins' Awaken the Giant Within, in which he discusses Neuro-Associative Conditioning, a process whereby we can change our "state" or behavior by associating "…unbelievable and immediate sensations of pain to our old behavior [or state] and incredible and immediate sensations of pleasure to a new one." By choosing to experience positive emotions as much as we can, we become a far more attractive person, drawing to us the people and circumstances we desire for ourselves.

Furthermore, some excellent research by Prescott Lecky, of which I initially became privy to when reading Maxwell Maltz' *Psychocybernetics*, claims that all emotions stem from just one – excitement. Intuitively, this makes sense to me. We take the raw emotion, excitement, put it through our experiential filters which transmute it into a refined emotion that best represents personal experience. One person standing in front of whitewater rapids feels exhilarated while the other fearful, based on each one's personal life experiences. While it is normally impractical to consider mature adults unconditioned by previous life experience, please indulge me here. Imagining two such individuals on the precipice of our whitewater rapids, begs the question, "Why should one feel any different from the other about this shared present experience from (more or less) the precise same vantage point?" This to me proves the validity of Lecky's premise, whether the base emotion is excitement or something more benign. What if, then, before allowing an emotion, like fear, to run amuck and derail our best intentions, we were able to pause between the base emotion and the refined emotion, such that we choose the most appropriate refined emotion to serve our desired outcome? Before crying, "Ridiculous," consider if, as Henley claimed, we are to be the masters of our fates, the captains of our souls, this MUST be possible.

DEAL WITH BLAME

Blame, once ritual, is now habitual. It dates back to ancient times when scapegoats were sought to take away the evil and ills from an individual or group through a ritual transfer of these to the scapegoat, who would then be cast out from the community or even killed. Today, it is a psychological game played out of habit for more sophisticated reasons than in ancient times. Because it is a habit, we can choose to change our blaming behavior.

There are essentially two types of blame; that which we may describe as appropriate: the blame we attach to ourselves or someone else when something is our fault or theirs, and inappropriate blame: that which accuses ourselves or others unfairly. It is this latter type of blame from which anyone wanting to live life successfully must refrain.

Why we use inappropriate blame

<u>To make sense of our world</u>

One reason why we blame others and ourselves inappropriately is to make some sense of our world. If our world is one in which we rely upon others to protect us, to provide our survival and security we may lie to protect that status, as often such protection is overtly or covertly conditional upon us adhering to our protectors' rules. This is obvious in a small child whose parents (often subconsciously) make it clear that their love and approval is conditional upon behaviors which conform to a set of rules, explicit or implied, which they have established. Admitting to the transgression of such rules raises the perceived prospect in the child of abandonment and, therefore, the child will blame its transgression onto someone or something else.

Johnny is five and his sister is three. Their parents always keep a jar of candy on the dining room table, partly to treat the children when they have excelled in keeping one or other of Mom's and Dad's rules. Both children know that the candy is out of bounds unless sanctioned by Mom or Dad. However, through his ego's need to satisfy his sweet tooth, Johnny would often "steal" a candy. In his childish carelessness, he occasionally left discarded candy wrappers where his parents would find them. On the first occasion Johnny was questioned about the sweets it took him a little while before he blamed his sister for his transgression, for which he felt suitably guilty. As time went by Johnny felt easier about blaming his sister. It was now a habitual response about which he felt less guilt than on the first few occasions.

A bonus for Johnny was that his sister, Mary, was too young to defend her position. At first she felt great anguish at being blamed and would even cry, her parents interpreting her tears as an admission of guilt and a sign of remorse. Nevertheless, she became used to being blamed. Even when she could defend her position later in her childhood, her protestations of innocence met with disbelief from those who mattered, Mom and Dad. Mary would be blamed for everything that went wrong. Her world became one in which accepting blame rightly or wrongly was the norm.

Later, when Mary noticed that adults, most significantly her parents, would say one thing and do another, her tendency to accept blame was reinforced. Mom would tell grandma on the phone that she was too ill to bring the kids over when clearly she was not. Dad would promise to be home from work early on Friday night so they could have an early dinner and drive out to the countryside but would usually come home late and drunk. Mary learned that this is what "good" people do, and she wanted to be a good person like Mom and Dad. To make sense of her world, she needed to be accepting of blame.

The Johnnies of the world grow up with the habit of blaming others. Like the child they were, they never accept full responsibility for their lives. They will turn, for survival and security, to the government, their boss, their doctor, spouse and even children, blaming each when something goes wrong.

The Marys grow up with an amazing capacity to blame themselves for the most removed events. An aunt living in a distant country, whom they had met but once many years ago falls ill. The Marys would punish themselves for not having written more often. You can tell a Mary in the grocery store. She is the one apologizing to everyone in line behind her because the cash register (for which she has no responsibility) has broken down just as her frozen peas were being scanned.

To avoid pain

We will blame others inappropriately to avoid pain, sometimes physical but mostly psychological. In some sense this is again linked with survival and security. In Chapter 5 under the heading "Contribution" we saw how modern man's pre-occupation with materialism has progressed beyond mere survival and security to comparative comfort. To admit blame threatens our reputation which is a psychological state of being. It is the picture of ourselves that we con the world into accepting. By appropriately accepting blame that picture becomes distorted, tainted. Players in the world, our boss for example, will see our imperfections, and so may decide that someone else (someone appearing less blameworthy) is more suitable for the promotion we had hoped was ours. This jeopardizes our physical wellbeing relative to others and our psychological wellbeing in a loss of self-esteem and maybe even self-belief. It is less painful, in the short term at least, to blame someone else.

To avoid confrontation

If we transgress and admit to it, we have to face the music. If the price we have to pay seems too high – imprisonment, financial ruin, loss of love, loss of status – and we can get away with scapegoating someone else, we may choose this path of least confrontation.

To persuade

Guilt is an effective weapon of persuasion. If we can successfully induce a feeling of guilt in someone for doing or not doing according to our demands, then they will accept the corresponding blame attributable if they behave contrary to our demands, and so we are able to manipulate them using that blame. Guilt is used by just about everyone who wants to persuade another that his view is right. Advertisers use guilt to persuade us that we are awful parents if we don't feed our children brand X breakfast cereal; religious leaders convince us that we are sinful people if we live outside of their particular doctrine; politicians use guilt to encourage support for their policies; charities use guilt to encourage the "Haves" to contribute to the" Have Nots"; financial institutions flaunt guilt to ensure that we buy policies to provide for our dependents; intimate partners use guilt to imply a withdrawal of love; and children have mastered guilt, enslaving us to them lest we make them feel abandoned.

The cost of inappropriate blaming behavior

While there may be a short term benefit in physical and emotional wellbeing from inappropriate blame, there is a longer term cost borne by our spiritual selves. The psychic energy expended in suppressing the guilty and other negative emotions associated with such blame is enormous. The use of psychic energy for this suppression means that we are not focusing its beneficial properties for our personal growth.

We may sometimes feel guilt even when we're completely innocent. Have you ever come through customs with absolutely nothing to declare, passing through the "Nothing to Declare" exit feeling guilty? I know I have. It is the prospect of being stopped and, therefore, wrongfully accused and thus appearing guilty (and with a public display, to boot, of ritual bag searching). Where does this misplaced guilt come from? Either from past deeds for which we were guilty and did not admit to being so, like Johnny, or a tendency to inappropriately accept blame, like Mary.

The pettiest arguments can be started and fueled by blaming behavior. One such futile argument between my wife and I occurred many years ago while I was taking a shower.

> Wife: "The toilet paper's all wet. That's your fault."
>
> Lennox: "It wouldn't have become wet if you had put it away in the first place."

Whose fault was it; mine for not noticing it and, therefore moving it from where it would get wet or my wife's for leaving it where it could get wet? Did it really matter? After all, we had enough other rolls of the stuff for even the greatest of toileting emergencies. It was not a deliberate act of malice or sabotage, and at, say 50¢ a roll, we were not financially ruined as a result. The worst-case scenario I can think of now is that it was our last roll, we both had diarrhea and spending another 50¢ on another roll would financially ruin us. So what? My main concern is who would get to the one toilet we had in our apartment first!

Try and think of an argument you've had in which the attachment of blame was not a core feature, subliminal or otherwise. I doubt that you can. Blame is the ego's way of ensuring its investment in being right is protected, even when being right is a delusion we have created to make sense of our world. Hence, the widespread existence of neuroses.

Reject inappropriate blame

Successful living depends on our not inappropriately blaming ourselves or others. It involves risking the consequences of sacrificing the short term physical and psychological benefits that are immediate and real when we scapegoat ourselves or another, and pursuing instead the more delayed and longer term everlasting benefits of spiritual growth from such sacrifice. What, then, must we do to kick the blaming habit?

Differentiate between responsibility and blame

If, while walking down the road, someone punches you on the nose because you laugh at them, whose fault is it? Opinion will differ between your fault for laughing unprovoked, the assailant for over-reacting and both of you for the reasons mentioned. So it is possible to apportion blame. It may have been an over-reaction in your world view but clearly not in that of the assailant. Therefore, to accept no blame for what occurred is behavior consistent with a denial neurosis. There are simply some people in the world who will use violence to communicate their displeasure at even the mildest slight. The blame for what happened should be shared in some proportion or other.

Whose responsibility is it? I believe responsibility for the punch lays solely with the assailant. He had the "ability to respond" to you in any number of ways; laugh back, smile, swear, give you the finger, ignore you, etc. He is in complete control of his response. You are responsible for laughing and how you respond to being punched on the nose. Hence, there is a clear distinction between blame and responsibility. Blame concerns the apportionment of guilt, responsibility, the acceptance of control over one's response to a given stimulus. Blame, therefore, looks back on an event, responsibility forward from it.

Apportion blame but never responsibility

It may be deduced from the foregoing that blame may be shared but responsibility cannot. Imagine that you are involved in an acrimonious separation from an intimate partner. It affects your estranged partner so much that they commit suicide, but first murder several school children who (to them) are representative of the children they always wanted to have with you but never did. Even in death the message from this person is clear. It is your fault. You are to blame. You may be inclined to accept some of the blame for what has happened. Looking back, you may admit that it was never your intention to develop a long term relationship with this person let alone have children with them, and that if only you were honest about this earlier in the relationship the events which took place may never have occurred. This acceptance of blame is appropriate and, indeed, healthy providing you learn from it, overcome the associated guilt and respond by changing your future behavior in similar situations.

The responsibility for the acts of multiple murder and suicide may not be shared. Your deceased ex-partner is fully responsible. They chose to respond the way they did. What if a different response was chosen, a positive response, in which your ex-partner understood that, "Now I know the truth about this relationship, I can fulfill my ambition with someone else who loves me and wants the same as I do." In this frame of mind he or she decides to buy a lottery ticket to help cheer them up. The lottery ticket turns out to be a jackpot winning ticket. How justifiable would you be in demanding the portion of those winnings which fairly represent your responsibility in your ex-partner's decision to buy the ticket through your act of ending the relationship? No doubt your millionaire ex-partner would claim full responsibility for the purchase of the ticket, reasoning that it was their decision to buy it, rather than your fault that they did.

Accept human fallibility

We need to accept that we and others are susceptible to error. To err is human, to forgive is divine. We must learn to distinguish between an individual and their behavior. A person who is intrinsically good should not be chastised for errant behavior. It is the behavior that needs to be taken to task.

Learn the lesson

One other way that we overcome blaming behavior is to recognize and learn the lesson(s) from the event which has given rise to our inappropriately blaming ourselves or another. For instance, imagine you're crossing a road when from nowhere a "speed demon" nearly runs you over, no more than ten yards from a pedestrian crossing. Do you blame the driver for speeding, or learn to practice a more appropriate highway code of crossing roads, including using a pedestrian crossing particularly when it is so close by?

CHAPTER 7

DISCARD LIMITING BELIEFS

"One of the reasons why people give up hope
is that they look at their contemporaries and imagine them
to be far worthier than they themselves are."

– Rabbi Nachman of Breslov

THE AWAKENING

I once believed in Santa Claus

The sanctity of manmade laws

The chivalry of ancient wars

And that you cheat to open doors

Let's now observe more lies for size

The tough guy sighs but never cries

A state won't spy on its allies

A man lives and then he dies

Oh, how it is to my relief

Now I decide what I believe

No longer am I so naive

I can decide what I achieve

– LAC

DISCARD LIMITING BELIEFS

- Education ends when I leave school
- My lot is determined by my social class
- History is incontrovertible
- Scientists know best
- Time and age are against me
- I am not a lucky person
- Opportunity knocks but once
- I am separate from all else

Often, our progress in life is limited by what we believe. What we believe is true only to the extent to which we believe it. Men seem to take great delight in telling women what poor drivers they are. I have heard several men reason that this is so because men tend to be more aggressive than women and, therefore, drive with a more positive and confident outlook. Statistical evidence conclusively demonstrates that male drivers are more accident prone than female drivers, yet many women are prepared to accept the conditioned belief that they are worse drivers than men. If we break the statistics down further they show that young male drivers are more dangerous than older male drivers. So, aggression behind the wheel is not a trait for successful driving on highways.

A limiting belief can become our reason, our excuse for not becoming all that we can become in some arena or other. If, for example, you believe that your color, sex, size, looks or creed prevents you from, say, being successful in business, this will become for you a self-fulfilling prophecy.

You will never give your all in that arena, subconsciously knowing deep inside that you are doomed to fail. The fulfillment of your prophecy will lead you to conclude, "See, I told you so. I never had a chance because I am…" Of course, the world is not fair. There may be obstacles created by differences between individuals. Recognize them. Let them be your teachers. Learn what you need to from them and press ahead.

We will now examine some common, but perhaps not so obvious, limiting beliefs which are so easy to regard as legitimate reasons for limited success.

EDUCATION ENDS WHEN I LEAVE SCHOOL

Can you recall the day you finally left school, college or university? The joy you felt for your academic achievements. The relief at never having to study again. Now, of course, you know that leaving institutionalized formal education simply marked your graduation from Freshman to Senior in the university of Life.

If we choose to we can learn from everything. All of our experiences are by design there to teach us something or another. The trick is to recognize the teacher and learn the lesson:

> The teacher's guise can take you by surprise
> As often each will wear a good disguise
> Some will ignore it and hasten their demise
> Others will absorb it and they're the ones who rise
>
> The lesson though not free
> Is a gift to you and me
> The price we have to pay
> Is to heed and then obey
>
> The lesson may be found in suffering and pain
> It may be taught while you're walking down a lane
> Or even at the end of the teacher's cane
> But rest assured it is never taught in vain
>
> Your reaction to this lesson may be to sneer
> But have no doubt, have no fear
> Your time will come, it may be near
> When the student is ready the teacher will appear
>
> – LAC

In this section we are going to consider some phenomena that, hitherto, you may not have seen as part of your continuing education. Show me a man who knows everything and I will prove him to be an ignoramus or a dead man.

Children

Children are among the greatest teachers we could possibly hope for. When testing an adult's sensibilities their naiveté and lack of social airs and graces yield many lessons. You can treat them to the most celebrated menu in the finest restaurant and they will embarrass you in front of the Head Chef by saying his peas are too hard. They will reveal every painful detail of how daddy picks his toenails while watching TV. They will even ask the neighbor next door why she wears the clothes that she does as mommy thinks they make her look like a tramp.

Our double standards and selfishness are possibly most aptly revealed by Tony Gough in his book *Don't Blame Me!* when he writes of an encounter he had with his six-year-old daughter:

> "Katie was watching a video just before her bedtime, and she asked Mummy to watch it with her. This was their time together. I suddenly rushed into the room and asked my wife to take a look at something I'd written. As she did so, Katie took the paper from Jan. Ignoring Katie's signal, we both chided her for her bad manners, whereupon she stomped out of the room up to bed. It was only later that my wife and I realized what we had done. One of our home rules is 'Don't interrupt!' and here I was, unthinkingly, interrupting her time with her mother. The fault was entirely mine, not Katie's. I went up to her bedroom and said I was sorry for interrupting her time with Mummy, and that I had made a mistake. I told her I was wrong to expect one kind of behavior from her, and another from myself."

So, the next time you want to discipline your child, first ask, "Is his behavior trying to teach me something?"

Adversity, suffering and pain

What would we not give to avoid experiencing these? Yet, as teachers they have no peers.

Pain is a gift. It is nature's way of alerting us to heed a lesson before we can move on. Growth comes from suffering and pain:

> "A person who is beginning to sense the suffering of life, is, at the same time, beginning to awaken to deeper realities, truer realities. For suffering smashes to pieces the complacency of our normal fictions about reality, and forces us to become alive in a special sense – to see carefully, to feel deeply, to touch ourselves and our world in ways we have heretofore avoided. It has been said, and truly I think, that suffering is the first grace."
>
> – Ken Wilber

In experiencing the bad, we are able to better appreciate the good:

> "The deeper that sorrow carves into your being, the more joy you can contain."
> – Kahlil Gibran

When William James wrote, "Life is made in doing, creating and suffering," he was not theorizing. He was telling the literal truth. In every culture you may care to examine you will find fables telling of great or trivial tragedy which was the catalyst for triumph over adversity. They express the absolute necessity for adversity in order that we may grow.

Aladdin was a poor, helpless child. Having lost his father, he was completely reliant upon his mother. A wicked stranger [fear] imposing as his late father's long-lost brother, convinces Aladdin and his mother of the lie. He dupes Aladdin into recovering a great treasure from the depths of a cave [Aladdin's descent into the cave signifying his downfall]. As Aladdin ascends from the cave [rises to the possibility of a successful outcome], his would-be uncle's agitated behavior awakens Aladdin to the truth. He summons sufficient strength to repel the demands of the imposter to give up the treasure before he exits the cave [That is, he overcomes fear to continue toward a successful outcome]. On realizing he had failed, the imposter flees, entombing Aladdin in the cave [Doubt and confusion]. Aladdin is saved by the genie [faith] in the ring among the treasure, discovered in the moment of greatest need.

On returning to his village, Aladdin is said to have given up his errant ways, shunning the vagabonds whose company he had kept [Peers who held him back].

The treasures [wisdom] he brought back from the depths of the cave were used to purchase food, clothes, furnishings and other comforts. No longer was he reliant upon his elderly mother. He became the provider [Signifying adulthood – emotional maturity].

One day, a royal procession was in progress and all were forbidden to see the sultan's daughter [They were conditioned to accept limitation]. Aladdin, however, catches a glimpse and decides he must marry the princess [In a moment he catches a glimpse of all he can become. No more is he conditioned to accept less]. He asks for his mother's help in winning the hand of the princess. She refuses, saying that he is mad and should forget this folly [settle down]. You are now all that you will ever be. Do not seek more as you are sure to ridicule and disappoint yourself.

Eventually convinced, Aladdin's mother seeks audience with the sultan and presents a dowry of the most magnificent jewels. The sultan, though inclined to accept, is persuaded by his minister of state to provide Aladdin with a greater test of his ability to keep the princess in the manner in which she is accustomed to. The minister's motive is fueled by his desire for his son to marry the princess [Scarcity mentality]. The challenge is amply met by Aladdin whose dream consequently comes true.

Aladdin becomes so loved and famed that his reputation spreads worldwide. The imposter who had led him to the treasures which are now the foundation of his success, hears of his fortune and fame, and thus becomes angry. He plots to surreptitiously gain the "Jewel in Aladdin's crown," Aladdin's lamp in which the most powerful of all genies resides. The imposter succeeds and once more Aladdin is left with nothing, for the imposter had even taken his wife [A Fruitful And Informative Lesson Urging Renewed Effort; F.A.I.L.U.R.E.].

He was ordered by the sultan to find the princess within forty days or face death [Typically, those who are your biggest fans while you are up, become your biggest critics and the source of blame when you are down]. Aladdin wanders aimlessly for three days and three nights in the desert. Near the point of death, he decides to say his last prayer [Great is the temptation to quit one step before realizing success]. In bringing his hands together he inadvertently rubbed the ring which had helped him out of the cave, and which, in his despair, he had forgotten about [Success is a formula. To repeat it, do not abandon the things which you know are going to lead you to it]. On request, the genie of the ring transported Aladdin to where his wife and the lamp were being kept [Out of the comfort zone into territory A]. Together, Aladdin and the princess successfully devised a plot to overcome the imposter and were soon back in the palace grounds [the height of success], and, of course, live happily ever after.

The Old Testament story of Joseph is one of several falls from grace that ultimately led to success with the clear message that adversity is a necessary phase in the process of success.

Joseph was his father's favorite son. As such he was envied and hated by his ten older brothers. They conspired against him, put him in a pit [one might argue a symbolic significance, similar to Aladdin's descent into the cave, denoting Joseph's downfall], and later sell him to Ishmaelite traders who on-sell him to Potiphar, captain of the Pharaoh's guard. Joseph worked hard and was faithful to Potiphar for which he was rewarded by being placed in charge of Potiphar's entire estate [You will be rewarded by being your best self no matter the circumstances].

Joseph was a very handsome man. Potiphar's wife had a great desire for him, but Joseph refused to dishonor his master by succumbing to her desire for him. Ego bruised, she wrongly accused Joseph of attempted rape. In his anger, Potiphar condemned Joseph to prison. In prison, through his goodness and wisdom, Joseph, though he remained a prisoner himself, was given responsibility over all the other prisoners [What seems adverse at the time may, in hindsight, be the source of your greatest triumph, especially when you retain your integrity, regardless].

While in prison, he interpreted the dreams of the Pharaoh's chief butler and chief baker who were sent there after offending the Pharaoh. The butler's dream foretold of his release and restoration to his former duties; the baker's of his impending hanging. Joseph asked the butler to remember him and show him kindness by mentioning him to the Pharaoh so that he may be released from prison. This the butler did not do until two years later when the Pharaoh himself had two dreams which all the magicians and wise men in Egypt could not interpret for him. The butler then remembered to mention Joseph to the Pharaoh, informing him of Joseph's successful interpretation of the dreams he and the baker had had in prison. Consequently, Joseph was summoned by the Pharaoh.

He interpreted the dreams to mean that Egypt would enjoy seven years of abundance and then suffer seven years of famine. He proposed a plan whereby one-fifth of all produce would be collected and stored during the seven years of abundance to provide in the seven years that followed. The Pharaoh was sufficiently impressed to charge Joseph with the responsibility of organizing and executing the plan. As governor of Egypt he was now subject only to the Pharaoh in all of Egypt [Bless those who curse you, pray for those who mistreat you – Luke 6:28].

The famine duly followed the seven years of abundance and was all over the face of the earth. Joseph's brothers in Canaan were forced to travel to Egypt to buy grain. When Joseph saw his brothers, who did not recognize him, he set them a number of tests to satisfy himself that they had repented from the sin which they had committed against him. When eventually he revealed himself to them, they feared his wrath. However, in a spirit of forgiveness, Joseph explained that if they had not done what they had, he would never have been delivered to Egypt and become its savior, and so the savior of all the world. His suffering and their part in it was, therefore, necessary.

Carl Jung said:

> "A whole person is one who has both walked with God and wrestled with the devil."

"Real life" provides us with the same plunge into adversity suffered by our fabled characters prior to their success.

I once read a book, *Makes Me Wanna Holler*, the autobiography of Nathan McCall. Nathan grew up in a black working class neighborhood in Portsmouth, Virginia. From around the age of 14 he became embroiled in gang culture. He did it all: gang wars, gang rape, drugs (pushing and abusing), alcohol abuse, shootings, gun point robbery, house breaking, auto theft. At the age of 20, he was sentenced to twelve years' imprisonment for his role in an armed robbery of a McDonald's restaurant.

Free spirited, he found prison life hard:

> "There were moments in that jail when the confinement and heat nearly drove me mad. At those times, I desperately needed to take my thoughts beyond the concrete and steel. When I felt restless tension rising, I'd try anything to calm it. I'd slap-box with other inmates until I got exhausted, or play chess until my mind shut down. When all else failed, I'd pace the cell block perimeter like a caged lion. Sometimes, other inmates fighting the temptation to give in to madness joined me, and we'd pace together, round and round, and talk for hours about anything that got our minds off our misery."

It did, however, afford him the time to reflect on his life:

"One day… I picked up a book featuring a black man's picture on the cover. It was titled *Native Son* and the author was Richard Wright. I leafed through a few pages in the front of the book and couldn't put it down. The story was about a confused, angry young black man named Bigger Thomas, whose racial fears lead him to accidentally suffocate a white woman. In doing so, he delivers himself into the hands of the very people he despises and fears."

"I identified strongly with Bigger and the book's narrative. He was twenty, the same age as me. He felt the things I felt, and, like me, he wound up in prison. The book's portrait of Bigger captured all those conflicting feelings – restless anger, hopelessness, a tough facade among blacks and a deep-seated fear of whites – that I'd sensed in myself but was unable to express. Often, during my teenage years, I'd felt like Bigger – headed down a road toward a destruction I couldn't ward off, beaten by forces so large and amorphous that I had no idea how to fight back. I was surprised that somebody had written a book that so closely reflected my experiences and feelings."

"I read that book every day, and continued reading by the dim light of the hall lamps at night, while everyone slept. On that early morning when I finished reading *Native Son*, which ends with Bigger waiting to go to the electric chair, I broke down and sobbed like a baby. There is one passage that so closely described how I felt that it stunned me. It is a passage where a lawyer is talking to Bigger, who has given up hope and is waiting to die:

> 'You're trying to believe in yourself. And every time you try to find a way to live, your own mind stands in the way. You know why that is? It's because others have said you were bad and they made you live in bad conditions. When a man hears that over and over and looks about him and sees that life is bad, he begins to doubt his own mind. His feelings drag him forward and his mind, full of what others say about him, tells him to go back. The job in getting people to fight and have faith is in making them believe in what life has made them feel, making them feel that their feelings are as good as others.'"

"After reading that, I sat up in my bunk, buried my face in my hands, and wept uncontrollably. I cried so much that I felt relieved. It was like I had been carrying those feelings and holding in my pain for years, keeping it pushed into the back of my mind somewhere…"

"Before long, I was reading every chance I got, trying to more fully understand why my life and the lives of friends had been so contained and predictable, and why prison – literally – had become a rite of passage for so many of us. I found books that took me places I'd never dreamed I could travel to and exposed me to a range of realities that seemed as vast as the universe itself…"

"Up to that point, I'd often wanted to think of myself as a baad nigger, and as a result, I'd tried to act like one. After reading about Malcolm X, I worked to get rid of that notion and replace it with a positive image of what I wanted to become. I walked around silently repeating to myself, 'You are an intelligent-thinking human being; you are an intelligent-thinking human being…' hoping that it would sink in and help me begin to change the way I viewed myself."

Of course, many of the characters he met inside were to have as profound an influence on him as did the material he read. One such character was Moses Battle, whom Nathan described as the Jailhouse Sage. One encounter with Mo was particularly profound, proving to be a turning point in Nathan's thinking and, therefore, his fortunes:

"Mo Battle taught me chess by explaining its philosophical parallels to life. 'You can understand the game of chess if you understand the game of life, and vice versa' he said. 'In life, the person who plots his course and thinks ahead before he acts, wins. It's the same with chess.'"

"One day, I made a move to capture a pawn of his and gave Mo Battle an opening to take a valuable piece. He smiled and said, 'You can tell a lot about a person by the way he plays chess. People who think small in life tend to devote a lot of energy to capturing pawns, the least valuable pieces on the board. They think they're playing to win, but they're not. But people who think big tend to go straight for the king or queen, which wins you the game.' I never forgot that. Most guys I knew, myself included, spent their entire lives chasing pawns. The problem was, we thought we were going after kings."

"The most important thing that Mo Battle taught me was that chess was a game of consequences. He said that, just as in life, there are consequences for every move you make in chess. 'Don't make a move without first weighing the potential consequences,' he said, 'because if you don't, you have no control over the outcome.'"

"I'd never looked at life like that. I had seldom weighed the consequences of anything until *after* I'd done it. I'd do something crazy and then brace myself for the outcome, whatever it happened to be. I had no control over the outcome and no control over my life. When I thought about it, that was a helluva stupid way to live."

"But on the chessboard, I eventually saw that I could predict – and, more important, control – outcomes if I considered the consequences of moves before making them. That gave me a whole new way of looking at things."

Not everyone who suffers adversity learns such powerful life-changing lessons. The change that makes the difference is in one's attitude of mind. One has to remain open to possibility and recognize whatever guise the teacher may be wearing. Again, from Nathan McCall's experience:

"I often recited the Scripture that Reverend Ellis had given me to read before I was sentenced: 'Everything works together for the good of those that love God, for those who are called according to His purpose.' *If that's true*, I thought, *maybe I can get something positive out of this time in prison*. It sure didn't seem like it. But it made me feel better just thinking it might be possible."

"I remember clearly that snowy February day in 1978 when I was released from the joint. My homies gathered on the sidewalk that morning and watched me leave. As I climbed into the car and my mother drove off, I cast a long, hard look at the prison, and tears began streaming uncontrollably down my face. I felt a strange mixture of pain and pride. I was mostly proud that I had survived, and I told myself, then and there, *I can do ANYTHING*."

There are many other stories of brave people who have taken adversity and molded it into something so sublime that it has touched the hearts and minds of peoples all over the world.

Bill Wright, a prisoner of war, whose abiding memory of that adverse moment in his life was the demand, "Name, rank and number?" took the experience and shaped it into one of the most popular television quiz shows in the UK, Mastermind. The quiz master, Magnus Magnusson, would ask the contestants, "Name, occupation and specialist subject," before grilling them in front of a studio and television audience.

Bob Champion overcame the ravages of cancer to ride Aldaniti, a horse plagued by leg infirmities, to victory in one of the world's most grueling horse race, The Grand National Steeple Chase. Bob Champion went on to be a successful trainer of race horses himself.

At 19 months of age, Helen Keller was struck by a life threatening illness which left her deaf and blind. Conscious of just a few basic desires and unable to hear the sounds of human voices, she lost all sense of the little speech she had previously mastered. Yet, Helen Keller went on to conquer the world. In 1904, she graduated from Radcliffe College with honors at a time when few women were encouraged to pursue further education. At the time, she was the only well-educated deaf-blind person in the world. One of her books *The Story of My Life*, became a bestselling classic. Her world tours campaigning, in particular, for the deaf and blind were international news items. Amidst her abundant legacy to mankind are numerous pearls of wisdom matched only by her living example:

> "Worse than being blind is to have sight and yet no vision."

The human spirit is truly remarkable. It is irrepressible. Every day people, just like you and me, improve their lives having dealt with the most adverse of calamities.

Emotions

Emotions have already been covered in Chapter 6. All I want to say about them here is that we often misinterpret them and so use them incorrectly. I say use them because they are a resource. I remember a colleague of mine being rebuked by a customer over the telephone. The rebuke in all honesty was comparatively mild. Yet, this colleague moaned all day about the way she had been treated.

I told her that it did not matter what the customer called her, but what she answered to that was important and that it mattered not what the customer thought of her, only what she thought of herself that mattered.

The following day when I arrived at work, the first thing she said was, "That customer yesterday is really ticking me off." I simply could not believe it. I told her that she surprised me as I thought she was made of sterner stuff. She replied "Well, you've never been treated that way by a customer." I had to educate her about the finer points of managing a pub in which one cannot hide behind a telephone; where confrontation is face-to-face; where customers' inhibitions are washed away by the consumption of alcohol; where their weaknesses are cast aside by that same alcohol. She had an answer for this too: "Well, when somebody upsets me I stay upset." Not wanting to continue the discussion I thought *WHY? Why are you investing so much in being upset?* Then I realized it is a damn good reason (excuse) to rely on whenever you lack the courage to face another irate customer. This colleague of mine could say to the manager whenever he asked her to cover the phones, "No chance. Don't you remember what happened the last time I was on the phones? I don't want to experience that again."

The emotion was her teacher. How to handle it the lesson. There will be others who react to her the way that customer did. Is it because of her manner? Does she need to change to elicit a kinder reaction? Whatever the answers, by responding the way she does she is allowing others to control how she feels, and by doing so never learns the lesson of self-control. She will never grow beyond the control of others until she faces and deals with the emotion.

What emotions are you hiding behind or running from? I guarantee, they are preventing you from becoming all you can become.

MY LOT IS DETERMINED BY MY SOCIAL CLASS

I must confess that the tone of this next piece is heavily influenced by my having grown up in England during the 1960s and 70s. The urge to make wholesale changes has been resisted. What follows provides a stark representation of the more subtle contemporary reality.

Civilized society is a well-structured organism. It is self-perpetuating, self-sufficient and selfish. Like any other organism, the human body, for instance, it has classes of organs which serve its needs in specific ways. To achieve this, its sub-structures must favor some organs over others. Therefore, it advocates, promotes and defends inequality within its sub-structures: education, wealth, employment, housing and so on. For its continued survival, society must convince its organs to willingly accept this status quo, to be relatively happy with the roles to which they have been appointed. It does so by discouraging individuality, preferring instead to promote the "common culture" and fostering the fallacious notion of the "public will".

The stupefying effect of the common culture, from which we inherit our cultural values, prevents us from pursuing the alternative and eminently more satisfying choice of personal freedom. Society tells us that the common culture gives us our sense of identity and that it unifies us, when in truth it causes us to differentiate between "us" and "them", "the haves" and "the have nots". All of "us" are okay while none of "them" are. It encourages division. Personal freedom enables the individual to judge others by the fruit they bare and not the bark they wear. It encourages unity.

Our place within society is given to us at birth. Once upon a time that place was fixed as in, for example, feudal England, during which the organs were, by and large, organized into four separate and distinct classes. At the pinnacle was a self-appointed elite, reveling in the glow of its self-professed supremacy. This class of organs was stuck in time. Their role was akin to our understanding of the appendix – it is there but no one quite knows why and for what purpose. Yet, when it grumbles, it may cause acute pain to specific parts of the organism. Change occurred around them and in spite of them. They were defined by title, tradition, discipline, privilege, etiquette and chivalry. They drew comfort from these characteristics, from their knowledge that all other organs envied their position and, perhaps above all, from knowing that if, by some "holocaustic" quirk of fate, enough in the queue ahead of them were to die, they would accede to the throne. Hence, the other term by which they were known, "The Ruling Class". Divine Right had it that they were born to rule over others. The tragedy is many still believe this. Do understand, I am not anti-royal, I am not pro-royal. If you like, I am "a-royal" (An appropriate double entendre). This continued belief spills over far from the shores of Europe:

"In America we pretend we're are all equal, but we know better."

– Stella Adler, The Art of Acting

The next class of organs were often referred to as the nouveaux riches, or new money. They were among the few social climbers whose economic and political power was generationally shallow. To their rancor, they were seen as shallow and churlish by the elite. That they had worked for their status was just not the done thing; one ought to have been born into status. One needed title, tradition, discipline, privilege, etiquette and chivalry to be accepted into elite circles. It was in the breeding. One either had blue blood or one had not. There is nothing a nouveau riche organ wanted more than to be recognized and accepted as the equal of the elite. Their economic and political power allied with whatever other influence they could muster was channeled into achieving acceptance. They would covet knighthoods, breed and race horses, buy houses in the country, become huntsmen, arrange marriages between their children and those of the elite – whatever it took. Others in this class, however, would rebel against the elite establishment altogether.

Next in society's pecking order were those organs magnetically drawn to an ideal which was not born of themselves, in the same way that sheep are drawn to the shepherd's ideal for them – pen enclosure. This was the great mass of humanity. Some were doing better than others, so were accorded the scant privilege of being known as middle-class. However, these organs were characterized by their need to daily eke out a living to at least maintain their position in the order of things. Essentially, therefore, all of these organs were the working class of organs. This is still true today. If you want to know whether you are in this class simply ask yourself, "Can I stop working for as long as I choose to, and at least maintain the position I am in presently?" If the answer is no, then you are a working class organ. If the answer is yes, you will be a ruling class or nouveau riche class organ, or God forbid, a disenfranchised organ.

Disenfranchised organs, then as now, were those who no longer contributed economically to the organism. They were wholly supported by it. Overwhelmed by the effort to respond to the demands of the organism to perform meaningful work, they would drop out of competitive existence, accepting in its stead a life of subsistence and reliant upon the alms of the Church and others.

Each class of organs saw itself as different from and even antagonistic toward the others. Hence, the terms "Class Conscious", "Class Struggle" and "Class Wars". Each would create derogatory terms to stereotype the poorest qualities characteristic of each other's class. Yet, there was an impressively strong glue which bonded the whole charade together. That glue is each class of organs understanding of and conditioning to PATRIOTISM – the subjugation of self to the state or to the monarchy, the subjugation of personal responsibility to a notion of collective responsibility.

In defense of society, Mahatma Gandhi said:

> "I value individual freedom but you must not forget that man is essentially a social being. He has risen to his present status by learning to adjust his individualism to the requirements of social progress. Unrestricted individualism is the law of the beast of the jungle. We have learnt to strike the mean between individual freedom and social restraint. Willing submission to social restraint for the sake of the well-being of the society enriches both the individual and the society of which one is a number."

However, Gandhi also said:

> "Civil disobedience is the inherent right of a citizen. He dares not give it up without ceasing to be a man."

The distinction we need to make is between individualism – self-centered egoism, and individuality – the expression of individual freedom. Society is essential for successful living. Contribution cannot be made without a communal body to serve. The danger of society is that it preys on our gullibility and eagerness to transfer responsibility to the extent that we may accept the artificial limitations it imposes upon us. We cannot live successfully while feeling inferior or superior to another human being because of their title or position. If we are going to honor and revere someone, let it be for their genuine service to others and not because of some superficial distinction.

Our stupefaction by society may lead us to justify a person's worthiness of honor and reverence by accepting everything they do as being a necessary public service. Their mere appearance before a crowd of the masses is sold as morale boosting and dignified; their parading in a procession before a public event, as magnificent and sacred; their speech to the nation on Christmas Day as the fairy atop the tree.

Arguably, this view of social class may be somewhat accentuated. Arguably, it may be understated. It does not really matter. The message is, do not allow an imposed label to stifle your freedom to become all that you can become.

HISTORY IS INCONTROVERTIBLE

There are as many interpretations of history as there are writers of history. Historians, like the rest of us, are influenced by politics, pride, greed, appearances, status and so on, which can consciously or subconsciously cloud the truth. Add these factors to the primitive means of record keeping in historical times and a different picture begins to emerge.

The USA's historical documentation of the Vietnam War will differ from that of the North Vietnamese. For one, the American record will reveal itself as the "good guy" and the North Vietnamese as the force of evil. Conversely, the North Vietnamese account will portray the roles in reverse. The same can be said, no doubt, of America's run-in with Japan during the Second World War, or of Britain's imperialist colonization of various territories in the Indies and Africa.

Even very recent history can be distorted, as anyone who has played The Telephone Game can testify. Have you ever witnessed an argument between two people and later heard one or the other reporting the event? The whole episode is tailored to suit their needs. Exaggeration, understatement, distortion, economy with the truth and damn lies figure prominently in the report. Their desire for accurate reporting is not a priority.

Compare reports of the same incident written in the tabloid press compared to the broadsheets. The facts often differ, and the emphasis on which facts are important invariably differ. On July 21, 1998, the British media reported on Transport Secretary, John Prescott's initiative to raise the equivalent of $1.5 billion for public transport from car users. The following convey the varying tones of three newspaper reports on the day:

<u>The Independent</u>

He came by tube, he left by car...

This report primarily focused on the negative aspects of the initiative on car users. Even the headline is used to incite the negative emotion of hypocrisy toward the Transport Secretary. The report highlights the proposed probable congestion of the motorway, city tolls, and taxes on workplace parking lots.

The Express

Prescott's driving ambition…

This is a more positive headline, reflecting the more positive tone of the report which focuses on the positive effects of the initiative on non-car users. It talks of the biggest shake up for 20 years, with radical changes that could revolutionize the lives of everyone in Britain. There will be more bus lanes, thereby improving public transportation and a significant reduction in road congestion.

The Sun

Is this Prescott's vision of Britain…?

Beneath this headline was a large color photograph of Chinese workers riding their bikes to work in Beijing. There were references to London becoming an English Beijing. The inference was clear. The report continued by saying that schools and firms must provide secure bike sheds and that the government would create an extra 8,000 miles of cycle tracks. The general tone of the report suggested the initiative was a retrograde step.

Each reporter was at the scene during the event, so why do their reports differ so widely? Each newspaper had its own "position" to defend (or bias to maintain); each had a readership profile to satisfy; and each reporter had his own views about the initiative, which, objectivity notwithstanding, influenced the tone of his report.

No matter what paper they read, most people believe what is printed to be the absolute incontrovertible truth. Rather, we should see all historical reports, recent and dated, as no more than an interpretation of the events on which they report, and accept that there will be other, perhaps equally valid, interpretations of the same events. If it is important enough to you, do your own research, find your own truths.

Malcolm X taught African Americans that their heritage was far more illustrious than that portrayed in much of the then contemporary literature, historical documents and Hollywood. Malcolm X talked of highly cultured ancient dark-skinned civilizations like Samaria in the Middle East and those speaking Dravidian in southern India. He demonstrated how the influences of politics and pride caused writers and film makers to portray Ancient Egyptians with much paler skins than they actually had, and how the same influences caused them to portray Hannibal, who with 90 thousand African troops conquered Rome, as white. He pointed the African American to the deeds of Nat Turner, Toussaint L'Ouverture, Jean-Jacques Dessalines and Henri Christophe. This alternative view of Black history was a revelation to many Americans per se, let alone African Americans. It instilled the latter with a sense of purpose, dignity and pride, and for some it was the catalyst for discarding the conditioned limiting beliefs about who they were and what they could achieve.

We can allow the records of our own personal history to limit our growth. Recently, I was talking to an acquaintance who was explaining that she had had a bad day.

> I asked, "Why?"
>
> She replied, "You had better consult the stars."
>
> Tongue in cheek, I asked for her birth sign. "Sagittarius".
>
> "Okay, give me five minutes." Five minutes later, I said, "I know why you're having a bad day. You're chasing things too hard, especially money. You have enough for your needs but you want to get more too quickly which is causing you great frustration."

This bogus answer had nothing to do with her star sign but much to do with the human propensity for greed. It was odds-on that my answer would strike a chord somewhere.

> "You're so right. My dad always tells me the same thing. It is because I was born premature and want to catch up."
>
> "Ugh? Surely you have a march on everyone else as you 'got out' early?"
>
> "No. I lost time in the womb. Well, this is how it was explained to me by my grandmother anyway."

I still cannot understand the logic of this. Nevertheless, she allowed an old wives tale about her personal history to become a limiting belief. An excuse, even. I do not blame her for this, but it is her responsibility to overcome it. We must all be vigilant against such limiting self-beliefs.

SCIENTISTS KNOW BEST

Scientists in the main, like tinkers, tailors, soldiers and sailors, are ordinary people doing ordinary things. They believe in survival and security and suffer from a scarcity mentality. They can be career orientated and, because they are ordinary, may become more concerned with looking good than being good. To progress they will, like many others in a corporate world, conform to the corporate culture and the corporate mission. They are not, therefore, the independent free thinkers that we are led to believe.

Scientists outside the realm of corporate life rely on grants to fund their research. Often the grants they receive are provided by organizations who have a vested interest in the results of the scientists' research. A hypothetical example would be a meat producer funding research into the comparative state of health of meat eaters compared to vegetarians. Funding organizations often want to exercise a degree of control over the findings of the research which their money is funding. If our hypothetical research project were to find that vegetarians are healthier than meat eaters primarily because they do not eat meat, would the meat producing funder want the findings published?

We see similar conflicts of interest arising elsewhere. Those responsible for the purchasing of medical supplies are influenced by the cost of a drug as well as by its efficacy. This is not necessarily right or wrong. It is just true.

Scientific research findings are often open to interpretation. The British government, advised by its team of scientists, took a different view to that of the French government, advised by its team of scientists, over the safety of eating British produced beef when the BSE (Bovine Spongiform Encephalopathy) – Mad Cow Disease – scare was at its height. Was this a political or scientific issue? Did the French government see an opportunity to increase the sales of its home produced beef products? Was the British government prepared to support its own meat industry regardless of the health costs to millions of people?

Scientists told us that the world is flat, that the sun and other planets in our solar system revolve around the earth, that leaches would suck poison from our blood and cure us, that it is impossible to run a mile in four minutes, that acupuncture and the use of herbs are fanciful "medical" practices. It is true also that scientists resolved these mistakes, too. The point is not that scientists are stupid, but rather we are, if blindly accepting their findings when they don't serve us. We too have a responsibility to check the facts.

The problem with most scientists is that they do not believe in miracles – wondrous phenomena that we do not understand. They reason that because we do not understand something, because we cannot see or measure it, it does not exist. This is particularly so when it comes to anything about the human being which may be called mystical. Telekinesis, out of body experiences, the power of prayer, faith healing and the like, simply cannot exist because we do not understand them, cannot or have not witnessed or measured them.

A small (but ever growing) minority of scientists care more about being great than looking great. They also believe in miracles. These are the scientists who know that the unknown (the miracle) is out there just waiting to become known. They are not limited to using their five senses to discover truths. Dr. Joseph Murphy in *The Power of Your Subconscious Mind*, tells of how great discoveries were made by Edison, Marconi, Kettering, Poincare, Einstein, Friedrich Von Stradonitz, Nikola Tesla, Agassiz, Banting and Blenk-Schmidt using their subconscious minds (or more correctly THE subconscious mind).

The scientist that believes in miracles is the one that makes the great breakthroughs, that turns hunches and intuition into worthwhile discoveries. We are all in danger of being less than we can be by labelling ourselves. In doing so, we limit ourselves to only those truths that lie within the confines of our label. We become guided by doctrine and rules. If the rules we are playing by change (or there happen to be more or fewer rules to the game than we are aware) we are unable to detect the change, for our vision is impaired by our adherence to the dogma, which becomes like a beloved, but doomed ship to a devoted captain. We believe it has served us so well that we are prepared to sink with it.

TIME AND AGE ARE AGAINST ME

Time is a concept which man has shaped to suit his lifestyle. In fact, seconds, minutes and hours exist nowhere in the universe other than in the mind of man. Those units of account are designed to change the nebulous concept of time into the manageable use of time. It is a brilliant mind game.

The most efficient predator on earth, the shark, does not need an alarm clock to know it is time to brush its teeth and go to work, or a Rolex to tell it that it is time for lunch. However, this mental unitization of time works well for man. But when you see a silver lining, expect it to be attached to a cloud. The cloud over time is man's abuse of it.

Every day, we all have the same amount of time – 24 hours. And since we generally do not know when we are going to die, no one can say you have got more time than me. Our abuse of time is manifest in a series of lies about not having time:

"It's okay for you. I've got no time to keep fit."

"When do I ever have the time to study?"

"All that planning takes too much time."

"I never have the time to spend with the children."

"I just don't seem to have the time to eat properly."

Need I go on? Whatever we find ourselves not having time for, we can be certain that someone else is. The truth, therefore, is that the thing is not a sufficient enough priority for us to make time for it. STOP! Listen to your internal chatter right now. Is it saying "You know, there's some truth in that," or is it saying "Yeah, but...?" If it is the latter, may I respectfully suggest that you get your BUT out of the way. When it precedes all you do, life stinks!

Age does not matter unless you want it to… unless you allow it to. There was a study conducted in the USA which I only vaguely recall. The researcher took a group of elderly people from their residential care home to isolated lodgings out of town. She surrounded them with music and memorabilia from a time when they were younger. The group exhibited a fall in blood pressure and general easing of ailments and conditions associated with ageing. Returned to their normal environment the conditions and ailments returned. Their mental condition affected their physical condition. Every time I attend a family gathering, this research is reinforced in my mind. I listen to the 6-10 year olds calling the 17-25 year olds old, and then hear the 17-25 year olds calling the 35-50 year olds old, who in turn regard the 60+s as old. In isolation they probably never consider their age so much. Age is relative. It can be related to other people's views of how you should be, or to how you want to feel.

If you consider yourself to be too old, you may find yourself using insufficient time as your excuse for non-achievement. Seize the day. Live as if dying is not an option. An actuary can tell us when, statistically, we are expected to die based on averages and norms. There are no average people and the only norm I know is christened Norman, but prefers to be called Normie!

If you consider yourself to be too young to achieve something, take care that it does not become your excuse for non-achievement. Tomorrow, I'll become great is not good enough unless you are using a particular age as a guidepost in planning your success which you are working toward right now. Be certain that whatever it is you think you are too young to be, do or have, someone else as young as you is, does or has. I know you have encountered individuals who seem wise beyond their years, who command sufficient respect and authority to run a major organization or, perhaps, have achieved the financial success in their early-twenties that is normally associated with someone in their mid-fifties. It is not age, but maturity that matters.

Examples abound in everyday life of so-called elderly people who have the energy and life force we attribute to someone half their age. They look ten or fifteen years younger than they are and behave accordingly. Then, of course, there are those examples of so-called young people who look and behave as though some quirk of fate has shoved them through a time warp, tragically ageing them beyond all notions of justice and equity. The truth is that each of us is responsible for our own thinking about time and age. If we want to be limited by them, we will be.

I AM NOT A LUCKY PERSON

This is a major limiting belief. It stops people from even attempting a task or endeavor. It is the clearest indication that an individual has not taken sufficient personal responsibility for their success. They relinquish their power by believing that good old Lady Luck is the sleeping partner of anybody else but them. What is luck anyway? To be lucky is to be favored by chance. Chance is a probability, and a probability is a likely or possible outcome.

To be lucky, therefore, is to achieve a likely or possible favored outcome. Can we affect likely or possible favored outcomes? That is to say, can we create our own luck? Imagine that today you have started playing golf for the first time. What do you think your chances are of getting a hole-in-one at a par 3 hole? Maybe you cannot define it precisely as a 3 in 1 or 1,000 in 1 chance because you lack the experience to know. Your first thought may be no chance! But I am sure you will agree that a practiced, skilled professional has a better chance than you. Is it because he is luckier than you? No, it is precisely because he is more practiced and more skilled than you. All the skill you need comes from practice, practice and more practice. But what about those born with a natural talent? We are all born with a natural talent for something or other. Unfortunately, too many people mistakenly believe their only natural talent is laziness. The natural talent excuse for non-achievement is an inherent part of the lucky excuse, i.e., someone over there is lucky because of their natural talent and I am not because I have no natural talent.

Remaining with sporting analogies, it is not natural for a human being to stand with the balance of a Tyrannosaurus Rex, contorting his body so that many parts are moving against each other in an effort to swing a rod of iron or wood in order to hit a ball of plastic coated elastic bands a few hundred yards for fun or money. Is it? We find skiing so difficult at the first time of asking because it is unnatural to us. Even the best sprinters have to develop techniques unnatural to them to reach the pinnacle of their chosen endeavor; even they have to practice and develop their skills. The human will is such that we are well prepared to overcome sometimes seemingly insurmountable challenges if we want to enough.

To summarize, there are four things we have to do to make our own luck:

1) <u>Believe in luck</u> – that is to know that practicing and developing your skills will increase the probability of a favored outcome;

2) <u>Know your outcome</u> – you need to know what it is you want luck to bring you. If it is a hole-in-one, you have to aim for the flag;

3) <u>Take action</u> – you cannot expect anything to happen unless you happen. As Woody Allen said: "Eighty percent of success is showing up." As a bit of fun and research for this section of the book, I asked everyone I know whether they play the National Lottery. About 60% said yes. Another

question I asked them was, "Would you like to win the Lottery jackpot?" Ninety percent said yes. Therefore, 30% of people who want to win the Lottery jackpot are not even participating. They are giving themselves no chance of winning. Further questions revealed that the 30% are not participating because they do not believe they can win it. While I agree the odds are stacked against them, this finding illuminates a principal reason why most people do not pursue what they really want to do to a successful conclusion as being a lack of belief that *they* can succeed at it. Success at it is what happens to other people;

4) <u>Practice</u> – it is through practice and improving your skills in your chosen endeavor that you load Lady Luck's dice in your favor.

OPPORTUNITY KNOCKS BUT ONCE

Accidents do not happen. Events that we call accidents, just like those we call luck, are created when the elements of serendipity, the faculty of making fortunate discoveries by chance; synchronicity, an apparently meaningful coincidence in time of two or more events that are casually unrelated; and grace, goodwill or the will of God combine. The combination of these three elements creates an opportunity. An opportunity is where favorable conditions exist for success.

We often hear of a person's success that: "He was lucky to be in the right place at the right time, if not for which he'd be just like you and me." In truth, we are all in the right place at the right time, yet unlike 'him' we fail to realize opportunity. This, I believe, is for one of two reasons:

1) We simply do not take the required action with the sustained commitment necessary to see the opportunity through to a successful conclusion. I'm sure, like me, you've had at least one idea (opportunity) which you absolutely knew could be successful only to put it on the backburner for a while, allowing it to fester in the daily routine of your life and then later to see your very idea selling successfully in the stores having been acted upon by someone else. Damn, how frustrating! These unfulfilled ideas, or missed opportunities, can be far more basic than a great scheme to bring financial success overnight. And, more often than this;

2) One or more of the three elements which combine to create opportunity is not present. The possibility of opportunity is around us all the time.

We must be aware of this in order to capitalize on it. We saw in Chapter 3 how penicillin could so easily have been discovered four years before Dr. Alexander Fleming was credited with its discovery, if only those involved in its near discovery had been awake to the possibility of opportunity. The best way I can find to define this awareness of possibility is to say that you should live expecting opportunity to knock. If you have a chance meeting, or are involved in an unusual (or indeed most usual) event and ask yourself, "What was all that about?" do not leave matters there. Think synchronicity, "Why here?" "Why now?" These questions may guide your thoughts to serendipity, "What else is there to this?" And, with the grace of God, you may find some unexpected answers that lead you to say, "What an opportunity," just like you have in the past. Only this time, you will take action if it's an opportunity that you wish to pursue. Whether it is or is not, at least you will no longer say: "He was lucky to be in the right place at the right time, if not for which he would be just like you and me." You now know the truth is that if you had taken any one of the many opportunities around you, you would be like him!

You now have a remedy for missed opportunity. If hitherto you were unaware that taking action is a prerequisite for capitalizing on opportunity, you do now. Some say that knowledge is power. I'm not sure. But I am certain that knowledge is the key to empowerment. You now have knowledge of the three elements which combine to create opportunity so are able to recognize it and indeed help to create it by introducing any one of the elements not present for opportunity to occur. So, be empowered. Go forth and seek opportunity.

I AM SEPARATE FROM ALL ELSE

Perhaps the greatest lesson we can ever learn is one taught by nature. It is the greatest lesson because once learned by all, the elusive state of utopia would exist on planet earth. The lesson is that everything in the universe is inextricably a part of everything else in the universe. The smallest ecosystems are a part of larger ecosystems, the ultimate ecosystem being the universe itself. Unity is characterized by interdependence. In the final section of Chapter 1, Learn to Love, we looked at the biblical and scientific proofs of this truth. Now, we are going to improve our intellectual understanding of it by looking at how we relate to other phenomena in our world.

We are to nature as an abusive husband is to his devoted and loving wife. His unfettered abuse is met with more unconditional love, in the hope that one day her love will change his ways. She may pray, "Father, forgive him. I know he loves me. Help him to overcome his burdens so that he may be free to love."

Forester, Richard St. Barbe Baker (1889 – 1982) wrote:

> "Almost everywhere in the world, man has been disregarding the Divine Law and the Laws of Nature to his own undoing. In his pride, he has rampaged over the stage of the earth, forgetting that he is only one of the players put there to play his part in harmony and oneness with all living things."

James Lovelock describes the truth about our relationship with all of nature:

> "The entire range of living matter on earth, from Wales to viruses, and from oaks to algae, could be regarded as constituting a single living entity capable of manipulating the earth's atmosphere to suit its overall needs and endowed with faculties and powers far beyond those of its constituent parts."

How, then, do we come to such a reverent understanding of our role in life's great play?

I believe there is a hierarchy of understanding. At the base level we have **cognitive** understanding which may progress to **emotional** understanding and finally to **spiritual** understanding.

We gather information through our nervous system and interpret what it means. Only when we understand what that information means do we move on to the next level of understanding. For instance, we see rain fall from the clouds. It germinates our crops which we see grow. Unless we had developed an understanding of the causal relationship between rain and crop growth we would never have developed farming to the extent that we have. So, seeing rain fall and crops grow led to a cognitive understanding, i.e., the causal relationship between rain falling and crop growth. Understanding that rain gives rise to crop growth and, therefore, our ability to feed ourselves may, in turn, give rise to an emotional understanding; a liking for rain.

Alternatively, if we spend a week planning a picnic with our best friends and it rains during the event, we may understand that rain is wet, which may lead to the cognition that the soggy sandwiches and uncomfortable clothing is due to the rain, which, in turn, may lead to our emoting a dislike for rain.

Over time, we will develop many cognitive and emotional understandings of rain, which may be associated with the way it looks as a droplet on the petal of a rose, the havoc it wreaks when driving in it, the postponement of sporting events it causes, the freshness it brings to a pine forest, the supply of water it brings to the faucets in our homes. The entire collection of emotional understandings we gain about rain may lead us to a spiritual understanding of it. Rain is water. Seventy percent of our physical being is water. It and we are one. There is no corporeal life without it. Our relationship with it is intrinsic at all levels: physical, intellectual, emotional and spiritual.

From a spiritual perspective, all of our experiences of rain (and all other phenomenon) are lessons to teach us the truth about our unity with it and them. When we achieve a spiritual understanding of all things we interpret our world from a different perspective. Our decisions are determined by unselfish spiritual criteria and not by the selfish physical, intellectual and emotional conditions that we have come to take for granted as rational. We understand that all things, no matter how good or bad they may seem at the other levels of understanding, are designed for our benefit and never for our disadvantage. We thank God for the food we eat, and thank the food for giving up its own life so that we may continue our physical existence. We do not just talk to plants, we have conversations with them. And, we develop loving relationships with our toothbrushes, and our clocks, and our pots and pans. The slightest occurrence brings a smile to our face. This is unity: a utopia in which we dare not cut off our nose to spite our face.

This, then, is an intellectual understanding of unity. Can we, however, raise human consciousness to a level sufficient to achieve utopia in our physical reality? We are each unique. As such we are an obstacle to the truth. Our past experiences color and cloud our understanding of what is at the physical, cognitive and emotional levels, preventing us from seeing the truth. Thus, we may each interpret stimuli at these levels differently.

Two people are given medicine. A likes the taste, B does not. A is cured of his ailment, B is not. In isolation their physical, cognitive and emotional understandings of the medicine will be very different.

Two people are taken on safari. They witness a pride of lions preying on a gazelle. The gazelle is chased down. Its throat is ripped out. Immediately, the entire pride feasts on the kill. Person A was brought up in a city far away. He had previously seen lions only in a zoo. He concludes that they are vicious and cruel and must be feared. Person B knows lions very well. The villagers where he lives often recount many folk tales about the lion's prowess. Seeing the kill, he concludes that lions are more graceful, powerful and proud than the most outrageous of all the folk tales he can remember about them. He is in awe of the lion. It is a beast to be respected.

Two people dine together. A spends the entire meal belching his approval of each course, while B suppresses the body's natural mechanisms to expel excess gas. A concludes that B, and everyone of the same culture, is without manners, without tradition and custom. In A's culture, belching is a way of showing approval for a great meal. The louder the belch, the more the enjoyment of the meal. B concludes that A, and everyone of the same culture, is without manners, is uncouth and uncivilized. B's are a stoic people who see most forms of self-expression as gaudy and irreverent. Neither will confront the other and thereby achieve a better understanding of him. Their silent disapproval becomes prejudice, which confirms their separateness as peoples.

At the spiritual level of understanding, there is only one interpretation of events. Each person understands that the lessons he needs to learn at the lower levels of understanding are different from those which others have to learn. And so, each person's part in the play is different, which makes for a great and exciting play:

> "Thanks be to God, for the world is a rich collection of everything, of which we are stewards of just a little, while others possess just a little else. Blessed are the moments in which our estates are shared, for then we have communion, and blessed are the moments in which our estates are ours alone, for then we may revel in the glory of our individuality."
>
> – LAC

To achieve a spiritual level of understanding from which the evidence of unity is clear, we need to overcome ourselves. We need to appreciate that what we do; our beliefs and feelings are merely representative of our precise part in the entire play. And what other actors do, believe and feel is representative of their precise roles in the entire play. No one is right. No one is wrong. In overcoming ourselves we will be free to love like the abusive husband who overcomes his burdens, and love is the key which unlocks the door to understanding.

To overcome ourselves, we must know the truth. To know the truth, we must overcome ourselves. This is life's most profound "chicken or egg" paradox. But, truth is the canvas of everlasting success, so we must each solve the paradox to achieve everlasting success.

Is a true understanding of unity a practical conclusion to our evolution or simply a destination to which we may only travel intellectually?

The Oxford English Dictionary defines utopia as an "…imaginary place with perfect social and political system; ideally perfect place or state of things." Of course, what is perfect and ideal for you may not be so for me. Utopia, therefore, must be a state of being within each individual. A place of infinite peace and harmony. The very expression of everlasting success, which itself comes from a spiritual understanding of the world, that is, a true knowledge of the unity of all things. Unity, therefore, is with the spirit of the beholder. It is a gift of everlasting success.

CHAPTER 8

REALIZE YOUR GENIUS

"Imagination is more important than knowledge."

– Albert Einstein

A BRIEF MOMENT IN TIME

Shining bright, bringing light to the world

It doesn't matter whether boy or girl

Come dance, come whirl and twirl

You precious gem, you precious pearl

Cosmic dust displaced

You joined the human race

Living life at pace

On the earth's surface

When you discover haste

You will reduce your pace

Bringing in its place

An everlasting grace

Now that you're on track

You'll shed that dragging sack

And you're never going back

To the mediocre pack

– LAC

REALIZE YOUR GENIUS

- What is genius?

- Keys to realizing your genius

- Falling short of genius

- A question of balance

WHAT IS GENIUS?

Again, I rely on the Oxford English Dictionary: "Natural ability or tendency; special mental endowments; exalted intellectual power, instinctive and extraordinary imaginative, creative, or inventive capacity; person having this." What is interesting about this definition is that it says nothing of the expression of genius. Genius is innate. No one recognizes this innate faculty until it is outwardly expressed. So genius lies within us all. A genius is an individual who has outwardly expressed or demonstrated the faculty of genius; an ordinary person who has accomplished an extraordinary thing. Everyone else is a genius-in-waiting.

How can I say that genius is a faculty innate in all of us? The indestructibility of matter and energy is proven. Rather than perish, it is transformed into other matter or energy. Water into vapor, natural gas into heat. The components of the air we inhale differ from those which we exhale. As well as being transformed, energy and matter are also transferred. The nutrients in decaying vegetation feed the soil and are used by the crop of grass which feed the cattle on which we may dine. Eventually we die and recycle the nutrients back to the soil. One such nutrient, iron, may be mined in years to come to make a bit for a drill. This matter and energy has been transformed, transferred and recycled since the beginning of the universe.

From the field of study known as psychoneuroimmunology (PNI or PENI) – the connection between our psychological function, nervous system and immune system – we learn that each cell has intelligence – a mind of its own – and that it is folly to talk of mind and body as separate entities. Cells are conscious and have awareness. They communicate with each other, just as you and I (cells in the body of humankind, so to speak) communicate with each other. Body affects mind as much as mind affects body. Diet, exercise, posture, breathing and relaxation are as important for a healthy mind as, say, positive thinking and positive emotions are for a healthy body.

A cell is matter, its intelligence energy. Like all other matter and energy, they date back to the beginning of the universe; transformed, transferred and recycled since that time. Part of a cell's intelligence is memory. Each cell (like you and I) is equipped with a memory which dates back to the big bang (and, who knows, maybe before). Ingenious discoveries are preceded by ingenious insights, which denote the activation of subconscious memory, which pre-exists our physical existence. When John the Baptist doused

Jesus, it is said that the heavens opened up to him. Some religious scholars have interpreted this as meaning that the memory of his pre-human existence returned to Him. He fully recalled His life as a spirit, including all the things that God taught Him, that is, everything there is to know about the universe. Jesus' knowledge enabled him to perform some very extraordinary feats. Jesus said "These things I do, you can do also." Thus, the innate genius in you knows everything that Einstein and even Jesus knew. It has the capacity to visualize and manifest great works like Shakespeare, Beethoven and Van Gogh. It has the answers that Stephen Hawking and others are striving to find in order to prove The Theory of Everything – TOE – that would describe all of the fields, forces and particles of nature in one seamless equation, of which, presently, God only knows!

Many people who have had near death, out of body experiences report that they saw many events occurring simultaneously in time at different places. These reports are later corroborated by the people involved in them. Our genius also knows the future. Dr. Joseph Murphy in *The Power of your Subconscious Mind*, explained such an experience personal to himself:

> "Many years ago, before the Second World War, I was offered a very lucrative assignment in the Orient, and I prayed for guidance and the right decision as follows: 'Infinite intelligence within me knows all things, and the right decision is revealed to me in divine order. I will recognize the answer when it comes.'"

> "I repeated this simple prayer over and over again as a lullaby prior to sleep, and in a dream came the vivid realization of things to come three years hence. An old friend appeared in the dream and said, 'Read these headlines – do not go!' The headlines of the newspaper which appeared in the dream related to war and the attack on Pearl Harbor."

The question to ask is, "How do I tap into this infinite intelligence to express my genius?"

KEYS TO REALIZING YOUR GENIUS

Healthy body – healthy mind

The most effective organizations are those which communicate well. Similarly, we are most effective when our cells have the most effective environment for communication. Therefore, the maintenance of a healthy body and healthy mind is the first step we may wish to take.

You are brainier than you know

Research suggests that we use somewhere between 1 and 3% of our brain's full potential, and that includes those who have demonstrated genius. Our understanding of how the brain works is still extremely limited. One thing we do know is that there are two sides to the brain, each dealing with different types of mental processes. The right cortex is the creative side and deals with rhythm, spatial awareness, imagination, daydreaming, color, dimension and the entire perspective of a problem or situation. The left cortex is the systematic side and deals with words, logic, numbers, sequence, linearity, analysis and lists.

Most of us are either right or left brain dominant. Studies of various genii have shown that they had a balanced use of their whole brain, showing an equal aptitude for creative and systematic mental activities. The following excerpt about Leonardo da Vinci is from Tony Buzan's bestseller *Use Your Head*:

> "In his time, he was arguably the most accomplished man in each of the following disciplines: art, sculpture, physiology, general science, architecture, mechanics, anatomy, physics, invention, meteorology, geology, engineering and aviation. He could also play, compose and sing spontaneous ballads when thrown any stringed instrument in the courts of Europe. Rather than separating these different areas of his latent ability, he combined them. Leonardo's scientific notebooks are filled with 3-dimensional drawings and images; and equally as interesting, the final plans for his great painting masterpieces often look like architectural plans: straight lines, angles, curves and numbers incorporating mathematical, logical and precise measurements."

This year I achieved "Patent Pending" status for an invention that has the potential to "Rock the World." I mention this for two reasons:

1. Hitherto, I did not regard myself as an inventor; a creator, yes, but not an inventor. I mean, come on, inventing is what da Vinci, Edison, Marconi, Watts and Fuller did. I'm just a guy who lives on a mountain in West Virginia. Now that I do absolutely regard myself as an inventor, I've given myself the command to invent at least one useful-to-others,

patentable and profitable invention every year. To ensure the optimal assistance from my subconscious, I've created a personal business card with the word "Inventor" among others on it.

Adding my newfound persona to my business card assists in its being programmed into my psyche. Talking about it, like now, and having others do the same (a prospect aided by my business card) reinforces the belief that I'm an inventor and, by association, a genius.

2. I did not wake up one morning and decide, "Today is the day I become an inventor; let me submit an idea to the U.S. Patent Office." I simply became disgruntled enough with the malfunctioning operation of a commonplace device of everyday life and thought, "There must be a better way to do this." This thought is no different than that I and millions of others have on a regular basis in similar circumstances. The difference on this occasion was that I *chose* and I *resolved* to back the thought with *action* until it was manifest in physical form.

So, if I am a genius, did I become one when I found the solution (idea), when I formed the idea into a drawing, when the drawing became a prototype, or will I become a genius only after the invention is recognized as a commercial success? I would argue most strenuously that the genius is manifest in the formation of the organized idea from the unformed, unorganized ethereal substance from whence all ideas come – infinite intelligence. Vincent van Gogh's paintings never sold for millions of dollars during his lifetime. Does this trifling fact, or the one that he was penniless and virtually unknown throughout his entire life render him a dullard during that time; or Starry Night (painted of the night sky from memory during the day from the room of his sanitarium) a tad better than my granddaughter's painting-by-numbers? She does stay between the lines, after all! We each have as open access to universal intelligence as did van Gogh or any genius of any age. The problem is that we intuit and do not recognize it, or simply choose not to act on the intuition. For me, Sir Winston Churchill, as with many observations, best summed up this malady:

"Men occasionally stumble over the truth, but most of them pick themselves up and hurry off as if nothing happened."

Engaging in a broad spectrum of study is said to improve one's ability to develop areas that may be considered weak, even if these areas are not among the ones being honed by study. This is so because new neural pathways develop between the neurons of the brain, increasing the ability of the neurons to communicate with each other. It would seem advisable, therefore, for creative people to engage in systematic activities as well as creative, and for systematic people to engage in creative activities as well as systematic, thereby creating neural pathways between the left and right cortices.

Access your subconscious mind

The subconscious mind is responsible for organizing the body's autonomic functions, those we don't have to think about: heartbeat, breathing, food digestion, excretion, fight-flight response, and so on. We ought to leave the subconscious alone to get on with the management of these biological functions. However, the subconscious is also responsible for mental functions such as perception, memory, reasoning and understanding. Rather than leave the subconscious to get on with these, we ought to make a conscious effort to access and influence these resources for it is in them that genius lies.

The best means by which I know how to elicit the support of the subconscious in attaining genius or any success include: goal-setting, visualization, affirmation, acting as if (I were the person I aspire to be), meditation, solitude, journaling, mentoring and teaching, painting, cross-disciplinary learning and physical exercise.

Subconscious perception

Paradoxically, we may learn about our genius from mental and physical disabilities. A neurological phenomenon, blind sight, has been observed in people who suffer damage to the occipital cortex (the region of the cerebral cortex to which the pathway from the eye and optic thalamus project). Damage here will lead to a blind spot in the field of vision corresponding to the damaged area. If subjected to visual stimuli, including bright light in the blind spot, the blind sighted person sees nothing. He is effectively blind in that area. However, Larry Weiskrantz lead a series of studies which have shown that such people are not truly without sight. Different visual stimuli were placed in the affected field of vision and the subjects asked to tell the investigating team what was there. Once they overcame the apparent absurdity of the task, their guesses were astonishingly accurate and much better than pure chance. It would seem that we have some subconscious mental process which allows us to "see" without the faculty of physical sight.

Subconscious memory

Whenever we communicate, we consult our memories without realizing that we're doing so. For instance, consider the following sentence:

> Robbie kicked the ball against the window and it smashed.

We do not have to think whether it were the ball or window that smashed. We know that the *it* refers to the window. Through experiences stored in our memories we know that windows smash, balls burst and that windows are more fragile than balls and, therefore, in a collision the window is likely to come off worse.

Again, in the following sentence there are enough memorized references for it to make sense without recourse to conscious thought:

> Jeremy and Jenny are playing chess and it is her move.

If we change one word, the sentence becomes incomprehensible without recourse to conscious thought and further enquiry:

Jane and Jenny are playing chess and it is her move. It is impossible to know which one's move it is because both Jane and Jenny can be referred to as "her".

Of course, conscious recollection is quite necessary, particularly in the case of what psychologists refer to as "episodic memory". For example, what time was it when I went to the bank yesterday? However, even here we seem to have a subconscious faculty that supports this obvious conscious process. Studies of amnesiacs have shown them to have subconscious recollection of episodic events where their conscious recollection has failed them. Their present beliefs and behaviors are influenced by the detail of events they are unable to consciously recollect.

Taking this phenomenon further, in a sense, our physical being has amnesia about the events which it has experienced prior to all of its cells coming together to form itself through conception and thereafter. (Remember, matter cannot perish. It is transformed, transferred and recycled). The intelligence in each cell that we spoke of earlier is endowed with a memory, of which we are not consciously aware. This memory (an energy which too cannot perish) must pre-date the cells' existence as a component of the body. While this notion may seem astounding, it is commonplace to talk about birds being programed to fly, turtles born on land being programed to return to the sea and so on. This programming comes from the field of infinite intelligence, which these creatures, like you and I, access through their subconscious being, and specifically, their subconscious memory.

Subconscious actions

Through repetition we delegate complex conscious tasks to subconscious automatization. For instance, walking, tying a shoelace, constructing written words, typing and driving a vehicle are all highly complex tasks. The most intellectually adept and motor-coordinated among us have difficulty in the conscious learning of these tasks. Once automated, the most intellectually inept and motor-uncoordinated among us make these tasks seem completely natural.

The importance of automatization is that it shows, with practice, fewer conscious decisions are required of us. Conscious decision-making relative to subconscious action is slow and time consuming. Therefore, the more mental and physical tasks we can delegate to the subconscious, the more proficient we become. For example, we often see the best goal scorers in soccer having an instinctive knack of being in the right place at the right time to maximize scoring opportunities. The accomplished goal scorer does not have to consciously decide what to do next as an offensive move is developing on the field of play. Instead, he unconsciously draws on the memory of what he has done many times before.

What I have learned, through study and practice, is that we are not only able to increase our proficiency by the automatization of the tasks we perform, but also through our psychic connection with others.

Role Modelling

As a child, I used to watch The Big Match presented by Brian Moore every Sunday afternoon. After the program, my friends and I would meet on a 70-foot long strip of turf sandwiched between a main road and an elongated block of apartments for which it was a sort of front garden. The Back Grass, as it was endearingly known, is where we copied all the "moves" we had seen the professionals perform on that afternoon's Big Match.

I remember one particular skill which fired my imagination – the overhead bicycle kick. The overhead bicycle kick is a technique in soccer whereby a player, suspended in mid-air, back horizontal to the earth's surface, makes a bicycle motion with his legs and connects with the ball. A spectacular and difficult feat of coordination. I had to master it. I practiced hard. Every opportunity I got, I attempted the skill. Even balls which, by their trajectory, were easier to head got the bicycle treatment. Eventually, I became very adept at the bicycle kick… so much so that I convinced myself that not even the best professionals could match my prowess at it.

In hindsight, I did something which, I have no doubt, made a huge contribution to my perfecting the skill. I constantly asked myself how would the player I first saw performing the skill do it? I went further and imagined I was him. For all intents and purposes, while practicing the skill, I became that person who inspired me to want to do it. My thinking changed. I was not *trying* to do it anymore. In the moment of execution, I was him and I knew how to do it. Ultimately, I could be myself in the moment of execution since I now had at least the same level of certainty about succeeding at bicycle kicking as did the person whom I modelled.

Writing this piece has transported me back in time to The Back Grass. The dreamer in me is goading me to go and practice some overhead bicycle kicks, while the realist in me has chimed in with, "REALLY… at your age, you don't need the hip replacement!" Sadly, perhaps, the realist has subdued the dreamer – for now, anyway!

Mastermind Councils

Napoleon Hill in *Think and Grow Rich* describes how Andrew Carnegie's staff of about 50 men was the foundation for his accumulated fortunes. The principle being that the sum of two minds is greater than the parts, since the synergy which together they create does not exist while they are apart. Napoleon Hill goes on to describe how he created his own imaginary council based on Carnegie's concept. Every night, over a long period of years, he would Chair imaginary council meetings between himself and the nine men – Emerson, Paine, Edison, Darwin, Lincoln, Burbank,

Napoleon, Ford and Carnegie – whose lives and lifeworks had most impressed him. Hill's definite purpose (which he stresses is important for the idea to be of benefit) was to rebuild his character.

I found this idea most appealing and have practiced it, on and off, for quite a few years. The commitment and discipline necessary to sustain this exercise is amply rewarded for those who persist. My own imaginary mastermind council includes Jesus Christ (infinite wisdom and unconditional love), Baroness Margaret Thatcher (decisiveness), Richard Branson (entrepreneurial flair), Sir John Harvey-Jones (big business acumen), Albert Einstein (intellectual brilliance) and Thomas Edison (persistence and creativity).

Interestingly, I have never met any of my council members in the flesh (though I once met a man who claimed to be Jesus!) Nevertheless, each member assumes the character and personality traits that their public personas suggest and that I imagine them to have. Not one of them is a "Yes man," so to speak. Each is a strong individual very adept at answering my direct questions. Often, the answers I receive from them are not what I want to hear, but I listen and weigh their advice, knowing that it is given from a position of their personal experience of life, an understanding of each situation I present to them and their desire for me to do well.

One night, I found myself procrastinating at a council meeting, not knowing what to do about a particular issue, when Mrs. T. (I thought rather rudely) interrupted Jesus, looked me in the eye and said, "Look, young man, if you cannot handle it, get out of the Chair and I'll take over." In an instant I found the decisiveness I needed to overcome my dithering.

As my values have changed over the years, so too has the composition of the council. There have been two leavers whom I have not replaced. They left amicably through the natural ending of their tenures.

To some, the role modelling and mastermind techniques I have described will be no more than fanciful trickery of the mind. So be it. To me there is a lot more to it than that. It is my contention that the subconscious is the mind of the spiritual self. It is as conscious to our spiritual being as the conscious mind is to our physical being. Spirit is the part of each of us that is connected to all things. And, from this is derived the reality of infinite intelligence. Hence, all subconscious (spiritual) minds are connected. Each person's conscious and subconscious minds, of course, interact. Because of this, it is possible for one person to enter the conscious thoughts of another.

It is commonplace to be thinking of someone when all of a sudden the phone rings and it is them on the line. Close friends and partners often know each other's thoughts. Family pets can know internalized emotions in their owners. A friend's late cat, Pet, always knew when she was coming home, regardless of where she was in the world. An hour before she would arrive, Pet would casually walk to the front door and establish camp. Five minutes before she arrived, Pet would get excited, walk about and purr.

Thought is energy, energy is imperishable. This is why the likes of Jesus, Einstein and Edison, although here before my physical presence on earth, are able to make a real contribution to my success through membership of my imaginary mastermind council.

Dreams

The language of the subconscious is Dream-Speak. It is a language of pictures and metaphors. In order to access the subconscious for genius we need to understand dream speak. I have a book on the meaning of dreams, but use it only when I'm really confused about a dream I've had. I, otherwise, prefer to interpret the dreams myself. I'm the one who knows the precise circumstances of my life and, therefore, the true context of the dream as it relates to me. It is rather like the difference between reading one's horoscope in a national daily compared to having one's personal astrological chart compiled using one's exact birth time and place. The former can only generalize.

In terms of the type of information we receive from dreams, I believe there are four categories of dream. Those in which:

1) A past event or development comes to light;

2) Problems are solved;

3) We are alerted to something happening right now; and

4) We are alerted to an impending event.

A past event or development comes to light

One morning, I was waking from sleep with the vivid memory of a dream. I was in a familiar bar in the City of London. The friend I was with turned and saw an acquaintance whom he greeted. I recognized this person to be an old friend whom I had not seen for many years. I went and stood directly in front of him with an impish smile until he recognized me. He did. That familiar, warm, engaging smile brightened the place. We engaged in a gripping embrace which at once crushed the pretentious air of success out of me. I broke down in tears. The last time this person, a mentor so dear to me, had seen me I was a shadow of the person I had hoped to become; the person I had become in my dream. The relief touched every cell in my body. He had known me as an introverted procrastinator, and was surprised at my metamorphosis.

Coming out of this dreamy state, I realized the dream was a metaphor for the magical power of decision. My metamorphosis arose solely from my decision to be great. I went immediately to Chapter 4 and added to the piece on Decision Making in the section "Executing your goals":

> "Once we decide, we become a different person, a changed person. Choosing sobriety in favor of alcoholism will change a person's destiny the moment the decision is made – that is magical. Deciding is analogous to pruning the dead wood from a tree. In doing so, we encourage the growth of new shoots in a different direction. They yearn to seek the light, whereas the dead wood no longer has the capacity to do so. We must continually prune to ensure new growth in our chosen directions, providing balance in our lives."

Problems are solved

I used to have a recurring dream every now and then. In the dream, I am waiting for a coach to take me to work in London. The coach cancelled. I run to the nearest train station from which there are frequent trains to London from platforms one and three.

Just as I arrive, I miss a train leaving from Platform One. I decide to go over to Platform Three. While equidistant between the two platforms, the next London bound train is announced to be leaving from Platform One. I turn and run to Platform One but miss the train all the same. While walking back to Platform Three, I miss a third train. Now, completely fed-up, I walk back to Platform One and ask an employee for the times and respective platforms for trains to London. Unsure of the times, he tells me that they are frequent from Platforms One and Three. Although I am none the wiser, the act of stopping to ask the employee for some relevant information reminds me that I have plenty of time to get to work. I now saunter over to Platform Three. A train duly arrives and gets me to work on time.

I only ever had this dream when I was at a crossroads or when I was anxious that a course of action may be wrong. To me, the dream was my subconscious expressing the view that I was on the right track – hence the stage on which the dream was cast, a railway station – and that I should relax and be patient in the knowledge that I had made the right choice, and the right outcome would occur at the right time.

We are alerted to something happening right now

A close friend was too busy building his business to go on vacation. His wife was invited to go on vacation with an old friend of hers, which he thought was an excellent idea. Several days into the vacation, he awoke from sleep in a cold sweat. He only vaguely remembered a dream but knew it had something unpleasant to do with his wife. Worried, he could not sleep the rest of the night, he telephoned her first thing the next day. She said she was fine, having a good time, that he should not worry and that she would see him in a few days. He thought nothing more of the experience.

A week or so after she arrived home, my friend overhead a telephone conversation that his wife was having with the friend she vacationed with. From this, he discovered that his wife had had a fling with a local waiter while on vacation. Angry and bemused, he questioned her about this. Once she stopped denying it, he found out that her misdeed took place at the exact time he awoke from his nightmare. In love with his wife, he eventually forgave her, blaming himself for being too involved in his business to pay her enough attention.

Six months later, his wife was out with friends from work and was due to stay over at one of their homes for convenience. Again, my friend awoke from a vaguely remembered dream which he knew was negatively connected with his wife. While thinking the worst, he did not want to jump to conclusions. A couple of days later, he casually said to his wife that he knew she was having another relationship and felt they should discuss it to determine whether it was appropriate for their marriage to continue. The calm, collected delivery along with the piercing eye contact disarmed his wife's desire to deny the truth. Again, he was right. Again, the time of his awakening coinciding exactly with the second infidelity. They agreed to separate and did so amicably.

<u>We are alerted to an impending event</u>

Another close friend related a dream that informed her of an event which was to unfold imminently. She dreamed of being in a large, beautiful, open spaced house which felt comfortable to be in. She wandered freely about the house enjoying the unique restful vibes of each room until, that is, she arrived at the attic. The trap door to the attic was bolted and padlocked. Everything about it shouted, "KEEP OUT!" It was decidedly cold and unfriendly.

She realized that there was something hidden in the attic which she was not meant to discover. But what could this mean in "real life"? A week or so later, she discovered her husband's bank statement and was surprised to see that he was $5,000 overdrawn. This encouraged her to investigate his personal financial papers, kept in the filing cabinet which they shared. In there, she found a letter from her husband's bank approving his request for an overdraft. The letter was dated two days after the dream she had had.

She interpreted the dream thus: The large spacious house with its warm, comfortable rooms represented the relationship she shared with her husband, which generally was open, honest and loving. The locked attic, of course, was representative of the secret overdraft, which she was not meant to discover.

Many would assume that the events described here are no more than coincidence, and that is their prerogative. They will never avail themselves of the guidance provided by the subconscious through Dream-Speak. They will never be touched by the many miracles that happen around them every day. Their awareness is closed to them. For them, seeing is believing.

If you get into the habit of analyzing your dreams, no matter how familiar, bizarre, mundane or irrelevant they may seem, you will come to a point where significant insights are gleaned from them. Eventually, you may reach a stage of heightened awareness in which you are so open to ideas that you begin to gain powerful insights from mundane occurrences hitherto unavailable to you: the way an apple falls from a tree; the growth of a bacterium on an agar plate; the flight of birds through the air; the way the wind blows at certain times of the day or year; the way a forest catches fire in a prolonged dry spell; your buoyancy in the bath tub.

Genius is about increasing our understanding of how the world works. The answers are out in the open, hidden only by our rejection of what is possible, our refusal to accept that all things are possible if we believe them to be.

Imagination

When I first came across Einstein's quote that imagination is more important than knowledge, I thought, "That sounds good," and that thought was the complete extent of my awareness of what I now know is a far reaching insight. What we cannot imagine, cannot exist for us. Conversely, that which we can imagine, absolutely can exist for us. Let me give you a playful, but powerful example. Think about something you did yesterday. Okay. Now, think about something you know you are going to do tomorrow. Have you completed the exercise? Yes? Well done. Welcome to time travel! That's right, welcome to time travel. You see, your perception of time travel has always involved your physical being. Who said it had to? Your physical being is only a very small part of who or what you are. Think about why you would want to travel in time. In most cases, it would be to learn about the past and unravel the mysteries of the future. Why do you need your body to do that? Archaeologists and historians unearth the secrets of the past all the time, not by getting into a *Dr. Who* Tardis, but by using their imaginations. Economists, politicians, fashion designers and planners shape the future all the time, again, by using their imaginations.

So, what is the benefit of this time travel to you? By visiting the past, you may discover things about yourself which you can use as lessons to improve your now. By visiting the future, you can shape your next now the way you want it to be. Remember, however, not to dwell in the past or the future as your life can only unfold now.

Now that you have accepted the reality of time travel through imagination, the possibility of physical time travel is brought that much closer. Classically, the concept of time travel has been inextricably linked with a necessity to travel beyond the speed of light. How fast do our thoughts travel? Thoughts are energy. We know that at the quantum level, energy sometimes shows up as particle and vice versa. So maybe, just maybe, there is another way we can look at transporting our physical mass in time, apart from travelling beyond the speed of light.

For genius to show up for you, you must be able to imagine that which you have yet to experience. Think the impossible, knowing that it is possible. Take each objection to its being possible and methodically satisfy it until none bars the way to its acceptance as possible. If there is any residue of doubt, proceed anyway. The view of the mountains gets clearer the longer you proceed toward them.

Meditation

Imagine yourself in a row boat on choppy waters during a violent storm. Your thoughts and actions are fixed on staying afloat – nay, staying alive! As the waves throw you in one direction you immediately take corrective action in the other. Water filling the boat is frantically scooped out. Your entire being is focused on surviving the ordeal as it unfolds moment by fearsome moment.

Now, imagine yourself in the same boat; only this time, on the calm surface of a sun kissed lake. You row with rhythmic, effortless stokes. The movement is so easy that it soothes rather than aches your muscles. Your mind, no longer focused on survival, wanders aimlessly from thought to thought. One moment you recall current challenges in your life, the next, wonderful times near and far. You remember the promise you made to take your children to Disneyland. Immediately, your mind begins to reconstruct the details of the trip.

In the first scenario, you were completely caught in the moment. In the second, the moment was caught in you. In the daily humdrum of our lives, we are caught in the moment, afraid to release our grip on the oars lest we lose control. Meditation is a convenient and hugely effective way of releasing the tensions of life. It affords a safe environment in which we can loosen our grip on the oars so that our minds are free to receive subconscious guidance.

Meditation is far more relaxing than sleep, during which our dreams stimulate cerebral and muscular activity, oscillating heart rate and blood pressure. In the meditative state the subconscious is predominant, allowing us to receive insights from the field on infinite intelligence. The insights fall into the same four categories as our dreams.

CLOSE YOUR EYES. Be still right now. Listen to the chattering of your mind. You know that you are experiencing the subconscious being of the meditative state when this chattering is absent. You realize that the excited individual twittering of birds is a harmonious conversation among many. The incessant ticking of the clock becomes a melodious lullaby accompanying you into the depths of subconscious existence. Your body seems weightless and, therefore, without burden.

You know that you have experienced the subconscious being of the meditative state when the 20 minutes you were meditating seemed like only 5; or by your deep, drowsy, rested feeling; or conversely, acute awareness immediately afterward.

Experienced practitioners of meditation say that regular meditation brings its calm into their daily lives. The subconscious and conscious minds seem to interact more readily, creating a smoother pathway for guidance and insight from the former to the latter.

In the timelessness of the meditative state you are able to view your world from a broader perspective. Each moment is in you.

"Be still, and know that I am God."
– Psalm 46:10

Genius is not a function of academic brilliance

Thomas Edison had 3 months of school education. His school master accused him of being addled (empty headed). Angry, his mother withdrew Thomas from school. His education continued at home with her.

> "Thomas Edison left school when he was twelve to sell candy on a railroad train. In between sales, he did experiments in the baggage car. Then he learned how to be a telegraph operator and began to invent things. He never stopped. By the end of his amazing career, he had invented the light bulb, motion pictures, the phonograph, had installed

New York City's electrical system, and had made improvements in almost every other means of communication in use today. He brought about a revolution in living: people now could work and read after the sun went down, and could hear each other over vast distances.

"This is the lively story of the genius who affected the twentieth century more than any other inventor."

– The story of Thomas Alva Edison, Margaret Cousins

In high school, several of Einstein's teachers said he was a waster; today, we'd say loser. His wastrel ways lead him to obtain a letter from the family doctor saying he was on the verge of a nervous breakdown. On presentation of the letter (and supporting documents) to the school's Principal requesting that he leave for medical reasons, Einstein was expelled.

At 16 he failed the entrance examination for a prestigious technical college in Zurich. A year later he passed the examination comfortably. Of the four students who graduated (a fifth failed) in the science course in Einstein's year at the college, he achieved the lowest scores.

Genius *is* a function of:

1. Hard work – "There is no other road to genius than through self-effort."

– Napoleon Hill

2. Persistence – "Everything comes to him who hustles while he waits."

– Thomas Edison

3. Faith – If you have faith as a mustard seed, you can say to this mulberry tree, 'Be pulled up by the roots and be planted in the sea,' and it would obey you."

– Luke 17:14

4. Curiosity – "A generous and elevated mind is distinguished by nothing more certainly than an eminent degree of curiosity."

– Samuel Johnson

5. Passion – "Search then the Ruling Passion: There, alone,
    The wild are constant and the cunning known;
    The fool consistent, and the false sincere;
    Priests, princes, women, no dissemblers here.
    This clue once found, unravels all the rest."

– Alexander Pope

6. Courage – "Screw your courage to the sticking-place, and we'll not fail."

– William Shakespeare

FALLING SHORT OF GENIUS

Not everyone will be recognized in the annals of history as a genius, but we all have the right to seek the genius within. And, what if we fail? In failing we must succeed. For it is only in failing that we do succeed. The least and utmost we dare expect is to be all that we can be, and know that, ultimately, we can only ever achieve this in an endeavor for which we have a passion, are prepared to work hard at and display courage in, in the face of adversity; ask daring questions of with an open mind; and KNOW, without evidence (keep faith), that we shall succeed at if only we persist long enough.

The following story is based on the life of a client.

Ever since she could remember, Anne had a passion for flowers. She left school at the age of 16 years. On doing so, she went to work in a florist. Her attitude was one of dedication laced with ambition. Her dream was to create and own her own botanical gardens.

She earned very little as an assistant in the store, but, nevertheless, saved 10% of her weekly wages. In 10 years of hard labor, her savings, including accumulated interest, amounted to $10,000. It was now that she began to wonder how the dream could become reality.

Meanwhile, her boss, whom over the years had become like a guardian, began voicing her desire to expand the business. Her conundrum was the lack of a partner. One day, while lamenting her situation, Anne piped up, saying, "What about me?" At first, her boss was amazed. Slowly, however, she warmed to the idea. Anne would be the perfect partner. She knew the business, was well versed in her boss' working practices, was proven to be honest and trustworthy, was extremely keen and hardworking, and had the cash to invest. After much discussion, a deal was struck. A second store was opened, over which Anne took personal charge. The original store was to remain in the sole ownership of Anne's boss with the second and subsequent outlets affording Anne a 40% stockholding.

A further eight years passed, by which time Anne's partner had had enough. She wanted to retire. Anne exercised her option to purchase her partner's share of the now multi-outlet business. She carried on for another five years and then sold out to a competitor. Anne was able to retire wealthy.

It's true that she never quite realized the genius of the botanical gardens. However, during our coaching relationship we both came to realize that the botanical gardens were akin to a "Lost-Leader", the future magnet that pulled her into a full and rewarding life that, without the magnet, would not have been. In the opening words of this chapter's poem, Anne shone bright and brought light to the world, regardless of not realizing the fullness of her genius.

A QUESTION OF BALANCE

Some say Hitler was a madman, others that he was a genius that lost his way. We often hear that the line dividing genius and insanity is a fine one. Examples of genii exhibiting abnormal or eccentric behavior abound.

Michael Jackson, one of the most successful pop music artists of all time was, off-stage, a completely different personality to his onstage persona. He was reclusive, shy, aloof and behaved bizarrely: wearing a mask; allegedly sleeping in an oxygen-filled glass case; and seemingly keen to live the childhood he professed was lost to his life onstage. Onstage, Michael Jackson was expressive, flamboyant, emotional and confident.

In later life, Einstein had the nervous breakdown he had earlier feigned while a schoolboy. Edison would mostly sleep on the floor of his workshop. He could spend days in there without eating unless his wife brought in meals.

Finally, we are all familiar with the story of Vincent van Gogh deliberately cutting off his ear.

These genii have indeed crossed a thin line – that which separates passion and obsession. It is a line that parallels the one separating genius and insanity. If ever you do realize your own genius, your challenge, then, it would seem, will be the healthy stewardship of your passion so that you retain a balance in your life without dampening your productive genius.

CHAPTER 9

WISDOM

"Wisdom is not communicable. The wisdom which a wise man tries to communicate always sounds foolish... Knowledge can be communicated, but not wisdom. One can find it, live it, do wonders through it, but one cannot communicate and teach it."

– Hermann Hesse, *Siddhartha*

WISDOM

Wisdom travels the ethereal plane
Coursing its way like blood in a vein
Touching us all like a shower of rain
The connection's not made by using the brain

It travels through mass
There's nothing it will bypass
Not even the dumbest thing, like an ass
Though from time to time you may think that it has

The effects are so great that we can be blind
But truth be known it's all in our mind
Just look inside and it you will find
That's in you and me and all of mankind.

And how do we know it, this wisdom of ours?
It comes to us all in the darkest of hours
It can be seen in the blooming of flowers
Or in the builder's erection of soaring towers

But most of all how do we get wise
Is there a notion that we can surmise?
A plan so grand that we can devise
Or does it befall us, just like a surprise

– LAC

WISDOM

- Wisdom defined

- Intuition

- Objectivity vs. subjectivity

- Judgment by the wise

- Wise decision making

- Toward wisdom

WISDOM DEFINED

Wisdom is not accumulated knowledge. It involves an understanding of how things really are. In some ways, it is a nebulous reality, elusive to scrutiny. Evidence of it may be found in mythology, proverb and visionary poetry. For example:

Mythology:

> "Many North American Indian myths concern the powers and exploits of the shaman. While, in some cases, the shaman inherits his role, it is more common for him to be summoned by the spirits, usually against his will, who drive him out into the wilds in great anguish until he undergoes an ecstatic experience, best described as enlightenment. He then accepts his vocation, having had all the secrets of the universe revealed to him, and having acknowledged his particular spiritual aids and guides."
> – Mike Dixon-Kennedy, Native American Myth & Legend

Proverb:

> "A proverb is one man's wit and all men's wisdom."
> – Lord John Russell

Visionary poetry:

> "All is best though we oft doubt,
> What th' unsearchable dispose
> Of highest wisdom brings about,
> And ever best found in the close."
> – John Milton

Another form in which we find wisdom indirectly defined is anecdote; upon which I will rely much in this chapter to demonstrate the availability of wisdom to us all.

Socrates, when dubbed the wisest man of Greece retorted: "Tis because I alone of all the Greeks know that I know nothing." We live in a world that conjures up more questions than answers. The more we find out the less we seem to know. This involves us in a never ending quest for answers.

With each discovery, we unveil a little piece of wisdom's mystery edging ever closer to a view of its fulsome naked whole, only to realize that we are further from the truth. This lustful affair with truth is the framework of our curiosity.

Wisdom is rooted in Truth. Truth is everlasting. But, in a world of constant change, how do we know what is everlasting? The cells of our bodies are born, live and die in a cycle which means that we have a "new" body several times a year; the temperature and climatic profile of a given geographical region today may differ from, say, fifty years ago; the evolution of a species ensures its change and adaptation to changes in its environment; scientific intervention in the natural order of things through, say, biogenetics, redefines what we know, revising our expectations of what is possible. Wisdom is the foundation upon which our knowledge of these and other things rests. To get closer to the foundation is to gain in wisdom.

INTUITION

The foundation of knowledge is intuition. Intuition is:

> "Instinctive knowledge or insight without conscious reasoning."
>
> – Collins Gem English Dictionary

The word Educate is derived from the Latin word Educare, a literal translation of which is to cause a thing to come out, to draw out, extract, elicit; the point being that education is not a process by which knowledge is put into the mind, although we may be forgiven for believing so. The teacher introduces a "new" subject, about which we know apparently little or nothing, and proceeds to inform us of it. However, we saw in the section "What is genius?" at the beginning of Chapter 8, that knowledge is already held within, just beyond our conscious awareness:

> "No man can reveal to you aught but that which already lies half asleep in the dawning of your knowledge."
>
> – Kahlil Gibran

Indeed, it is interesting to note that seventeenth Century scientists such as Newton, Hooke, Faulkner and Halley generally thought that their work was no more than rediscovering laws which the ancients (Greeks, Egyptians, etc.) had known in much more detail. Contemporary archaeological findings on the Ancient Egyptians' understanding and application of planetary systems concurs with their views.

Wisdom, therefore, is a phenomenon emanating from the subconscious. We also learned from Chapter 8 that the subconscious may be accessed through dreams, imagination and meditation. This, perhaps, is why wisdom is synonymous with the sage, who tradition has it, lives a peaceable, contemplative lifestyle.

We too are subject to moments of wisdom which manifest in the actions we take, giving wisdom a practical value and application in everyday life. Such moments may bypass us in our obsession for proof: "I'll believe it when I see it"; when wisdom often demands that we believe it so that we may see it. How often has your intuition told you one thing only to be overruled by your need for observable proof, later to find on reflection that trusting in your intuition would have been the right thing to do? This is particularly so of relationships and business dealings.

You see, the challenge is that your physical senses, while aiding your rationality, also trigger emotional responses, encouraging you to act emotionally.

Imagine that you've just had a wonderful meal in your favorite restaurant. You are full to bursting. You cannot possibly eat another morsel. But wait, the dessert trolley comes rolling by and those profiteroles, or the chocolate cake with cream, or pancakes or apple pie and cream or whatever else it is that you know you can never resist, draws your attention. You can see it. You can even smell it. The taste is already in your mouth, along with the satisfying feeling of devouring it. Oh joy, "Give me that big piece right there!" If you were acting rationally (and not emotionally), you would not have the dessert, plain and simple. Your rational reasoning would be that to have any more food would:

1. Make you uncomfortable for most if not the entire rest of the evening;

2. Possibly induce heartburn;

3. Lead to flatulence;

4. Overwork your digestive system;

5. Possibly cause constipation;

6. Compromise any weight control plan you may be observing;

7. Be unkind to your heart; and so on.

The power of your emotional response triggered by your physical senses has outweighed your rational response also triggered by your physical senses. So, when reacting to your physical senses you cannot rely on your rational response overriding your emotional response in the moment of truth. A more reliable proposition is to trust in your intuition. It can only give you answers that are best for you.

OBJECTIVITY VS. SUBJECTIVITY

Our faculty for objective reasoning is accompanied by that for subjective reasoning. The inappropriate application of these faculties to any given situation may lead us into conflict and strife. An argument is a good example of this. In a typical argument, the adversaries are beset by emotions and tend to allow their respective emotional states to override their respective objective states. This takes the argument down a subjective path on which the argument cannot be satisfactorily determined, since subjectivity is in the mind of the beholder. We all view things differently. Therefore, arguments over subjective matters are futile. For instance, it is difficult to express an objective preference between an apple and an orange. One is preferred by one person over another largely dependent upon taste, smell, touch, aesthetics and even sound; some preferring the squelch of the orange to the crunch of the apple, all of which are subjective measures of preference. So too with human relations. Like fruit, we are all very different. Whether you prefer one person to another because of their intellect, height, color, qualifications, dress sense, etiquette, education, socioeconomic grouping and so on, is completely subjective, and a function of your own personal preferences. It is impossible, therefore, to categorically (that is objectively) say that any one person is "better" than another. Only from a personal, subjective perspective are you able to so judge.

What is subjective may become objective within strict parameters. Returning to our basket of fruit, the orange becomes the fruit of objective choice when one wants to use it for an orange soufflé, whereas the apple becomes the fruit of objective choice when one wants to make an apple pie. Yes, this is blindingly obvious, but we don't always use oranges for orange soufflé and apples for apple pie when we transfer this logic to other aspects of human behavior. The employer hires an employee because that employee is cute, rather than competent; the jock gets to play on the team because his father is coach, rather than for his talent; Company A wins the contract from

Company B because Company A's Purchasing Manager is buddies with B's Sales Manager. These decisions are not being judged, but rather brought to light to highlight the interplay between objective and subjective faculties and how using each incorrectly may lead to failure and regret.

When we are unable to objectively say that one person is better than another, perhaps we ought to refrain from judging others, since the basis of such judgment is the other person's characteristics, which are subjectively preferred (or not). One may wish to argue that one's value system is somehow superior to another's, so allowing that one to make such judgments. If so, such a person may wish to observe his ignorance for it is like saying that oranges are superior to apples with no reference other than personal preference. It is mere subjective preference which is okay, but let us see it for what it is and then rest easy with the resultant outcome of our choices based on subjectivity alone. An appreciation of this wisdom enables us to better understand, tolerate and even embrace others for the uniqueness they bring to the table of humanity, while relaxing our abhorrence of the differences that make them unique.

JUDGMENT BY THE WISE

Despite the foregoing, our tendency is to judge others. But, as wisdom has it:

> "Do not judge or you too will be judged. For in the same way you judge others, you will be judged. With the measure you use, it will be measured to you."
>
> – Matthew 7:12

That is to say, judge, but be expected also to be judged in return, by the same criteria. Hence, if you judge others by their race, sex, age, technical ability, intellect, and so on, you too should accept being so judged. I'm sure you know as well as I do many who like to "dish it out," but cannot take it in return.

A wise person sees himself in others and others in himself while retaining his uniqueness (personality) and sense of himself (self-image). In his decisions (judgements) involving others, he has the capacity to ignore the illusory distractions of their superficial differences and, thereby, judge while standing on firm ground rather than in quicksand. That is, he does not discriminate on the grounds of personal prejudice. Judging from this place does not make our judgments infallible. The occasional earthquake will shake the ground on which we stand, forcing us to a different place altogether – a different paradigm – the view from which is (by definition) different and from which we would not make the same judgments we did from the previous place. This is a corollary of personal growth and, thus, a fundamental consequence of any quest for successful living.

He sees himself in others

While writing this section of the book, I had occasion to travel to central London on a train where my peace was disturbed by a group of boisterous schoolboys. Just as my tolerance level rose to the point of intervention, one of the boys exploded a stink bomb. The pungent smell tickled my nostrils and danced in my throat. It proceeded to drown my entire being, triggering the memory of my own schoolboy antics, even to the extent of exploding stink bombs in public places to upset stuffy adult sensibilities. I laughed about it. How else would one expect a group of schoolboys, with energy to burn, to behave? I moved carriages at the earliest opportunity and continued on my journey in peace.

He sees others in himself

When I first set up in business as a consultant, eager young people would approach me to find out how I got started and whether I could advise them on how to do the same. In my first career as a banker, I would not give them the time of day. All I would see was what they all had in common: no money, no business plan, no means of repayment and no collateral, equals no chance. This is what I was trained (conditioned) to see. Thankfully, as a self-employed business person, I could see something else they all had in common: a dream. A dream which is all I once had. A dream which equaled every chance. My colleagues and I were exceedingly generous with our time for these dreamers, for we knew with a little help and direction maybe one in every one hundred would realize the dream. Sufficiently rewarding odds for the expenditure of our time, we thought.

He retains his uniqueness and sense of himself

The wise person's decisions are selfless in so far as he is not part of the decision making equation. For instance, it is not uncommon for a person who has had very little wealth to vote one way in an election, and so doing, criticize, judge and condemn others for voting differently, only for the same person to vote with those whom he had been used to criticizing, judging and condemning because he has come into money. A wise voter knows what is best for the nation – the world even – and casts his vote accordingly.

One may agree with the shifting voter and that's okay, but remember we are seeking wisdom – everlasting truth. If he loses all his money, will he change his voting habits back to what they were? Perhaps. The wise person does not allow circumstances to determine who he is and how he should behave.

There are numerous other situations in which we allow our selfishness to mask the truth. We have ex-smokers condemning smokers, converted vegetarians criticizing meat eaters, born again Christians belittling agnostics, the slim sneering at the overweight and so it goes on. The new reality that anyone involved in any of these changes is experiencing is wonderful; not least because it is a goal achieved or, in their eyes, a progressive step in their personal development. However, in the great scheme of things, it may be a step away from the truth:

> "Why do you look at the speck of sawdust in your brother's eye and pay no attention to the plank in your own eye?"
> – Matthew 7:3

WISE DECISION MAKING

When I was younger, I often found myself perplexed by decisions made by those who had authority over me – parents, teachers, bosses; decisions that affected my life. It was a constant torment. "How could they do that?" Today, it is no different. Decision makers continue to perplex those affected by their decisions. What is different for me, however, is why such perplexity may arise. If the decision maker is acting with integrity and in the best interest of those who are affected by their decision, why do decision maker and affected not always agree over the wisdom of the decision? Simply, the two see things differently.

When integrity is being exercised by the decision maker, the differences in view are due to differences in information held by the two parties. The closer are their views of reality, the more palatable will be the decision.

Imagine you are the executive chairman of Widget Incorporated, the largest widget manufacturer in the world. The company is nearing the end of its best ever financial year. Your board of directors approves a 10% across-the-board pay raise for all employees, effective from the beginning of the next financial year, in recognition of the important role they continue to play in the company's rising fortunes. Three weeks prior to affecting the pay raises, you learn that the main raw material, naffe ore, used in the manufacture of widgets is to rise 50% in price as a result of an arbitrary decision by the cartel of countries – ZENON (Zone of Enterprise for Naffe Ore Nations) – rich in naffe ore.

Widgets are a basically homogenous product in a very competitive market. Furthermore, a highly substitutable product, round-to-its, are selling at the same price they have been for the last two years, about 5% more than the current price for widgets.

You decide to hastily dictate a company-wide memorandum before leaving for an urgent meeting of widget manufacturers to discuss the current challenge facing the industry. It reads:

"Notwithstanding previous indications, pay increases for this financial year will be in line with the industry average which is expected to be 0%. This news will be disappointing to some of you but the decision has been taken with the company's best interest at heart. I know and expect that we will all pull together to ensure the success we have enjoyed continues."

In the absence of the vital piece of information about the imminent price rise in naffe ore, you could forgive a number of staff for reacting negatively to your memorandum. You want to act responsibly. You know that the pay raise cannot proceed under the new market conditions, but feel inclined to say the very least until the industry decides its joint response to the price rise in naffe ore. Your company's individual plans will largely depend upon this.

Let us now say that having received the information about the price increase, you felt it was possible to delay making an announcement until after the widget manufacturers' meeting, by when you imagine that the industry direction and your company's own response would be clearer. Even so, you still decide that a 0% pay raise across-the-board is the most appropriate action to safeguard the wellbeing of the business. You could now dictate the following memorandum:

"Notwithstanding previous indications, pay increases for this financial year will be 0%. Within the past few hours, ZENON has announced an arbitrary increase of 50% in the price of naffe ore. You do not need me to tell you that naffe ore, for which there is no substitute, is by far the largest component used in the manufacture of widgets. We have calculated that the revised price of widgets will be 15% higher than competing round-to-its, which have remained stable in price for some two years. This puts us at a major competitive disadvantage."

"At a hastily convened meeting of widget manufacturers it was agreed that we should all take appropriate measures to protect the long term future of widget manufacturing. Your board of directors is undertaking a full review of the company's cost structure. The savings we expect to find will, at best, be minimal since the success we have enjoyed is partly due to the diligent management of overheads."

"The last thing we want to do is to start making redundancies, thereby reducing our capacity to manufacture widgets, and so jeopardizing our principal position in the marketplace. In the circumstances, I am sure you will agree that the decision we have made, though unpalatable, is the most sensible for the long term welfare of the company."

"I know and expect that we will all pull together to ensure the continued success of our company. That, after all, is the Widget Incorporated way; a way that has seen us through many difficult times in the past. Any feedback you may have would be appreciated and should be made through the normal channels."

Now that your employees have a view of this "reality" which is closer to your own, it would be only the most unyielding of individuals who would be aggrieved by the decision you have made.

If you are a professional salesperson, you are likely familiar with the (often annual) practice of territory realignment and compensation plan reviews. These measures are usually taken for sound business reasons, one of which is NOT to stick it to the salesforce. However, they can have the consequential effect of the salesforce having to work harder to achieve the same results as the previous year. As this consequential effect is what the salesforce experiences directly it can elicit the perception, "We've just been screwed!" Why this is the number one perception of the salesforce to which it applies is that the decision makers have failed to provide the necessary information to allow the affected the opportunity to view things from the decision makers' perspective. Resentment, curtailed communication and a fall in performance ensue.

If better quality information would prevent the misunderstanding by the affected and, assuming that decision makers do have the best interests of the affected at heart, why do decision makers not improve the quality of information they provide? The reasons are several:

Poor communication skills

It may simply be that the decision maker knows no better. It does not occur to him to place himself in the other person's shoes, so to speak. He, therefore, has no idea of the emotional trauma his decision has on the affected and, so, will be ignorant of his ability to evoke a more positive emotional response from that other person.

Weakness of Character

A decision maker with little moral fiber will fear that the affected will threaten his position by challenging his decision and by so doing, his authority, should he provide them with sufficient information to do so. Such a decision maker is one who mistakenly believes that privileged information provides his power. In fact, the information he has which others do not, serves at best to provide an illusory buffer around his self-doubt. This decision maker is esteemed by controlling others.

Paternalism

This decision maker wants to be responsible for everyone. He wields his authority in a way that limits others' ability and desire to take responsibility. His manner discourages others from taking ownership of what they rightfully should.

TOWARD WISDOM

The journey toward wisdom is an evolutionary process; evolution being the sum of finite revolutionary events over a given period of time. Each revolutionary event furthers our understanding of how things really are. Examples of such include the discoveries of fire, atoms, living cells, the laws of gravity, the speed of light, X-rays, the general and special theories of relativity, microwaves, telephony, electricity, subatomic particles, the expanding universe, the big bang theory of creation, the laws of physics not prohibiting time travel, evidence of primitive life in a meteorite believed to have originated on Mars.

Our evolution toward wisdom is an evolution of the mind. It runs parallel with our physical evolution. As we evolve physically to maximize our advantage in a changing environment, so too are we evolving mentally to maximize our advantage in a world we as yet do not fully understand.

Where will this evolutionary process take us? Right now there are still many more questions than there are answers. Until and unless we truly know fully the mind of God our curiosity will continue to fuel our journey. In some sense, maybe in every sense, what we are dealing with here is our ability to handle change. Hence, the wisest among us are those most adept at handling change. In a single lifetime (perhaps) the best we can hope for, the wisest we can become, is to believe as Socrates did and that is, regardless of how smart we become, to know what little we know.

CHAPTER 10

SACRIFICE
THE ULTIMATE PRICE

"Nothing can resist the human will that will stake even its existence on the extent of its purpose."

– Benjamin Disraeli

SACRIFICE

Sacrifice you say
On such a gay day
I want to run, I want to play
It's spring time in early May

Sacrifice the Lamb
Not this raging, roving ram
I want my tea and toast and jam
And when I'm hurt I want my mom

Sacrifice for what?
I refuse, I cannot
I've so little time to do a lot
But now I'm tired and want my cot

Sacrifice to please
You say this as a tease?
It's not just done with sublime ease
It's difficult like shelling peas

Sacrifice for Love
Oh please, God above
As if life isn't hard enough
Without this sacrificial stuff

– LAC

SACRIFICE: The ultimate price

- A perspective on sacrifice

- Delayed gratification

- Lead thyself not into temptation

- Kick the habit

- A lesson from nature

A PERSPECTIVE ON SACRIFICE

The general understanding of sacrifice is to give up something. Christ on the cross is the ultimate sacrificial icon. Other, more usual acts of sacrifice include going to war for one's country, forsaking one's career for the benefit of the spouse's, leaving a progressive career to look after the children, abstaining from life's "pleasures" to achieve athletic excellence and remaining faithful in a relationship.

In truth, a sacrifice is always something that we make so that we may receive something else of greater value, with two exceptions:

1. Sacrifice forced upon us as the "sacrificial lamb" in some bizarre ritual; and

2. Sacrifice due to our own weakness born out of mental dis-ease. And even in this weakened state we find there is a payoff. The "victim" who wants a reason to resist taking responsibility for his life is able to blame another for his lot. We are mentally dis-eased to the degree to which we are not in control of our emotions. If, then, we sacrifice because we are made to feel guilty, this is our weakness, the payoff for which is the appeasement of our guilt.

If asked, what is the greatest sacrifice we can make, many of us would reply to die for someone or some worthy cause. Is it, however? If one believes in life after death and one is right, then life goes on. Further, most subscribers to this view believe that life after death will be better. If one does not believe in life after death, and one is right, one will remain dead. In either case, who is to say that giving ourselves unconditionally in this life to another or to a worthy cause, come what may, is not a greater sacrifice? In the same way, suicide is not a brave act. The payoff is relief from the problem(s) that one is beset with. Surely, it is braver to choose life and strive to overcome the problem(s).

The greater benefit received from our sacrifice may often appear to accrue to others, and this is true if we fix our gaze on the material benefits alone. If, for example, we believe that we have life because of Christ's sacrifice on the cross, the material benefit – sentient life – has clearly accrued to us. However, the benefit to Christ was a spiritual benefit, both intangible and immeasurable, and, therefore, understated.

Similar benefits accrue to soldiers of war, parents, and others who apparently sacrifice something for the benefit of others. Feelings of pride, satisfaction, joy and so on from seeing or otherwise knowing that their sacrifice has aided the progress of someone or something they hold dear are the intangible, immeasurable feelings of success; their success in aiding the others' success.

As a parent, what material value would you place on your child's first step; their first utterance of mommy or daddy; their first (and probably last!) acting role in the school play, in which they nervously, though bravely, recited their lines by rote; or the day they themselves became parents? Indeed, some of us are able to accept a lowly lot in life, being at ease with our under achieving, knowing that we get a second and subsequent chances through our children and even our grandchildren. Their success is somehow ours.

Sacrifice is made to either rid ourselves of the symptoms of mental dis-ease – guilt, pity, anger, etc. – which is our payoff, or to obtain a benefit of greater value than that which we have sacrificed. This benefit may be calculated in material or non-material currency. Our success may be measured by the extent of our sacrifice. The most successful people, then, would be those who, in their lifetimes, have made the greatest sacrifice for the benefit of others, notwithstanding any benefit (material or non-material) that they themselves may receive. In support of this position, Pilot Officer, V.A. Rosewarne, recounted in a letter to his mother that was subsequently published in the London Times on June 18, 1980 how a person's life can only be justified by the extent of his sacrifice in so vast and ageless a universe.

Success viewed in this way provides us with a whole new perspective on what it really is. No longer are we inclined to see it in purely financial terms. The likes of Mother Teresa, Gandhi and Martin Luther King, Junior spring to mind as readily as those of Carnegie, Rockefeller, Bill Gates and Warren Buffett.

Using sacrifice as our measure of success, Jesus Christ would appear to be the most successful person known to mankind. It is appropriate, therefore, that his crucifixion is the icon of sacrifice; and thereby, success.

What are you prepared to sacrifice to achieve your success?

DELAYED GRATIFICATION

The principle of delayed gratification, being the postponement of an immediate reward for the sake of some more important reward in the future, is <u>the</u> quintessential lesson in sacrifice. It can be observed on many levels: in waiting to be served in a popular restaurant; in waiting until the end of the week for a paycheck; in years of study to achieve qualifications; in saving a portion of one's income to build a retirement nest egg; in foregoing television to write a bestseller; and in giving up a perceived corporate security to build a business of one's own.

Delaying gratification requires discipline, desire, patience and a fervent belief in your future. If you believe that you will amount to little, you will see little point in delaying gratification, and so will choose not to, instead opting for instant gratification. It is easier to delay gratification when we have a strong sense of purpose. When we believe in ourselves, know what we want, trust we can have it, and associate great benefits with achieving the gratification we have delayed, we are more inclined to wait for it.

What is it we wish to gratify? Simply, our desire for success; our desire for happiness. We must here confront another paradox. Happiness is a NOW experience. It is impossible to feel happiness in the future (or, indeed, in the past). Yet, we know for our next and subsequent nows to be satisfying we need to sacrifice something in this now. Therefore, the sacrifice itself can be a source of satisfaction. One's suffering tangible material privation now by saving money for the future, for example, is superseded by the intangible psychological benefit of peace of mind in subsequent nows, which benefit is also experienced in this now. When the subsequent nows are reached, we have the added material benefit of the object of our sacrifice, in this case financial resources, which, incidentally, has a bonus added by way of the peace of mind also experienced in the subsequent nows.

The perceived value of the delayed gratification must outweigh the value of instant gratification for us to commit to it. We will indulge in instant gratification the moment this is not true, perhaps spending what we would otherwise save. If our desire for instant gratification is great, we may endeavor satisfying it by "mortgaging" our future gratification. For instance, borrowing money to spend now and paying it back from future income. In acute cases, we may even fall prey to compulsion and addiction.

LEAD THYSELF NOT INTO TEMPTATION

Most of us do not suffer from such chronic addiction and, thus, may be unsympathetic toward those prone to severe addiction. We may even judge them with an air of superiority, seeing them as weak, out of control and unable to deal with life's difficulties the way we (who are made of sterner stuff) are able to. Though commonplace, is this belief justified?

An addict is a devotee. A devotee is an ardent follower, who is a faithful person. To be faithful is to be loyal. Therefore, to be addicted to a person, place or thing is to be loyal to the same. Our responsibility is to decide whether the addiction is a well-placed or misplaced loyalty. One way of deciding is to determine whether it promotes one's wellbeing or not.

Addiction also suggests harmful and unbalanced behavior. The hurt inflicted on self, family, friends, career, credibility, integrity and values is easy to detect in the blatant addiction to drugs, alcohol or gambling. However, there are subtler addictions which are more widespread and which almost certainly affect you and me. Such addictions include caffeine, greed, money, power, laziness, busyness, tiredness, fitness, illness, partners, children, friends and so on. This is probably a good time to remind you to suspend your disbelief. "How can my partner, my children or my friends be an addiction?" To the degree to which you attach yourself to them and see who you are through them, you are addicted to them.

The crux of the matter is that most things in moderation are not harmful to us. Problems arise when we take them to excess, which is the point beyond which the activity can be described as beneficial (i.e., it promotes personal growth), since the opportunity cost of pursuing the activity is higher than the benefits derived from it. The points at which alcohol, tobacco, over-the-counter drugs and caffeine cease to yield a net benefit are readily defined. One indicator for alcohol consumption is published by The U.S. National Institute on Alcohol Abuse and Alcoholism (NIAAA). Interestingly, their limits are well below those we would associate with the archetypal alcoholic.

For example, men are said to be at increased risk when consuming more than four units of alcohol per day, and women when consuming more than three units of alcohol per day. One unit is roughly equivalent to 12oz of beer, 8-9oz of malt liquor, or 5oz of wine. The potential risks of exceeding these limits are raised blood pressure, liver damage, cirrhosis of the liver, cancers of the mouth and throat, and psychological problems, including depression. So, in general terms, a man swilling over three pints of beer a day, and a woman quaffing four glasses of wine a day are endangering their health. If aware of this information, they continue to as they have been, they are, by definition (their actions are detrimental to their personal growth) addicted to alcohol and are, therefore, alcoholics. A point of clarification: I speak of excess being the point beyond which the addictive activity can be described as beneficial – the promotion personal growth – because the addict may regard continual stupefaction from sober reality as a benefit, since coping with that sober reality is something they don't do well. Clearly, however, their perceived benefit, rather than promoting meaningful growth, is an agent for senseless death.

While dated, it is interesting to note that according to the June 1987 edition of *Management Today*, 75% of people with a drinking problem are in fulltime employment – the so-called functioning alcoholic. A more contemporary statistic from The NIAAA claims that 1 in every 13 American adults abuses alcohol or is an alcoholic, with several millions more engage in risky drinking habits.

People who drink seven or more large cups of average strength coffee per day risk broken sleep patterns, restlessness and anxiety. These conditions are so physically and emotionally draining that they may take more coffee thinking it will help the symptoms, only to exacerbate them. Some cases of chronic anxiety have been discovered to be no more than the effect of high caffeine intoxication. When the drinking habit is broken the anxiety levels subside.

The limit beyond which an activity can be described as beneficial is rather more subjective when it comes to really subtle addictions like relationships, spectator sport, exercise, shopping, working, lying or watching television, to name but a few. This, however, does not render these activities any less detrimental to our wellbeing where the safe limit has been exceeded. The danger of addiction to these activities, like the blatant addictions, is that we leave ourselves little or no time to pursue anything else, to enjoy a balanced, rounded life. Instead, we may become a spectator at life, watching others "get on with it" while we watch from the sidelines. This is particularly so of excessive TV and spectator sports. It is not unusual to hear a TV addict, the so-called Couch Potato, complain that he is prevented from doing X, Y or Z for lack of time, when, in truth, the instant gratification of watching TV is more appealing to him than, say, learning a new skill, enhancing relationships by spending <u>communicative</u> time with loved ones, or improving his health with an exercise regime.

People with such addictions feel good or bad depending on how well their favorite team performs or on how well their stage hero's life turns out. Being away from these addictions can induce withdrawal symptoms similar to but milder than those experienced by blatant addicts.

We fail to recognize the magnitude of the harmful effects of subtle addictions for two principal reasons:

1. Their subtle nature makes them very difficult to detect. Their victims do not wander around with red, rolling eyes or in an exaggerated stupor; and

2. They are socially acceptable. Those who succumb to them are a great majority, making them even more difficult to detect and, thus, more acceptable.

A person who resorts to running up credit card debt on retail therapy, or indulges in comfort eating when depressed is more acceptable to society than one who resorts to excessive drinking or gambling when challenged by the same condition, while the effects on each one's family may be indistinguishable.

Addiction can be encouraged by our lifestyle. The busyness of our lives may encourage us to eat a lot of prepacked, precooked, off-the-shelf meals which tend to have a high salt content. Salt is, of course, essential to our wellbeing. However, excessive amounts can be detrimental to good health, causing high blood pressure, water retention and other ailments. Choosing to eat in this way, we become accustomed to the taste of excessively salted foods. Even when we eat freshly prepared foods we over-salt as the food, otherwise, seems tasteless. We are eating more salt than is good for us. If we are knowingly doing this and continue we are addicted to it.

A classical feature of addiction is denial. Many drinkers and smokers are convinced they don't have a problem, even though they consciously and consistently choose to exceed consumption limits known to be detrimental to their health. Others do admit the problem and yet continue, gripped by their addiction, to trade their health and other benefits for it, proclaiming, "You only live once!" as if life can only be expressed through their addiction and that any other expression thereof would be mere existence.

Awareness is 90% of responsibility. Alcoholics Anonymous tells us that we first must admit to addiction before we can be rid of it, and that we are never cured of it, but must work daily to overcome its attractions. I will tell you the same thing about subtle addictions. If you really want to maximize your potential, recognize them in yourself and be honest about how well they serve you.

If you are still unconvinced of your addiction(s), please do accept the following challenge. Choose an activity which you regularly engage in – drinking, smoking, comfort eating, watching a particular soap opera, attending a particular sporting occasion, meeting with friends at a particular time and place – and refrain from doing it for one month. How do you feel right now about the thought of it not being in your life? How will you feel during abstinence from it? Can you already feel the onset of withdrawal symptoms? If you do have the courage to rise to this challenge you may experience other, perhaps more rewarding, activities replacing that which you have (temporarily) abstained from. Absence is said to make the heart grow fonder, in which case you may find that your abstinence has reaffirmed your commitment to and enjoyment of the activity from which you have abstained. Either way you will benefit from the challenge. Go on, accept the challenge. I dare you!

KICK THE HABIT

Once we recognize and admit to the addiction, our next challenge is to overcome it. In order to do so we must see it for what it is, not what it appears to be. One challenge here is that society loves its labels. Labeling is an effective and convenient way of making sense of things, bringing order into a world of disorder. So, to label an addict an alcoholic, a gambler, a junkie, a smoker, etc. is convenient and aids communication in a broad sense. However, each addiction is underlain by emotional dis-ease. The manifestation of this dis-ease – the addiction – is symptomatic of the cause – the dis-ease.

The afflicted person accepts and adopts the label, seeing his emotional problems as being associated with, but not essentially the cause of his addiction. The emotional pain of overcoming the addiction may be so great that we self-sabotage. For example, changing from one diet to the next without allowing sufficient time for the first to really take effect; or eating a piece of cream pie because of the weight loss we have achieved, only to succumb to a second and then a third. Before we know it, the habit has been rediscovered along with the instant gratification and apparent relief it brings.

Understanding the true nature of the addiction gives us a better chance of overcoming it. It better prepares us for the emotional turmoil that ensues when any attempt is made to overcome it. Knowing that our emotional dis-ease is at the route of the addiction means we can treat this cause in preference to the symptom(s). To stop drinking, then, may not be enough. We must seek to cure our emotional dis-ease. Stopping the drinking without curing the underlying problem is analogous to driving a car with exposed spark plugs only in dry weather. In such conditions it is fine. Once the rains come the car will not operate since the spark plugs fail to fire in the wet conditions. If we attend to the problem and enclose the spark plugs, the symptoms of not operating in wet conditions disappear.

A LESSON FROM NATURE

When I was a little boy, I would often spend summer days doing my level best to distract a community of ants from whatever labors they seemed intent on pursuing. I would erect barriers before them, step among them, pour water over them and even frizzle them with a magnifying glass! My efforts, however great, served only to delay the inevitable completion of the ant's task.

It appears that once an ant embarks upon an undertaking, it is single minded in its efforts; so much so that it will succumb to no distraction. It may even ignore the work of others in the pursuit of its idea. It will hurry and scurry until its idea becomes physically perceptible to other ants. Once others see the benefits (and only if they see there truly are benefits) of the one's idea they will sacrifice all else and become equally engrossed in the completion of the task, such task being for the common good of the ant hive.

M. Maeterlinck in *The Life of the White Ant* describes an episode whereby a worker ant whose abdomen and both hind legs had been cut off, continued walking on her four remaining legs, dragging her entrails behind her so that she could save a cocoon. The ant refused to die until the cocoon, which (Maeterlinck believed) to her represented the future of the hive, was safe and secure.

One species of ant gorges itself on the honeydew of a Colorado indigenous oak. Those that successfully gorge themselves to an expansion of five or six times the normal size are "promoted" to a position of esteemed responsibility whereby they are further gorged until they are eight times the normal weight. Once this is achieved, they cling to the roof of the nest and remain hanging there until death; their sole purpose being to regurgitate the honeydew to feed their fellow citizens. It is not expressly clear what the gorged ants gain from this, although it would appear to be in the inherent sacrifice of the one for the benefit of all.

I am not sure whether God intends for humanity to become as selfless and giving as the ant appears to be. If so, we have not yet grown to realize the fruits of such a morality as that shared by ant communities. In our present selfish state let us at least endeavor to harm no other in the pursuit of the self-gratification we call our goals.

The ant has achieved a pure commune-*ism*. Not one in which all are supposedly equal, but one in which each knows her role and performs it selflessly for the benefit of the community above personal gain. Observers have noted that in community ants display a great intelligence, but alone, uninspired by the "collective mind" they lose three quarters of that intelligence. Perhaps there are lessons beyond sacrifice that we may glean from the ant.

CHAPTER 11

WHEN ALL IS SAID AND DONE

"We are such insignificant creatures on a minor planet of a very average star in the outer suburbs of one of a hundred thousand million (100,000,000,000) galaxies."

– Stephen Hawking

THE RIGHT PERSPECTIVE

I live at…

Nice Cottage

5 The Street

Any Town

Florida

USA

Northern Hemisphere

Planet Earth

Third Rock from the Sun

Milky Way Galaxy.

Oops! I forgot the zip code

– LAC

WHEN ALL IS SAID AND DONE

The universe is vast – maybe infinite. But like fleas in a jar, we have an overinflated perspective of our scale. We are egotistical enough to see ourselves at the center of the universe, the most important element of it, and that may even be true. Yet, shadowing this super ego is humanities alter ego, the antithesis of the super ego that would have us deny our responsibilities as co-creators with the Creator. It has us trapped in a universal gravity of excuses, which effectively holds us in an orbital motion around Planet Fear in a galaxy of failure.

While it is true that the most insignificant element in the universe is as equally important as the most significant, since we know, from quantum physics, that if it were possible to remove the smallest subatomic particle from the universe, the universe would collapse. However, the universe we should strive to be the center of is our own internal universe. When we achieve this, all things are possible for us and we give birth to them in the universe external to ourselves: mind manifests matter – in the multifarious forms and glory of our choosing.

Within our own internal universes, most of us spend too much time thinking about things that need little thought, and too little time thinking about things that need great thought. When discussing someone's life who is nearing death, it becomes sharply evident that we, mostly, do not regret the things we have done but, rather, the things we failed to do.

> "I expect to pass through this world but one;
> any good thing therefore that I can do, or any
> kindness that I can show to any fellow-creature,
> let me do it now; let me not defer or neglect it,
> for I shall not pass this way again."
>
> – Stephen Grellet

It is never too late to seize the day. So, now that you have come this far in life, what next? Well, life begins here! All that has gone before is history. You may use it to your advantage, use it as an excuse not to change, or just see it as a pleasant or unpleasant collection of experiences in the annals of time to fondly reminisce or recall with fearful trepidation. What you do choose will be your choice. In an age in which our vision is boundless, do not see how far you can go, go how far you can see. The rest will unfold when you get there.

Your future may lie in whatever you're doing right now, and then it may not. To determine whether what you are doing right now is the key to your future, ask yourself three questions:

1. If not this, then what?

2. If not now, then when?

3. If not me, then who?

Hopefully, you will be inspired by the answers to these questions. If not, do not despair. At least you are closer to an understanding of what is going to inspire you to success. In your search I want you to be mindful of one reality; you are already an unequivocal success. Allow me to take you back in time by your age plus nine months. You and 400 million others set out on an arduous journey. One that was all uphill! A journey that epitomized all that we understand by the term *survival of the fittest*. 0.05mm long, you travelled at 3 to 3.5 mm per minute.

Ejaculated into the acidic conditions of your mother's vagina, you relied on the safety in numbers that your 400 million companions provided. Many died in the acid antechamber before the journey truly began. You and the survivors competed furiously for the right to Life. A right determined exclusively by nature's seemingly cruel though purely honest Law, *survival of the fittest*. You knew that only one of you could gain that right. However, your genetic programing instilled in you the knowledge that it, despite what was at stake, was a team game in which whoever gained the right to Life was merely a representative of all; a first among equals. Without the masses the ultimate victor would stand no chance of success. In that regard the spoils are shared. And so, we have Life's first paradox: we journey through life together alone.

Millions of you passed through the cervix into the uterus where you were nourished by the alkaline mucus of the cervical canal. Refreshed, you battled on up into the fallopian tubes, a 45-minute journey that only 2,000 – 0.0005% – of you survived. At this stage, you would all perish unless ovulation took place so that one of you could fuse with an egg. Fortunately for you, in particular, and for your 400 million companions in general (as their struggle was not in vain), ovulation did occur, and YOU fused with an egg; and so Life began anew. It is noteworthy that in that success the distance was determined. All you needed to do was decide how quickly you were going to cover it.

When deciding what the future will hold, be comforted by your overwhelmingly successful history. You are a 1 in 400 million success. The chances of winning the lottery jackpot are 1 in 14 million. Therefore, there is a 36 times greater chance of winning the lottery jackpot than there is of being born. Congratulations from one success to another.